No One Is Fatherless

365 DAYS of *Opa Dan's* Two Cents' Worth of DAILY DEVOTIONALS

Live in such a way that those who know you but do not know God will come to know God because they know you.

When one of your Special Forces Teammates of 20 years sends this to you, it means a great deal.

DANIEL KOSTRZEBSKI

EDITED BY — Carol Kostrzebski

No One Is Fatherless can be ordered on www.nooneisfatherless.com

For orders over 10 copies or if you have questions please reach out to SALES@BECKARY.COM

 Copyright © 2021 by Exponential Publications, LLC
Lancaster, Pennsylvania

Bible verses are from the NIV translations of a Bible mobile app.
(Edition: NIV 50th Anniversary, version 8.0.2 // 2020-09-08_16-38-07-1914 // 2019 Tecarta, Inc.)
Some phrases have been bolded for emphasis.

Select names have been changed for privacy purposes.

Cover/Book Designer: Michael Douglas

All Rights Reserved. No part of the book may be reproduced or transmitted in any form
or by any means, electronic or mechanical, including photocopying, recording or by any
information storage and retrieval system without written permission from the publisher,
except for the inclusion of brief quotations with credit given in a review.

Printed in the United States of America

ISBN 978-0-9740303-2-6

Foreword
by Pete Beckary

My brother Albert and I have had the honor to know Dan for many years. He and I connected through music as high school bandmates—Dan on piano and me on tuba and bass trombone. Al and Dan met in elementary school, graduated high school together in 1981, and remain friends to this day. According to Al, Dan was best known as a good guy with a one-of-a-kind *machine-gun* laugh that would erupt without warning. Dan was a highly valued team player in sports and well-liked by everyone. We both considered Dan to be one of those special people you never forget.

When my life hit a rough patch a little over ten years ago, I reconnected with Dan. I learned that Dan would reach out to God for guidance and often found that His timing was perfect. Dan was a great source of support during this trying time, and we connected regularly by phone. Over the course of numerous calls, I learned more about his Special Ops service. I was so moved by his amazing stories, I told him, "Dan, we need to tell your story!" His immediate response was to share his story as a witness for God's glory! Dan wanted to share his testimony of God's grace upon his family and his life. It's a story about a soldier, his faith, and how that faith grew in confidence when he did what God guided him to do.

Several years had passed, and while I all but forgot about that conversation, Dan was keeping to his faith in daily devotionals to his family and others shared here in this book. He continues this practice today. Through this daily devotional, Dan shares his life stories—both personal and military. He talks of triumphs over adversity, the consequences of his own life choices, and how through the grace of God he's been reunited with his entire family. He's cultivated a unique connection with them through sharing a daily Bible verse coupled with his own hard-earned wisdom.

Thanks for taking this journey with us. Enjoy Opa Dan's two cents!

Pete Beckary
Publisher

A Purpose

A tribute to God "our" Father! This book details an earthly father's determination to stay connected with his Lord and his family, to be a spiritual leader in daily devotionals to keep Christ the center of our family's lives. Each day at some point, depending on where everyone in the family is, the family is to read "Dad's Two Cents." This dad believes that by doing his best to obey what God asks him to do, he will prove God right. God does not lie. I share this experience with the world in hopes it brings other families closer together in Christ, too, experiencing great joy, peace, and love with their families. Our Father in Heaven intends and desires joy for all of His children, just like most mortal dads do with their children.

The title of this book comes from one of the many fine Southern sermons from Brother Kenny Rogers. I listened attentively on Father's Day as Pastor Kenny Rogers was giving guidance on the father's role in the family as a spiritual leader. My thoughts immediately drifted to those who don't know their fathers or others, still, whose fathers have passed away. During my military experience, I mourned for my brothers and sisters who did not return home to their children. A version of this happened within my own family. I was recently informed by my daughters that they were led to believe—and truly thought—I was dead for much of their childhood, growing up with their mother in Germany. I assure you that this book is written by a father who is a witness of true love and forgiveness represented by our Lord, Jesus.

In the age of Google knows all (what do parents—or even preachers—know anyway), and the mere fact that this dad was never known for his patience in child rearing, I listened to my pastor's sermon on Mother's Day. He shared a story of his prison ministry in which he distributed hundreds of Mother's Day cards for the inmates to fill out and return to him to be mailed. When Father's Day came, he again attempted to distribute cards in the same manner and was unable to give away one card. This sermon hit home with me, as I would rarely have daily, weekly, or even monthly communications with my four children. However, my wife Carol would. Many sermons to follow would emphasize the "godly man's" role to lead his family spiritually throughout his life—not just when the kids are young and living at home. I realized quickly that I was lacking in these efforts and looked for a way to recover in that role. Truth be told, I was headed toward loneliness and depression, and I knew it. I had relationship issues within my so-called "family"—all of them.

Like many fathers, I was far from perfect. Some would describe certain aspects of my fatherhood as a complete failure. My daughters Kim and Lynn were estranged from me for most of their childhood. Their mother Dawn and I divorced early in our marriage, and she returned with our children to Germany—her homeland—when they were two and four years old. I didn't see them again until 2004. Kim was 20 years old, and Lynn was 18.

I had served in the military since I was 18 years old. I was full of energy and ready to go to battle. However, my youthful oats got the best of me and I was married at 19, with a daughter on the way (Kim). After a brief break in service, I joined the Army again with my second daughter soon on the way. By the time I was 22 years old, I had my own family. Just before

I left for Special Forces training, my lack of attention to my family brought about a quick divorce. This split led to Kim and Lynn returning to Germany with their mother to start a new chapter in their lives without me.

With my travels and Special Forces training in the great state of Texas, I met a wonderful woman whom I would soon marry. For 30 plus years, I've shared my life with my precious wife, Carol. Carol made the leap of faith with a young man, divorced with two children and just beginning his career in the U.S. Army Special Forces. Go ahead and figure the odds on that marriage lasting very long.

I made it through the Special Forces Medical Training and was quickly assigned to the 5th Special Forces Group at Fort Campbell, Kentucky. Three weeks after the birth of our first son, Shane, I was deployed to Saudi Arabia for eight months. The first Gulf War had begun. No cell phones to communicate with home. Just handwritten letters, few and far between. Carol and I made it through round one. Then two weeks after the birth of our second son, Blake, I was deployed to Somalia for eight months. This deployment also featured handwritten letters as our only form of communication. Somalia was full of small conflicts (compared to the Gulf War) across the country, which led to the battle of Black Hawk Down. Our detachment had just left the country a couple of weeks prior to that horrible day. Carol and I had, thankfully, survived a second round of being separated for an extended period of time. I was not home much at all, though. There were deployments far away from home and training at various locations on different military bases. This was the life of a Special Forces soldier. My memories of changing diapers or rocking my children to sleep are few and far between.

Carol and I were by no means described as Bible thumpers. While we were raised in the Christian faith, we were young and lacked the biblical disciplines later learned in our walk with Christ. As a young Green Beret in the Army, eager to prove my warrior skills, I must confess I struggled with balancing my priorities between that and my new family with Carol, Shane, and Blake. So now with this shaky Christian foundation and past of many cracks and bends, my children are all grown. Is it possible in Christ, that all things really are possible? Can we all be a family?

I would not be writing this book if the answer to the question wasn't a resounding, "Yes!"

During one of my recent trips to Austin, TX, with Carol, our 23-year-old Uber driver asked us what one thing we could attribute to our lasting marriage. We both replied immediately at the same time, "Jesus Christ." For today I declare that there is an abundance of communications daily. There are joyous plans for the future of a growing family with Christ as their focal point each morning. This is a victory won. Not a single battle, but a real-deal testimony of a miracle that highlights forgiveness, which is the cornerstone of our faith in Christ Jesus, our Lord.

But how did I achieve this? First and foremost, I had to take action and make time for daily scripture reading, with prayer to follow. It took many years for this father to read the Bible cover to cover and put my heart into it. Much of the time while reading the Bible I did not realize why I should be reading the Bible, I just had a calling to do it. I recall in my talks with God, He would direct my thoughts to the famous Nike commercial with Michael Jordan: "Just Do It!"

You see, I had been saved.

Having a Catholic upbringing, I was keenly aware of Jesus. I was taught to believe and worship as a young boy in the Catholic Church. Even so, I was born with an inherent, uninhibited desire to take risks. I could easily get into some joyful trouble, no harm meant to anyone, of course. As a young Private First Class on a wild night in Nuremberg, Germany with the men of my unit, I sat alone in a park. I was calling out to Jesus for help. I felt myself getting out of control. The alcohol, the women, and the environment I was in were going to take me down hard if I didn't get help. So, there I sat.

A man approached me at sunrise on a Sunday morning and handed me one of those church cards about being "saved" (written in German and English—what are the odds of that?). I read it and followed the directions to their location, which was in the city center just behind me. I knocked on the door and a woman answered, "Can I help you?"

I showed her the card and said I need Jesus. She asked me to follow her inside. This was a small chapel, not the big monster church you often see in Europe. I believe it may have been a Baptist missionary. I was a clueless, lost sheep. A man inside asked me if I would "receive" (not believe—I already did) Jesus Christ as my Lord and Savior. I said "Yes," and we recited the Sinner's Prayer together on our knees under a big wooden cross. My eyes teared up in a moment of tremendous relief. I looked at this man and asked, "Is that it—am I saved, all said and done?" He told me that I was now in God's hands. I knelt for a good bit alone next to the cross, then quietly left, knowing something had changed. I wasn't sure just what it was. I got out my old Bible back at my barracks and started to read it—cover to cover was the goal. I did this in secret, of course, so the other troops wouldn't label me as a Bible quack.

As the years passed, I got out of the Army and then back into the Army, with rough times along the way. As each episode, each chapter played out, my conscience was telling me to "stop and listen to the Holy Spirit." I could not, I was a young and powerful paratrooper by 1985. Now with my second daughter, Lynn, I felt unstoppable. I was a lean, mean killing machine full of pride. It wasn't long before I was divorced, estranged from my daughters, paying child support, and not communicating with my former wife. I was still a believer, and I still read my Bible on deployments in secret, often pausing to say a quick prayer and wonder, "Is this the way to live?"

Not long after my separation from my first wife, I met Carol in 1988. Carol was very sweet and innocent, not familiar with the military at all, let alone Special Forces. I was truthful with her from the moment we met at that night club in San Antonio, TX. I told her I had two daughters and was going through a divorce. That truthfulness up front was the beginning of a very fruitful, godly marriage. That Bible reading I was doing was already making an impression on my character. Be truthful and honest!

As time would tell and this book will reveal, "Because God said so," was my childhood approach to being so lost and all over the place (spiritually and otherwise), as my Father, with great patience, blessed me so. Many years later, I acquired a smartphone, and the

NIV app became my daily reach. Devotions to ponder and to pray about, then talk to Jesus like I talk to the folks at work. I committed to communicating each morning and day with Christ, telling Him everything on my mind. Carol would catch me with my lips moving, and I would tell her I was just going over some ideas with Jesus. When I was home, we would all go to our local church as a family on Sunday. This eventually led to Carol and me becoming Sunday school teachers together, though, admittedly, I sometimes still loved to be by myself in the woods. Perhaps in a tree stand with my little pocket Bible and just reading. Total peace. No bombs, no bullets, and no people to interrupt my thoughts with our Creator. Baby steps, my brothers and sisters—we are talking years leading into decades. God sent me multiple godly friends, churches, and pastors to come full circle and be able to articulate God's promises come to life. All this happened the hard way for me, of course (spiritually stubborn). This is so I would not forget (God's plan for me to write about this someday, perhaps). No father wants the hard way for his children and neither does God our Father. With daily devotions to ponder on my NIV Bible app, the practice eventually turned into "Hello Family" each and every morning, my two cents' worth to share with my family group on WhatsApp wherever I was on the globe each and every morning.

The title of this book is also a reflection of our family's challenge dealing with a dad who can be very opinionated—perhaps as the result of a successful, pride-filled Special Forces military career. Currently, Carol and I lead a Sunday school class, which our youngest son, Blake (29 years old now), recently attended while visiting us. When I shared that I was taking on the challenge of giving my two cents' worth to the family via WhatsApp Group Message, Blake's response was, "It's more like 50 cents, Dad." This led to a burst of smiles and laughter, myself included. After many years of reading books written by Max Lucado (used as a lead study in our Sunday school class), the daily scripture readings continued. "Hello Family" was on a roll with sincere prayer, praises, and meditation inspired by a Bible phone app at the beginning of each day.

March 1991: Just arriving home after getting off the plane following the Gulf War, I hold my first son Shane. I have a bottle and am in amazement at how he has grown. He is already communicating.

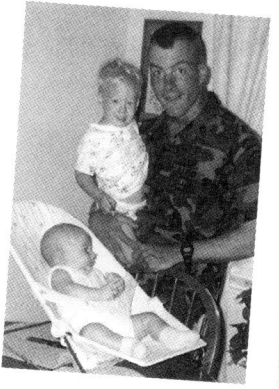

May 1992: Just arriving home from Fort Benning, GA, after finishing Ranger School (class 6-92). Upon completion, I was awarded some big honors; coming home to a couple of "little rangers" was the warmest honor of them all.

A PURPOSE | 7

DAY 1

A father to the fatherless, a defender of widows,
is God in his holy dwelling.

PSALM 68:5

HELLO FAMILY: Look hard at this scripture and pause. "Fatherless"? I can attest there was and is a period in most of our lives that even though we had a father, we also had issues in life, including confrontations and relationship struggles, that left us feeling fatherless. How critical it is not to lose yourselves to the world thinking you are not relevant, not important, not secured, not loved by a "Father." Later scriptures warn of worldly teachings and ways for "itchy ears" (2 Timothy 4:2–3 NIV) that will be counter to the reality of joy coming from a Christ-like relationship with the Father above, our God. None of us is ever Fatherless — no matter what — to God. Most all fathers wish to see their children experience joy from our making and effort, just as our Lord Father God does. However hard we earthly fathers try, I assure you we are no comparison to the love and guidance of God our Father. Love you all!

DAY 2

The LORD is my shepherd, I lack nothing. [2] He makes me lie down
in green pastures, he leads me beside quiet waters, [3] he refreshes
my soul. He guides me along the right paths for his name's sake.
[4] Even though I walk through the darkest valley, I will fear no
evil, for you are with me; your rod and your staff, they comfort me.

PSALM 23:1–4

HELLO FAMILY: "The LORD is my shepherd…he refreshes my soul." How much money is spent on vacations in an attempt to refresh our souls? There is no greater peace than a one-on-one relationship with our Lord. It is the best vacation every day! Stay close to the Shepherd and the wolves can't get you. In a dog-eat-dog world moving at the speed of sound, do you ever stop and listen to absolute silence? Make the time to do just that. Find that place to study and communicate with Christ. Love you all.

DAY 3

"Ask and it will be given to you; seek and you will find; knock and the door will be opened to you."

MATTHEW 7:7

HELLO FAMILY: Scripture such as this — and there are many that reflect this theme — are the promises of God. Prayer gives hope, answered prayer gives strength, and confidence in your faith. When we go to Church (worship), we are a witness to those who testify to their answered prayers, which strengthens everyone's faith. As I observe my grandchildren, I am reminded of a father's likeness to our Creator, God the Father. Their children ask and seek. Odds are their father delivers. So, when you read that we are created in the likeness of God, remember this scripture. Then prepare for the words of Jesus that we must enter the Kingdom of Heaven with a childlike heart. Know that we as adults must pray like a child to God the Father, in total faith and honesty. Love you all.

DAY 4

*Know also that wisdom is like honey for you:
If you find it, there is a future hope for you,
and your hope will not be cut off.*

PROVERBS 24:14

HELLO FAMILY: Wisdom is like honey...oh how sweet it is. So, **pray** for it specifically, even if we are not really sure what it means — like me, try it and the joy in your life will flow beyond measure. Pray specifically, ask God to bless you with wisdom. The Bible speaks of great wealth and joy coming from wisdom, a promise from God. Love you all.

DAY 5

> But whatever were gains to me I now consider loss for the sake of Christ. [8] What is more, I consider everything a loss because of the surpassing worth of knowing Christ Jesus my Lord, for whose sake I have lost all things. I consider them garbage that I may gain Christ [9] and be found in him, not having a righteousness of my own that comes from the law, but that which is through faith in Christ—the righteousness that comes from God on the basis of faith.
>
> PHILIPPIANS 3:7–9

HELLO FAMILY: This scripture writes of the change in values and having Christ as priority #1 in our lives. When time is made to read, pray (get the Holy Spirit in the fight too), and worship, our values are transformed. Doing what is "right" for others becomes our normal behavior rather than being so focused on selfish endeavors. You will transform in a godly way and blessings will follow with a sincere heart. Love you all.

DAY 6

> Let someone else praise you, and not your own mouth; an outsider, and not your own lips.
>
> PROVERBS 27:2

HELLO FAMILY: Yes indeed, eat humble pie for breakfast every morning. The "pride comes before every fall" warning comes with every boast we hear. Why do we think these scriptures are written like this? Why not be excited and boastful about our talents and successes? Simply put, it may really irritate people when a person walks around bragging about themselves. Speaking from personal experience, talking smack can get the juices flowing big time. It is all fun and games at first. When it is not contained, it can cause a punch in the chops. We all are good at something. Some of us many things, yet really horrible at other things. What is really special is when we use our God-given talents to bring joy to others and we are told how good they are, fully knowing we are not that great but we took the time to do our best and joy resulted for all involved. That is the magic of working together in the family of Christ. That's the power of God's love. Love you all.

DAY 7

"I have the right to do anything," you say—but not everything is beneficial. "I have the right to do anything"— but I will not be mastered by anything.

1 CORINTHIANS 6:12

HELLO FAMILY: We have "the right to do anything," so do things that cause no harm, especially to ourselves or anyone else. Do good for yourself and others. Love God. Read about Him. Learn about Him through the scriptures, prayer, and communications daily. Why? Because we have the right to choose to do these things. Chances are if we do not, we may be without a solid foundation to deal with the temptations of this world, and there are many. Live a life standing for something and not falling for everything this world comes up with. Love you all.

DAY 8

My son, do not despise the LORD's discipline, and do not resent his rebuke, [12] because the LORD disciplines those he loves, as a father the son he delights in.

PROVERBS 3:11–12

HELLO FAMILY: Well, well, well my children (and we have all been children). We all have fond memories of some fatherly discipline. All of us who have had a father remember a moment in time when he came down hard on you out of love. Yep kids, it hurt me more to do and say some things, fully knowing it was going to really shake up your world in that moment, but it was all done out of **love**. Discipline from God may come from a back injury or a torn hernia to humble our pride enough to get us out of the weight room and back into church. God has a way of getting our attention, just like our parents did and do. Our Father has control over such measures in our lives. I am blessed for having a Father who knows me well enough to know what is best to bring me joy, even when some discipline is in order. Love you all.

DAY 9

Therefore, there is now no condemnation for those who are in Christ Jesus, [2] because through Christ Jesus the law of the Spirit who gives life has set you free from the law of sin and death. [3] For what the law was powerless to do because it was weakened by the flesh, God did by sending his own Son in the likeness of sinful flesh to be a sin offering. And so he condemned sin in the flesh, [4] in order that the righteous requirement of the law might be fully met in us, who do not live according to the flesh but according to the Spirit.

ROMANS 8:1-4

HELLO FAMILY: We hear this term, "being saved." Accepting and receiving Jesus as your Lord and Savior. This scripture explains how and why. The law refers to the rules by which the different religions burden the populace under their control. Jesus walked among us in the flesh to demonstrate how to beat the system(s) of these rules, to simplify a relationship with God and make it real — to get personal and to have a relationship with God the Father, through our Lord Jesus Christ. When we truly understand this, we will see Christmas in a whole new light — celebrating Christ's birth makes for a merry Christmas, indeed. Love you all.

DAY 10

*Trouble and distress have come upon me,
but your commands give me delight.*

PSALM 119:143

HELLO FAMILY: Our Bibles reference many godly men and women who dealt with major distresses throughout their lives. This is a calling to reassure us all that life is full of great challenges, but we should never despair. Always stop, take a knee, say a prayer, and keep marching in good faith when storms surprise your walk. Everything that happens to the children of God happens for a reason: to greater glorify the God we serve. The blessings will come. We are promised by God. Do not ever despair. Love you all.

DAY 11

Jesus replied: "Love the Lord your God with all your heart and with all your soul and with all your mind." [38] This is the first and greatest commandment. [39] And the second is like it: "Love your neighbor as yourself." [40] All the Law and the Prophets hang on these two commandments.

MATTHEW 22:37-40

HELLO FAMILY: The act of "love the Lord your God" is shown with **time**. Time in **prayer** (talk to Him), **scripture reading** (take the time to read His advice), and **worship**. To receive the joy of fellowship and be a witness to the miracles of others and their experience receiving grace. So, you ask, "What is love and how do you do it?" As Christ did. He came to earth to spend time with us and to show us the way. Christ came with words of encouragement to motivate us and give us hope in our faith. Christ served humanity in person with many healing miracles, to glorify God with a simple physical touch. Then, Christ gave His final gift: His life for our salvation, the forgiveness of sins. Love you all!

DAY 12

An honest answer is like a kiss on the lips.

PROVERBS 24: 26

HELLO FAMILY: Makes me think of our former president Donald Trump. America was desperate for a straight-talking, straight-answering president and Trump took America by storm. This scripture validates the sweetness of being honest. Speaking truthfully and directly, speaking with compassion and love builds your relationships to a whole new level. Having a reputation within the family of being honest and truthful is vital to the trust between each other and will bring joy even in times of struggle, working through the challenges of life. Love you all.

DAY 13

For the love of money is a root of all kinds of evil. Some people, eager for money, have wandered from the faith and pierced themselves with many griefs. [11] But you, man of God, flee from all this, and pursue righteousness, godliness, faith, love, endurance and gentleness.

1 TIMOTHY 6:10-11

HELLO FAMILY: Recognize that when money is worshiped, it can quickly take the place of the priority of prayer, scripture, and worship. Here are warnings to us all to flee from this! Stay humble, keeping the faith and the use of money to love one another. This allows God's blessings to flow through you to others as guided by the tug of the Holy Spirit. Recognize that joy comes through love and service to others. Let the love of God rule your life. Let the love of money go and be a "man of God" who trusts in the Lord our God. Love you all.

DAY 14

Surely the righteous will never be shaken; they will be remembered forever. [7] They will have no fear of bad news; their hearts are steadfast, trusting in the LORD.

PSALM 112:6-7

HELLO FAMILY: "No fear," or as my mom says, "No worries." My son-in-law Damian says, "No stress, Dan." Fully understand what it means to be God's children and who God the Father is. We are reading about God, who is way more powerful and capable than anything we can imagine — even Aquaman! No matter what happens, you can keep calm and know that you are serving a purpose every waking moment of your life. That purpose is to glorify God as His child. So do it with honor and be calm. Serve God and live joyfully. Even with the frightening news of unfortunate events in the world, keep your cool, remain joyful, and remember the might of the God we serve. As the future unfolds before us all, listen to the guidance of the Holy Spirit. He advises us each step of the way, lighting our paths. Love you all.

50-CENT BONUS

My daughter, Lynn, nearly brought me to tears this morning. She said, "This is the window where the children wave goodbye." We had just taken my granddaughter, Leonie, to her new preschool. The little children line up along the window to wave as their parents depart for a few hours. This reminded me of a lesson in our Sunday school book written by Max Lucado. It references this same goodbye, of a parent's difficulty leaving the child in school for the first time and the deep struggle of leaving your child with strangers (to the children, for sure). Even after the first time, it is still hard and will always be, even as we all grow up. This experience shared by us all is love — real, sincere LOVE. This pain of separation also occurs when we separate ourselves from God our Father. Then as time passes, we return, and the little smiles await in the window. The waves begin and then there are tears of joy, and hugs and kisses for a child back in the arms of their "Father," their guardian. It is written that we are created in the likeness of God. Know this when you engage in your prayer and your communications with our Lord Jesus. Our Lord also feels the same great joy with our smiles and eagerness in sharing our "day in preschool." What amazing joy we share loving each other in this way. What an amazing experience to live being loved. Blessings, kisses, and hugs for such a wonderful week. AND we will all be together in Christ. In His time. For eternity. The best joy ever, together. Love you all.

December 2018: My daughters Kim *(above)* and Lynn *(right)* out and about enjoying the blessings of being together during the Christmas season.

December 2018: Some of the best times are with both my daughters, just us. I was running around town, shopping, of course. My girls will appreciate that comment. I love them so.

DAILY DEVOTIONALS | 15

DAY 15

This is how we know what love is: Jesus Christ laid down his life for us. And we ought to lay down our lives for our brothers and sisters. [17] If anyone has material possessions and sees a brother or sister in need but has no pity on them, how can the love of God be in that person? [18] Dear children, let us not love with words or speech but with actions and in truth.

1 JOHN 3:16–18

HELLO FAMILY: "With actions and in truth." Let everything about ourselves be spoken by all those around us, in our actions, and with our honor. As a member of the family of God, our legacy is about our actions, our truth, and how we live our lives. What will your family, friends, and community say about you? It won't be what you said to them. It will reflect directly on how you treated them all. This loyalty, integrity, and distinction will bring great glory to God as it has with many of the men and women who serve around us. Tim Tebow comes to mind as I recall his successes in college, boldly wearing John 3:16 under his eyes and other Bible verses as he played. He continues to be a prime example of a godly man to this day. Love you all.

DAY 16

I will extol the LORD at all times;
his praise will always be on my lips.

PSALM 34:1

HELLO FAMILY: Well, look at today's scripture — it rings of today's challenges in a troubled world. Yet we are called upon, "at all times," to glorify God. Even when unfortunate circumstances happen, praise the Lord. For God is in control always and knows the gifts He has blessed all of us and our family with. As we have been reading, brothers and sisters, God only commands that we love one another. With actions of love, we move through the challenges of life, all the while praising God with our lips. As I type this message, I am a witness to this happening in our family, and in confidence, I raise my hands in praise to our Savior Jesus! Love you all.

DAY 17

The fear of the LORD is a fountain of life,
turning a person from the snares of death.

PROVERBS 14:27

HELLO FAMILY: "The fountain of life." I am surrounded in my work by the most honorable men of the Special Forces community, whom I am blessed to have served and continue to serve with still in the communities from which we came. These men with whom I have lived, survived, and worked for decades, endured both hardships and triumphs in life. In our fifties now, we are in a situation to find that Fountain of Youth. Where the same rush of power, speed, and wit carried us through great victories and battles, we watch this new generation of our Special Operations men and women boldly defending our great nation. We all have and continue to feature a common thread—to conquer **fear**! As followers of Christ, we are challenged not to fear the spiritual battle that rages in every soul. Do not fear the call of our Lord Jesus, who offers us a sanctuary with the same "rush" of power found in a relationship serving in the Army of God. So many of our very close comrades have suffered. Some have even taken their own lives. We do call out to fear as a cause, perhaps fear of not being able to control the future. I ask us all to call out to Christ and invite the divine intervention of God to defeat the tribulations, the rages of war, and the challenges of relationships before us, whatever they may be. It is a choice to receive Christ and "join" the Army of God (just as is done when many volunteer to serve in our country's most demanding and dangerous jobs), serving Christ as your Commander. All mankind is free to choose everlasting life. Love you all.

DAY 18

Therefore I want the men everywhere to pray,
lifting up holy hands without anger or disputing.

1 TIMOTHY 2:8

HELLO FAMILY: "Therefore I want the men everywhere...." In other words, be comfortable in your own skin and praise God openly (hands up) for everlasting life. My pastor references this theme on many occasions when there seems to be a sense of sleepiness during a great and powerful sermon. "Can I hear an AMEN?" he calls out in a loving way. For surely in church we can take action on this scripture. In the presence of our brothers and sisters gathered together in worship, raise our hands in prayer. This scripture calls upon your motivation and confidence to exercise your enthusiasm in faith and joy openly. Lift our hands to the sky without fear and praise to our Lord in prayer, in good times and bad, as we are called upon to do. Then go forth and love one another, as taught by Jesus. Love you all.

DAY 19

The LORD watches over the foreigner and sustains the fatherless and the widow, but he frustrates the ways of the wicked.

PSALM 146:9

HELLO FAMILY: "Frustrates the ways of the wicked." After watching Aquaman and seeing how he was constantly frustrated by his attacker, I cannot imagine having God the Almighty being the source of the frustration. Yet we see examples of personalities in the daily news, our workplaces, and even in our churches of people in a state of constant frustration. These frustrations are not coming from God at all. These examples are clearly present for us all to observe at every level of society as a need to follow the teachings of Christ and repent from allowing ourselves to become frustrated. From our local communities to national politics, tabloids, and social media notifications we have delivered to our phones. The choice to avoid frustration is made by the one who reads and understands this scripture. God has preserved a manual that has survived thousands of years: our BIBLE. The Basic Instructions Before Leaving Earth. Read it and stop getting frustrated about things over which you have no control. Love you all.

DAY 20

"You have heard that it was said, 'Love your neighbor and hate your enemy.' [44] But I tell you, love your enemies and pray for those who persecute you,"

MATTHEW 5:43-44

HELLO FAMILY: This is a call to battle. This commander's intent is a great challenge for many. What earthly commander would call upon the greatest, strongest, and most battle-hardened units under his control to do the opposite and not totally beat and defeat the enemy? Some folks out there have cruelly gone to great efforts to hurt members of my family, and the shocker is they are family themselves! Can you imagine? Of course you can. In our families, the battles rage for a multitude of reasons I don't even need to list. Our words are the harshest for those with whom we are closest. Family, friends, and neighbors receive the wrath of our selfishness and toil. I found it easier to just go off by myself and avoid human contact altogether, in an attempt to avoid an angry outburst directed at anyone who enters my line of fire. This is not healthy at all. Our Lord calls upon us not to build this fire inside of our minds, our emotions, or our quests to even the score. Or far worse, to do more harm. We are called by our faith to be forgiving soldiers in the Army of God. This scripture goes even further. We are to love our enemies. I am learning as of late, as you grow in your faith, you will not fear the enemy. You will bring joy to the lives that cross your path. Peace will fill your day as you call upon the Holy Spirit to light your way. Love you all.

DAY 21

One person gives freely, yet gains even more; another withholds unduly, but comes to poverty. [25] A generous person will prosper; whoever refreshes others will be refreshed.

PROVERBS 11:24-25

HELLO FAMILY: Back to trust in God. Prosperity is the American dream. Many risk it all to breach her borders. They will pay outlandish prices to make it to America to potentially live in financial greatness. Coming from a background of financial struggles, it was out of the question for me to give money away to anyone else. Being stingy was a way of life, so to speak. Making ends meet, putting food on the table and gas in the car can be stressful to the provider of the family. It can and will take a toll on many fathers, as it did on me. There came a point in my faith that I was at rope's end, in tears, trying to figure out how to manage it all. Not only financially with all the bills, but to prosper in my family relationships as well. Finally, it got so bad that I just broke down and went to my knees. There came a point that I just gave in and I tithed. I started following these three pillars: Prayer, scripture reading, and going to church each Sunday. I didn't really have a clue, but there I was in the experience of a lifetime that was starting to unfold and not even realizing it. God was in control. Fact is, I could only control my behavior. Opportunities began to open, and I grew in my career in ways that I could have never imagined. I am a witness and, in this devotion, I declare that I am "refreshed." Love you all.

DAY 22

For he has rescued us from the dominion of darkness and brought us into the kingdom of the Son he loves, [14] in whom we have redemption, the forgiveness of sins.

COLOSSIANS 1:13-14

HELLO FAMILY: "Forgiveness of sins." Accepting Christ as your personal Lord and Savior is a must. For one to be adopted into the Kingdom, the inheritance of God's grace is in this forgiveness. Christ will be your advocate and your lawyer before God on Judgment Day. Your sins are covered by the great and final sacrifice of Jesus, the Son of God. Love you all.

DAY 23

Though I walk in the midst of trouble, you preserve my life.
You stretch out your hand against the anger of my foes;
with your right hand you save me.

PSALM 138:7

HELLO FAMILY: "You save me." Well, from personal experience, this scripture rings loud and clear early in my faith as a soldier during the first Gulf War, as well as during my time as a member of the Special Forces detachment ODA 525. We may all survive the anger of our foes at some point in our lives; we just never may realize when God stepped in to save us. Perhaps work related or not, whether it was a traffic jam that slowed you down enough so you would avoid a massive vehicle accident, you just never know. What you must know as a person who has accepted Christ as your savior is that God is in charge, and He has you securely in His hand. God has a purpose for you living here. We are to be joyful as children of God and to be Disciples in sharing where our joy comes from: a personal relationship with Christ. Our family agreed to pray together the Lord's Prayer at high noon, every day, wherever we may be. Being away now on a work trip, knowing my wife and family are praying together is a precious moment to share together. Maybe other families can do this, too. Love you all.

DAY 24

Praise be to the God and Father of our Lord Jesus Christ!
In his great mercy he has given us new birth into a living hope
through the resurrection of Jesus Christ from the dead.

1 PETER 1:3

HELLO FAMILY: "He has given us new birth into a living hope…" The key word here is "living." Know that hope never dies when you are in Christ. As your daily struggles and challenges confront you, call on the living Lord Jesus Christ to make good fortunes to come from these challenges. Your confident faith in Christ and the Holy Spirit to respond to your prayers for assistance will make you a witness. A witness to share to all who will listen. Love you all.

DAY 25

An honest witness does not deceive,
but a false witness pours out lies.

PROVERBS 14:5

HELLO FAMILY: A trained ear will hear a pause to answer when the question is sent. This pause is the potential creation of a not-so-true response, and yes, even an outright lie. Parents have this trained ear—I assure you—and the body language that follows is quite amusing, too. As adults, do we not understand that God our Father has the same trained view of our souls, our hearts, and our sincerity? Best to be wise and honest with ourselves. The person we view daily in the mirror is exactly who God observes. Take a good look at your reflection and review your faith in Christ, who loves you dearly. Love you all.

50-CENT BONUS

"Does not deceive." This can be applied to Donald Trump's "Fake News" accusations. The fact is today reporters have been busted out big time. Honesty is about telling the story as it is and not choosing to tell just one side of the story. Allow the recipient of the witnessed reported account to decide. People pick up on those who are dishonest, especially when someone or the media is reporting on a story every single day. How we "speak" or "witness" situations establishes our lasting credibility in our relationships with the very people we are with on a daily basis. Our Bible teaches us to build a character of honesty and integrity. Say what you mean and mean what you say. The wise see through these lies and twists of words, just as our Lord does. Love you all.

DAY 26

For everything God created is good, and nothing is to be
rejected if it is received with thanksgiving, [5] because it is
consecrated by the word of God and prayer.

1 TIMOTHY 4:4-5

HELLO FAMILY: The Bible starts in the first chapter of Genesis with God's creation: the world as we know it, which includes us. The emphasis is that God's creation is "good." No need for any changes, special paint jobs, modifications, remodeling, etc. Relax, it is good. Early in this chapter we are warned of "later times" and the secular world of humanity moving the mark, the standards surrounding what is "good." We now have people making major modifications to their bodies, even to their gender. We have a "climate change" generation recognizing that what God created as good is in conflict with our human desires for electricity, Google, and fast cars. This scripture affirms God's blessings of all things created by God, including "us." With pure and sincere hearts, we pray as God's children, to receive blessings from each other and for each other, "in thanksgiving." Love you all.

DAY 27

*The righteous person may have many troubles,
but the LORD delivers him from them all.*

PSALM 34:19

HELLO FAMILY: Wow, this is a great follow up: "but the LORD delivers him from them all." In a nutshell, we can't help ourselves from ourselves. God knows we are human. We get caught up in the snares of temptation, greed, and of fleshly desires. This can stress us to no end. There isn't enough time, money, or friends to put out the fires all around us. This is why He sent His son, Jesus, to show us the way, to teach us how to accept ourselves as we are—no modifications needed. Believe that God will deliver us all, no matter what we get ourselves into. Love you all.

DAY 28

*"Therefore I tell you, do not worry about your life, what you
will eat or drink; or about your body, what you will wear.
Is not life more than food, and the body more than clothes?
[26] Look at the birds of the air; they do not sow or reap or store
away in barns, and yet your heavenly Father feeds them.
Are you not much more valuable than they?"*

MATTHEW 6:25-26

HELLO FAMILY: The secular world has created your worth based on a set of monetary values. What you wear, what you eat, what you drink, your home ZIP code, the car you drive, the credit cards you carry, the tattoos you display, the phone you have, and we could go on and on. These false forms of worth are stressed upon us every waking moment. No escape from social media, movies, commercials, music lyrics, and more. But what really matter in the end are your spiritual values—your faith, beliefs, and actions therein. Where is your heart? Faith in Christ frees you from the chains stressing you to keep up with the social status of our secular culture. Free yourself and your heart. Relax and experience a relationship with Christ, His unconditional love. Get your family on board and reignite relationships with your spouse, family, and true friends. Your spiritual family awaits you at church. Love you all.

DAY 29

A hot-tempered person stirs up conflict,
but the one who is patient calms a quarrel.

PROVERBS 15:18

HELLO FAMILY: I am guilty! This one speaks of siphoning the joy from the limited time we have with loved ones, especially family. A heated argument at the dinner table or during an extended family event could even spoil Christmas morning for the whole family, kids and all. Nobody experiences joy when a hothead is being grumpy and demanding. Keeping your calm is the key to good mental and physical health for all of your relationships, which will give you joy in the long run. A relationship with Christ trains your thoughts to recognize these trigger points of anger, enabling you to find a solution before it is an issue. Recognizing, identifying the problems in your heart is the first step in knowing what to pray for. So ask for help and call on the Holy Spirit to fill your day with the light of Christ. Love you all.

DAY 30

For sin shall no longer be your master, because you
are not under the law, but under grace.

ROMANS 6:14

HELLO FAMILY: "Not under the law, but under grace." When we really get the concept of a relationship with Christ, we recognize there are no conditions, no requirements, and no tests to pass. Your decision to accept Jesus Christ as your Lord and Savior grants you the adoption papers and inheritance from God, unconditionally. You are "in the will." Your heart, conscience, actions, speech, and relationships with loved ones will change. Joy comes from service to others, making their day. You are no longer living your life by the law of the land, rather, by the joy in a relationship with Jesus who will guide your every moment. Love you all.

DAY 31

You will go out in joy and be led forth in peace; the mountains and hills will burst into song before you, and all the trees of the field will clap their hands.

ISAIAH 55:12

HELLO FAMILY: "You will go out in joy." We see "joy" mentioned again. So, define joy in your life. Joy is not defined as being frustrated to the point of cursing, hating the driver in front of you, or being miserable to loved ones for whatever reason. **JOY** is letting it go, not being upset. Forgiving others instantly. Calmly managing the challenges set before you with confidence, fully knowing that when you call upon our Lord, He is there. A peace of mind knowing that God will always meet your needs. The confidence that Jesus is there with the Holy Spirit to light your way. We should always pray for wisdom and discernment to guide our decisions. Love you all.

DAY 32

It was good for me to be afflicted so that I might learn your decrees.

PSALM 119:71

HELLO FAMILY: "It was good for me." Pain, afflictions, and troubles always get our immediate attention. Pain will put you in bed for days on end. Like pain from a parachute accident or a car crash. The list goes on. These are and were the times that I was stopped in my tracks and decided to pick up the Bible and read it from cover to cover, somewhat out of boredom in the early days, I must confess. And look at me now. Our Lord and Savior has a plan for each of us who has confessed Jesus as our Lord and Savior. Being that I am a stubborn mess at times, selfish and not always a good listener, my Father has to get my attention and guide me by the tug of an ear—sometimes both ears. (My grandkids get that treatment at times, all in love). Know once again that God is in control and has the Holy Spirit lighting your path at every moment. We just have to open our eyes and let the light shine in. Love you all.

DAY 33

God did this so that, by two unchangeable things in which it is impossible for God to lie, we who have fled to take hold of the hope set before us may be greatly encouraged. [19] We have this hope as an anchor of the soul, firm and secure. It enters the inner sanctuary behind the curtain,

HEBREWS 6:18-19

HELLO FAMILY: "It is impossible for God to lie." As we all grow older, we sometimes question whether our parents were being entirely truthful. When I would question my parents (my job as the oldest son of five), I would often get the response, "Because I said so." It is funny how now, reading the Bible as my Father's words test my soul, I hear this again and again–"Because I said so." God provides us guidance and direction for our own good–to bring true joy into our lives. Trusting in His direction gives us a hope to cling to when we find ourselves struggling on His unique path for us. With His guidance, we can find light in those struggles and joy only He can provide, because He said so. Love you all.

DAY 34

"Truly I tell you, anyone who will not receive the kingdom of God like a little child will never enter it." [16] And he took the children in his arms, placed his hands on them and blessed them.

MARK 10:15-16

HELLO FAMILY: "Like little children." As youth, we were free spirits. No worries, no stress, no knowledge of the future or worldly issues. Mom and Dad had it all under control. As adults, we are challenged in our faith to trust God, just like when we were children trusting our parents. When my parents answered a question, it was because they said so and there were no further questions. When we study God's Word, it is that way also, because God said so. Pause and look at children, their innocence, their excitement for life, and their vulnerabilities. Children basically believe what they are told. Jesus spoke these words with authority, be open to the scriptures you read, like a child and allow the child in you to accept His teachings. Love you all.

DAY 35

Guide me in your truth and teach me, for you are God my Savior, and my hope is in you all day long.

PSALM 25:5

HELLO FAMILY: "Teach me...my hope is in you all day long." If there is a teacher, then there is a student. The students have their homework, they are tested, graded, and they are rewarded, or not. What kind of students are we? What grades do we hope for? Jesus gives us strength, willpower, and **hope** for every day. Like children in school, parents encourage their kids to be good students and get great grades. We "hope" our families are getting good grades too, maybe even scholarships at the University of Christ. Love you all.

DAY 36

Do nothing out of selfish ambition or vain conceit. Rather, in humility value others above yourselves, [4] not looking to your own interests but each of you to the interests of the others.

PHILIPPIANS 2:3-4

HELLO FAMILY: "Selfish ambitions." This is a hard one. I have been guilty of being very selfish in many ways over the years. Many times in my bursts of anger and frustrations, the word "I" would be involved. I was offended and often ended up lashing out at the people I loved most. We need Christ to remind ourselves daily not to be like this. To not lash out with words that discredit our faith in Jesus. Jesus was never selfish. Jesus gave His life for all of us. This scripture is about looking out for others and their interests, what is good for them. It applies to relationships, whether they are established or not. It all comes down to motives—what is in it for us? When our own interests come into mind first, know to pause for prayer and ask yourself, "What would Jesus do?" Love you all.

DAY 37

So this is what the Sovereign LORD says: "See, I lay a stone in Zion, a tested stone, a precious cornerstone for a sure foundation; the one who relies on it will never be stricken with panic."

ISAIAH 28:16

HELLO FAMILY: "Panic"? Do you know if you have experienced panic? In much of our military training, panic is a situation instructors attempt to put you in to test you. Like having your hands tied behind your back and your ankles tied together and told to jump into a ten-foot-deep pool. There are many experiences in our lives that can create a stress level that can push you beyond thinking clearly and making very unwise decisions. We all need a "precious cornerstone." We want to build our lives on beliefs and values that have been proven to last a lifetime. Like a brick mason who looks for the perfect corner brick to begin his mastery, we are all called to Jesus. We build our lives on the teachings of Christ so we can live fearlessly and prosper. Prayer, scripture, and worship are the pillars of the wise. Find that cornerstone and start building. Love you all.

DAY 38

For in this hope we were saved. But hope that is seen is no hope at all. Who hopes for what they already have? [25] But if we hope for what we do not yet have, we wait for it patiently.

ROMANS 8:24–25

HELLO FAMILY: "We wait for it patiently." I see a little humor here, because I know of children who have no patience. That's me I am talking about. Jesus said to enter the Kingdom as a child. A big part of this scripture is rooted in having faith—having the faith to be wise enough to know what to hope for and having the faith to know that it will happen in God's time and not ours. This is the key to a joyful life. All I can say is that I hoped one day to have a nice place to entertain my family. Fishing for Shane, hunting for Blake, camping for Kim, and a kitchen for Lynn. It came in God's time and what a blessing it is. Love you all.

DAY 39

> ...*Being strengthened with all power according to his glorious might so that you may have great endurance and patience, [12] and giving joyful thanks to the Father, who has qualified you to share in the inheritance of his holy people in the kingdom of light.*
>
> COLOSSIANS 1:11-12

HELLO FAMILY: "Inheritance of his holy people in the kingdom of light." Inheritance and Kingdom of Light! Look at this now—have you ever really been in the dark? Real darkness will strike panic in your life. Now imagine that darkness for eternity. As a member of a family, you may find yourself working through all kinds of challenges, even adoption. The adoption process will bring a family through great sacrifices and tests of patience. There will be emotional highs and deep lows during this time. By accepting Jesus, the Son of God, as our Lord and Savior, we are in fact adopted by God the Father. There is a process to everlasting life. There was a huge price to pay for this adoption: Christ. Just as there is a huge price ($$$) in the adoption process today to be legally brought into a family. What a blessing it is to have the Father adopt us, so we too can enjoy eternity in the Kingdom of Light. Light being truth, love, and fulfillment in knowing that you are cared for by the Creator, for eternity. Love you all.

DAY 40

> *Fight the good fight of the faith. Take hold of the eternal life to which you were called when you made your good confession in the presence of many witnesses.*
>
> 1 TIMOTHY 6:12

HELLO FAMILY: "When you made your good confession in the presence of many witnesses." This is a public declaration that you have accepted Jesus as your Lord and Savior. When a person at church accepts Jesus as their Lord, it is the most moving moment many of us know. Our Pastor declares that the angels in Heaven are cheering loudly as another soul is saved. If you look around at the church members present in the congregation, there is not a dry eye. This celebration is then followed by a baptism in the near future if not during that particular service. The fight comes when you have to make Christ a joyful priority in your life, making the time to pray, read God's Word, and stay in the good fight of the faith. Harness the Holy Spirit. It was the Holy Spirit that moved you to publicly announce your acceptance of Jesus as your Lord. Prayer, scripture, and worship is the battle to be won. Love you all.

DAY 41

The fear of the LORD is the beginning of knowledge, but fools despise wisdom and instruction.

PROVERBS 1:7

HELLO FAMILY: "Despise wisdom and knowledge." You must pray for wisdom in order to make sound decisions for you and your family. You must learn about our Creator. Jesus is the path to a joy-filled eternity. You gain knowledge of that in seeking instruction from God's Word, the Bible. Fear can be taken out of context here. It is not a *panic* state of fear. It is a *reverence* of knowing the greatness of God and who He is. The **I Am**. The one who holds our souls in the highest regard. We are God's creation along with the earth we live on. Respect this totally and follow His commands. Love you all.

DAY 42

You will be enriched in every way so that you can be generous on every occasion, and through us your generosity will result in thanksgiving to God. [12] This service that you perform is not only supplying the needs of the Lord's people but is also overflowing in many expressions of thanks to God.

2 CORINTHIANS 9:11–12

HELLO FAMILY: "Generosity." Giving to charities, tithing at the church, helping your neighbor…the list goes on. When God blesses you, the blessing should pass through you and not stop. The Dead Sea is so named because water (life) flows into it and stops "dead." There is no outlet for the Dead Sea. Think about your blessings and keep them flowing. There are too many examples of people who have done exceptionally well with God's blessings but didn't do anything with them. People are depressed with millions of dollars in their bank accounts. They spend time and money on doctors to medicate them and listen to their problems. Still then, there are those who take their own lives in despair and depression, who were unable to find true joy in their lives. A consistently growing relationship with Christ will bring joy, and He will comfort us in our times of need. Generosity is one of the many blessings that will help keep our joy flowing. Love you all.

DAY 43

"Have I not commanded you? Be strong and courageous. Do not be afraid; do not be discouraged, for the LORD your God will be with you wherever you go."

JOSHUA 1:9

HELLO FAMILY: How many dads would like to tell their kids, "I will be with you wherever you go"? How comforting is that for a child going off to a school full of a bunch of bullies. Dads can't be everywhere, but our Lord is. Be bold and pray with a sincere heart. This past year, month, week, day, hour, minute, or second when you called out to God in prayer, He was there every time! He is still there today, waiting and listening. Stop a moment and recall your answered prayers. Be courageous and continue your lives in prayer. Read the Bible and worship our Lord Jesus. Just remember, your "Dad" likes to hear from you when there are no emergencies too. Love you all.

DAY 44

Do you not know? Have you not heard? The LORD is the everlasting God, the Creator of the ends of the earth. He will not grow tired or weary, and his understanding no one can fathom. [29] He gives strength to the weary and increases the power of the weak. [30] Even youths grow tired and weary, and young men stumble and fall; [31] but those who hope in the LORD will renew their strength. They will soar on wings like eagles; they will run and not grow weary, they will walk and not be faint.

ISAIAH 40:28-31

HELLO FAMILY: "Increases the power of the weak." Yes, when we do wear down, we need time to heal. Know that your faith will strengthen you. Be joyful **always**! Your faith in Jesus will give you strength through all the challenges that enter your days. "His understanding no one can fathom." Many times as kids in the back of the car, my siblings and I would ask "why" questions, wearing down the patience of my parents. The tone in my dad's voice warned of a potential detour to the side of the road to remind us (and our behinds) about how to behave in the car. We will never be able to "fathom" all the ways of our Lord in getting His point across to us. This is where faith comes in, understanding the patient strength of God. Like a child we are to follow the guidance of our Lord. Why? Because He said so. Pray for wisdom always and make wise choices in life. Know that the wise can get very irritated when time is wasted but are also patient and forgiving in their ways. Don't waste yours. Read and study the word of God. Love you all.

DAY 45

To him who is able to keep you from stumbling and to present you before his glorious presence without fault and with great joy— [25] to the only God our Savior be glory, majesty, power and authority, through Jesus Christ our Lord, before all ages, now and forevermore! Amen.

JUDE 1:24-25

HELLO FAMILY: "To Him." We have all kinds of blessings, so many (you were all born American citizens, for one) that it's easy to fall into the trap thinking we earned it or are entitled to these blessings. Always remember, it is your faith in Jesus Christ. That voice of the Holy Spirit, guiding your efforts and controlling your tongue. This is building the character you have as young, righteous men and women of a family unit. A family that reads scripture, prays together, and worships Christ is a family that will limit their stumbling. Have a blessed day, y'all, and don't forget about our daily Lord's Prayer at noon. Love you all.

May 2017: A picture of faith, a public announcement to all who see it. A declaration of sorts for a wavering soul that was finally able to stand on the Promises of God.

DAY 46

Preach the word; be prepared in season and out of season; correct, rebuke and encourage—with great patience and careful instruction. [3] For the time will come when people will not put up with sound doctrine. Instead, to suit their own desires, they will gather around them a great number of teachers to say what their itching ears want to hear.

2 TIMOTHY 4:2-3

HELLO FAMILY: "With great patience, and careful instruction." This speaks of a careful choice of words in any relationship, especially when speaking about the word of God or when teaching others about Jesus. This entire scripture speaks of an upcoming point in time marked by cold relationships; emotionless, selfish accommodations; and a lack of love. Sometimes there are environments hostile to God's Word. We are already witnessing, as Americans, the bitter hatred in our country when Christian values and ideals are openly spoken. So many are fixed on the hate that dwells from hell itself, they get absolutely upset hearing anything remotely supporting Christianity. As our families grow closer in the love of Christ, pause and recognize the joy that is shared for each other. Recognize what the warmth of family company brings to the moment—a filling of any void of loneliness or insecurity. In a time where sound doctrine, or *logic* as I like to say, spins the news cycle, pitting Americans against each other, enjoy this experience with Christ and His teachings regarding the family. Keep those false worldly ways and teachings of what "itchy ears" want to hear out of your lives. Love you all.

50-CENT BONUS

As I have mentioned early in the book, when you surrender to Christ and accept Him as your Lord, tests follow to determine how fast you shall be fed. When fed too quickly, babies can choke and get seriously hurt. I believe the same applies when growing spiritually. As we grow, our parents lead us along, based on how well each of us receives a lesson or two. We are not just dropped into the deep end of the pool with a pair of scuba tanks on our backs and expected to be experts in scuba skills. First, let's just see if the kid likes water. Being saved doesn't necessarily mean you are going to be a preacher, Sunday school teacher, or youth leader next week. You may like driving trucks, playing ball, cooking, or cleaning up. There are all kinds of ways to serve, and God knows your place way ahead of time. Like any parent, God wants our joyful service and support in helping the family get along. So, for the record, I was that little boy in the highchair who shoved just about everything I was being fed onto the floor. At times, I would spit the food into my hand and wait for my parents to turn away just long enough for me to feed the puppy at my feet. That was me—I was never in danger of choking on the food, but I sure didn't take any joy in getting fed. It took some time before I figured out that there was dessert after a good meal.

DAY 47

Therefore encourage one another and build each other up, just as in fact you are doing.

1 THESSALONIANS 5:11

HELLO FAMILY: "Encourage one another." Love with your words. Building joy and hope in one another creates excitement, gives hope for the future, and crushes depression. The excitement of getting up with a purpose to help others brings great blessings to all involved. One derives *encouragement* from the knowledge that help is on the way, and that encouragement falls into Dr. Gary Chapman's love language known as "Words of Affirmation." Always be encouraging in your dialogue with others. Ask, "What can I do to make this situation better?" It will even uplift those in listening range. Every relationship is lifted, and the blessings will surely come for all. Y'all have a super day! Love you all.

DAY 48

For God is the King of all the earth; sing to him a psalm of praise. [8] God reigns over the nations; God is seated on his holy throne. [9] The nobles of the nations assemble as the people of the God of Abraham, for the kings of the earth belong to God; he is greatly exalted.

PSALM 47:7–9

HELLO FAMILY: "For the kings of the earth belong to God." Oh, yes they do, and most of them don't realize it. It is by God that men are in their current positions and that we all are here to serve God. As it is written, God's hand is in the placement of our world's leaders. The leaders of war and conflict between nations. God's plan? I say yes, because the Bible tells me so. A thought to ponder. Serving as a Christian soldier in the Middle East, one can only imagine the spread of Christianity to an area where the mention of Jesus Christ as our Lord and Savior is totally against the law. God has a way to spread the good news and eternal hope of His Son, Jesus, to areas where God's Word is outlawed. We are so blessed to be in God's hand, as a child of God, through our Lord, Jesus. Love you all.

DAY 49

Instead of your shame you will receive a double portion, and instead of disgrace you will rejoice in your inheritance. And so you will inherit a double portion in your land, and everlasting joy will be yours.

ISAIAH 61:7

HELLO FAMILY: "Everlasting joy will be yours." The "inheritance." Ask yourself, "What brings me joy?" My dad told me yesterday how happy he gets when he hears about my youngest sister Mary and I out in the world together. Mary and I have traveled to visit family in Germany together. This brought him immense joy. When children share with their parents the plans they make with their siblings, parents grin from ear to ear, because family is about unity, coming together in support of one another. As brothers and sisters in Christ, in our church communities, we make plans together. Plans for baptisms, outreach programs, movie nights with the kids, and even camping trips, to name a few. Imagine God's smile as he gazes upon His children working together in peace and joy. In different chapters of our lives, different things bring us joy. So, take a moment to identify your joy button and move that mountain. In Christ all things are possible. Love you all.

DAY 50

If we are faithless, he remains faithful, for he cannot disown himself.

2 TIMOTHY 2:13

HELLO FAMILY: "Faithless." If one accepts Jesus as their Savior, can they be faithless? I dare say yes. Many of us accept Jesus as our Lord, **but** our faith is still as small as a mustard seed. Faith without works, effort, and devotion is not putting into practice "faith." So here we may be, in the family of Christ, not so joyful, and still caught up in the race of this world. At some point, we were moved by the Holy Spirit to receive Jesus into our hearts as our Lord and Savior—even baptized! Yet we have let the fire fizzle. Our Sundays are just another day to make money for someone else to spend. Fear not, our Lord does not disown us. When we received Christ, we became family for life, eternally. All we need to do is just come home. Love you all.

DAY 51

Since you are my rock and my fortress, for the sake of your name lead and guide me.

PSALM 31:3

HELLO FAMILY: "For the sake of your name lead, and guide me." In order to be led, you must surrender your path, your goals, and your wants to whatever or whomever is leading you. **This is hard!** We are inherently selfish, self-centered, and self-aware of our "likes." Just look at Facebook and other social media platforms. We want new cars, babies, puppies, shades, tractors with buckets, vanities, healthy kids, money for travel. We want our youth back, healthy joints, jobs, great evaluations, bonuses, and the list goes on. What is the answer? What is the sacrifice? Who gets stepped on, fussed at, or ignored in your quest to get what you want and have things your way? This scripture says to **stop** and follow Me (Christ)! Give Me a chance, what do you have to lose? Allow Christ to lead the way. By reading God's Word, your thoughts, decisions, and priorities will transition and peace will follow. Love you all.

DAY 52

"Greater love has no one than this: to lay down one's life for one's friends."

JOHN 15:13

HELLO FAMILY: This scripture is very fitting for those in the military who leave home, some never to return. This subject makes many emotional. As service members recall leaving home on many occasions, locking in the memory of their loved ones, their wives and children come to mind the most. Then there are the memories when fellow service members don't come home, and the family shows up at the unit, kids and all, asking about their dad or mom. And yet, today we still have men and women signing up of their own free will, fully knowing there is a distinct possibility that they will go to combat in a foreign hostile land far away. Who would sign up to go to battle? Who would sign up with the knowledge that they will experience absolute misery, pain, and starvation? That's just in the training. Then full mental and physical combat, with repeated deployments to places of potential misery? Then I think of Jesus, knowing the details of torture he would endure at the hands of mere mortals. This is the shocker I have trouble comprehending. Jesus has the nuclear option at any time. He is God, yet He gives His life as the final sacrifice for humanity. That's this scripture, y'all—it's the real deal. The ultimate act of service and sacrifice! Know that Jesus is Lord. Love you all.

DAY 53

He replied, "Because you have so little faith. Truly I tell you, if you have faith as small as a mustard seed, you can say to this mountain, 'Move from here to there,' and it will move. Nothing will be impossible for you."

MATTHEW 17:20

HELLO FAMILY: When we take time to stop and ponder, do we ever wonder what we want in life? Do we know what to pray for? Do we know where to move that mountain with our faith? What are the possibilities with our faith? We watch and think about a life that moves so fast and furious at times that there is no thought to prayer, worship, or taking time for God's scripture reading. A life with no self-reflection in a dog-eat-dog world can be empty. Those moments when we regain consciousness, we are planning our next chess move in this game of life. It can be a daily grind, spinning circles and reacting to crisis after crisis. Why not stop and take the time to pray about where your mountain should be moved? Remember that every day is a gift and it is up to us to choose to keep Christ front and center as we go through the day, looking to him for guidance in all we do. My mountain is the task getting all this on paper and making it a book for my children, grandchildren, and great-grandchildren to read every day. Now that's a mountain for me. You may not know this, but I graduated high school with a red circled 65 in English! With faith in Christ, all things are possible. Love you all.

DAY 54

The one whose walk is blameless is kept safe, but the one whose ways are perverse will fall into the pit.

PROVERBS 28:18

HELLO FAMILY: Well, the reward for being blameless is safety from the pit of doom. I recall the phrase "this is the pits" being used in my younger days. Back then you were doomed for using curse words, to put it lightly. So, other words or phrases of expression were used to publicly announce great dissatisfaction in situations that would upset the soul. This is one of those scriptures of wisdom. Simply put, do your best every waking moment to keep God in your thoughts and actions and be honest with yourself and others. When God is not in the forefront of our thoughts during decision making, a void is created. A void where the devil can work his way into a course of action pretty quickly. That's when the pit of doom gets a little bit bigger to trip into at some point or another. Keep the words "What would Jesus do" close to your heart. Love you all.

DAY 55

Share with the Lord's people who are in need. Practice hospitality.

ROMANS 12:13

HELLO FAMILY: Who are the "Lord's people"? The blessings of worship services with your church family opens your eyes to other believers and their own tribulations. This church body of people have been referred to by my pastor as our "spiritual family," otherwise known as the Lord's people. In many ways, being in church among our spiritual family allows us to learn about each other: the joys, the challenges, the victories, and the struggles. Life is lived together in prayer, worship, and study of God's Word. This family is very blessed. We are healthy and able and willing to be there for each other. We help others in our communities in hospitable ways, bills are secretly paid, and ramps are built at homes where sick family members are given easier access to get in and out. So many humbling actions by those willing to serve and to be neighborly. It occurs daily. Relationships in service to God with other Christians at church builds unity. Sharing our joys and pains, helping each other, celebrating with each other, and praising God for answered prayers becomes a way of life. You are not alone. Know that this is the key in God's plan for us: to experience joy here on earth, no matter what challenges come our way. Share and worship with the Lord's people. Love you all.

DAY 56

Defend the weak and the fatherless; uphold the cause of the poor and the oppressed.

PSALM 82:3

HELLO FAMILY: "To Free The Oppressed!" That is the motto of Special Forces. In Somalia working as a Special Forces medic, one of our taskings was to provide medical care to facilities that housed orphans. Full compounds of fatherless children were all around us. Many children were very sick and in need of immediate care. Caretakers were overwhelmed by the need for food and clean water to drink for themselves as well as the children. These children somehow were surviving on next to nothing. In the brief time we had, teams of American soldiers would bring food, water, and medical supplies. Myself and other Special Forces medics would set up treatment areas and get to work.

This scripture also describes many Americans right here at home. We see our homeless populations exploding in various states across our nation. How we approach those in distress is a test every time. Everyone needs to pray for wisdom in making strategic decisions regarding policies and allocations of limited resources. These scriptures do not say how these people ended up this way. It just says that they are there and we should defend them. They are everywhere. Love you all.

DAY 57

As for you, the anointing you received from him remains in you, and you do not need anyone to teach you. But as his anointing teaches you about all things and as that anointing is real, not counterfeit—just as it has taught you, remain in him.

1 JOHN 2:27

HELLO FAMILY: "And you do not need anyone to teach you." What? Jesus is the ultimate teacher? Read scripture and you will learn that you need no other. School is in session every waking moment while reading the history of the world followed in the Gospels. Through this study, prayer will take on a whole new meaning in our lives. We learn from our Teacher how to depend on God, with His thousands of promises. We learn to listen to the Spirit that lights our paths. Perhaps we can truly enjoy our waking up to a hot cup of coffee and a great Bible reading to boot. That's the excitement I really enjoy—having a Bible app surprise me each and every morning. What does God's Word have for us to learn today and pray for about tomorrow? Love you all!

DAY 58

The Lord is good to those whose hope is in him, to the one who seeks him;

LAMENTATIONS 3:25

HELLO FAMILY: God is good all the time. "Hope" for our future, hope to the "one who **seeks** him." So, get this and take action. To have **hope** for a joyous life and to **seek** the Lord for us and our families' futures, there needs to be repentance. Repentance is to "turn away from," or go in the opposite direction of sin, the things that hurt us. Sin hurts us and the loved ones around us. In seeking our Lord, we gain strength, we see light at the end of the tunnel of darkness; we attain hope for a future of joy through Christ and His strength. Jesus resisted temptations as an example of hope. It can be done! The Bible mentions shaking the sand off our sandals and walking away. It says that many of these sins can haunt us and our family for generations (grandparents, parents, children, grandchildren). We want godliness, joy, relationships with Jesus, and an immense sense of peace and truth in our daily lives. Get away from the entities (sins) that are hurting you, that make you sad and regretful, and seek Him. Turn to Christ, to the truth, to sanity, and to those who worship Him. To seek Christ is to pray, read God's Word to understand your path to joy, and worship Him always. Love you all.

DAY 59

For he will command his angels concerning you to guard you in all your ways;

PSALM 91:11

HELLO FAMILY: Angels guarding you in all your ways? Sign me up now! Can you imagine for a moment how many angels there are watching over all of us? This is a **promise**—one of the many our Word of God reveals to those who have faith in our Lord Jesus Christ, who believe like a child. I recall many movies and TV shows that depicted angels being there for folks in their time of great need. Christmas movies are some of my favorites, depicting angels that look like us mortals providing those words of wisdom to save the season. Think about our own lives. Ever have a car accident, suffer a bad fall, or go to war and have bullets and bombs dropping all around you? There are many tribulations out there. We all are destined to experience tribulations at some point or another. Knowing that an army of angels is there to guard you is a blessing for sure. In God we trust! Love you all.

October 2017: Here, we have a family crew in Germany together! From the bottom right: my son-in-law Damian with my granddaughter Leonie, my sister Mary Beth, my wife Carol, my "new" daughter-in-law Katie. (My son Shane was sick from allergies.) From the bottom left: me and then my daughters Lynn and Kim.

DAY 60

Now there is in store for me the crown of righteousness, which the Lord, the righteous Judge, will award to me on that day—and not only to me, but also to all who have longed for his appearing.

2 TIMOTHY 4:8

HELLO FAMILY: If there is a crown of righteousness, then there is an anchor of wrongness too. In my days of attending the Combat Diver Qualification Course (CDQC), when you did not do it *right*, you and your swim buddy dragged around a big heavy metal chain with a metal anchor on it. Wrong decisions in a military dive may not only cost you your life, but the lives of your fellow military members around you. Taking a stand to be righteous, to make selfless decisions, to hold on to the values that build character, are choices we must make. There are those who stand up for righteousness and those who fall for everything. Lives can be meaningless without a firm foundation to build upon. Our scriptures give us God's Word and guidance to make the right decisions. So? We pray for the Holy Spirit to guide and light our steps, so we don't stumble and fall. Love you all.

50-CENT BONUS

When you accept Jesus as your Lord and Savior, be prepared to get fed by godly friends. In one of those **career** moves, which wasn't the best for my military career, I requested a move to Fort Polk, LA. I wanted my wife Carol and the boys to be closer to her dying father. Carol's dad was just diagnosed with Lou Garret's disease. Getting to observe the last months of my father-in-law's life, I was able to witness love in ways I had never witnessed before, firsthand. I was seeing the Bible come to life and didn't realize it while it was happening. Carol's dad knew he was dying, and I was able to witness him talk gently and with such a tone of grace. He didn't just grab a quick hug, he held and embraced his children, my sons every time in their presence. He spoke with authority his relationship with Jesus and shared that daily in a most precious way. It was something God knew I needed to witness and experience.

Upon my arrival to Fort Polk as the leader of a new team, I met SFC Monty Flanigan, a fellow Green Beret from the 5th Special Forces Group. The only grudge I had in meeting this guy was that he wasn't from my Battalion—the 1st AKA Ranger Battalion of 5th Special Forces Group. Early on in our work, I noticed Monty deeply studying a King James Version of the Bible with feverish intensity. He expressed a deep passion for God's Word and had been recently baptized at a local church. I figured that was a good thing, because I had read the Bible cover to cover at least twice now, though nobody knew about it. When Carol's dad died, Monty offered to say a prayer at the funeral. It was the most heartwarming and comforting prayer at the service. My entire team was present, and we were astonished. That year,

Monty would read the bible during our breaks in our "cubicle." We worked together preparing for the next field exercise at the Joint Readiness Training Center, Fort Polk, LA. Monty would read the Bible out loud. Memorizing scripture in our office created "God talk," including everybody's two cents' worth. Nobody complained, and as soldiers in the line of work that we did, it was much appreciated. Soon, Monty invited Carol and me to a Baptist church where Monty served. He was going to lead a prayer service on a Wednesday night. Carol and I did not attend church while at Fort Polk, but she would take the boys to the church on the weekends when she went back home to visit her mom. We always had the best excuses for missing church, with visiting family close by and fishing trips with the kids. We did, however, go to that service to which Monty had invited us. It was quite an experience. Fire and brimstone preaching from a fired-up preacher-in-training in the pulpit! I told Monty he was the greatest, but since I was spiritually stubborn at the time, I declined every future offer to enter that church the rest of my tour at Fort Polk.

As time passed, Monty and I eventually returned to the 5th Special Forces Group at Fort Campbell, KY. I was assigned to ODA 515 in 1st Battalion and Monty was assigned as a 1st Sergeant at the 5th Special Forces Headquarters. Being in separate units under the 5th Special Forces, we made an effort to make time to catch up together and share the family news. I was about to retire upon my return from a deployment to Uzbekistan. I would share with Monty how eager I was to start a new chapter in my life outside of the military. Monty was continuing in his service to his country and to God as an active member in a local Baptist church in Clarksville, TN. He is and always will be a beloved friend and comrade in arms. Upon my return from that planned deployment to Uzbekistan and preparing to leave the Army, September 11, 2001, changed my life and the lives of a nation. I was reassigned to the rear detachment of 1st Battalion to assist and coordinate troop movements, resupply, family assistance and whatever was needed in the war on terrorism effort. Monty was doing the same at the Group Headquarters and we began working closer than ever before in these efforts. This man of God was one of those friends God puts right in your face to witness and learn from. Just as it was with Carol's dad. These men of God were put in my path as examples of how to lead a Christ-like life and so that I may someday share how my path developed as a witness to God's glory through them.

DAY 61

> *"I have swept away your offenses like a cloud, your sins like the morning mist. Return to me, for I have redeemed you."*
>
> ISAIAH 44:22

HELLO FAMILY: "Return to me." In other words, come home! Amazing as it is, forgiveness is the key to our faith. For God, through Christ, forgives our every shortfall no matter how horrible our past. Many of us drag around a great deal of guilt for the situations into which we got ourselves. A huge anchor of misery can haunt us for many years, perhaps a lifetime. That guilt keeps us from the promises of God's Word and an understanding of this very scripture. We can create a lifestyle that ensures every waking moment is busy beyond belief—a new family, busy career, fitness workouts, or taking night classes—just to keep our minds off our guilt. The Holy Spirit pleads with us, "You really are forgiven." It does take action. We must face the guilt and ask for forgiveness so we can communicate with love. No one is Fatherless, and God is always there waiting for our return to everlasting joy and salvation. Love you all.

DAY 62

> *"Do not be like them, for your Father knows what you need before you ask him."*
>
> MATTHEW 6:8

HELLO FAMILY: "Do not be like them." Why? Because those who are not in Christ are not sharing our Christian values. We are called to believe fully, like children. It is not necessary to worry about and question every single piece of drama in our lives or the lives of others. As Christians, our focus is on the cross, putting our beliefs into practice. That may mean less TV or perhaps less social time. Treasure our lives as a quest to know Jesus better and better each day. You know that Christ came here for us. We know that we are God's creation, perfect in God's eyes. No **need** for tattoos. No **need** for special diets. No **need** for practices, fads, or drunken activities that put us at risk to temptation that can harm us. Godly living takes great care of our existence. Our body is a temple for the Holy Spirit to dwell in and from. Do not be like those of the world. Be like Christ. Love you all.

DAY 63

The earth is the LORD's, and everything in it, the world, and all who live in it;

PSALM 24:1

HELLO FAMILY: Growing up around Letchworth State Park and the Genesee River with flowing creeks, ponds, and farmland is a blessing beyond words. Four seasons of amazing views to take in, and deer, turkey, and every critter one could imagine is near. The grandeur of it all, to take in each and every day was a front row seat to God's creation. Yes, that was my childhood playground. Many of us are blessed to have places like this to live or visit and explore, to witness God's creation. He has blessed the earth with spectacular waterfalls, high mountains, and so many other beautiful forms of nature around us — and us ourselves. We are also exposed to the amazing birth of life with wildlife, farm animals, and various pets. This reproduction among all these animals is such a godly experience, and to have the privilege of witnessing the birth of a human child will melt your heart with joy. This earth has many sights that display God's glory, His creation and plan for our planet to continue in the circle of life. These experiences are opportunities to witness God's work. If we appreciate and study the actual workings of the human body, how we heal, grow, think, and make plans, we are in for a real treat. Stay close to God in prayer, scripture, and worship. Stay close to God throughout your daily life. He is our Father. Love you all.

DAY 64

"Repent, then, and turn to God, so that your sins may be wiped out, that times of refreshing may come from the Lord,"

ACTS 3:19

HELLO FAMILY: **Wow!** What a scripture! "Repent" means to turn away from the things that harm you. B.I.B.L.E. (Basic Instructions Before Leaving Earth). Receiving Jesus Christ as your Lord and Savior is a jump into cool water, feeling refreshed in ways you will never be able to describe. Have you ever been really hot? Ever finish a long run, cut grass in 100 degrees, bale hay in a dusty field of heat and humidity, or work in a metal building fixing equipment that creates more heat when it runs? When you get that chance to take a break and grab an ice-cold glass of water to pour down your throat, ahhh. There is no better refreshment, so you think. Wait until you get totally submerged being baptized! The experience of coming up and out of that water entirely refreshed inside and out...there is no comparison. There are many temptations out there that harm you. So, turn away from them and turn to Christ and scripture and study God's plan for living a righteous life. It is refreshing to witness a joyful life for yourself. Love you all.

DAY 65

> *For no matter how many promises God has made, they are "Yes" in Christ. And so through him the "Amen" is spoken by us to the glory of God.*
>
> 2 CORINTHIANS 1:20

HELLO FAMILY: Let's talk about those promises, all 7,487 of them to be in the ballpark. Seriously, think about all of the countless and huge promises. All irrevocable, because of who God is, unchanging. He sees the end from the beginning (James 1:17). He is faithful. God can be trusted to keep His promises (Hebrews 10:23). He is strong. God does not overpromise and underdeliver. God is able to do whatever He promises (Romans 4:21). He cannot lie...He does not break promises (Titus 1:2). And there are thousands more. Confidence in our faith is key. **Believe**, like a child in the bond of this relationship. Yes, in Christ, all things are possible. Love you all!

DAY 66

> *A wife of noble character who can find? She is worth far more than rubies....[28] Her children arise and call her blessed; her husband also, and he praises her: [29] "Many women do noble things, but you surpass them all." [30] Charm is deceptive, and beauty is fleeting; but a woman who fears the L{\sc ord} is to be praised. [31] Honor her for all that her hands have done, and let her works bring her praise at the city gate.*
>
> PROVERBS 31:10, 28-31

HELLO FAMILY: Read and realize this scripture was written about 3,000 years ago! Let that sink in and know the value in reading God's Word. There have been situations in our lives when we've come to the conclusion that God was blessing us through our wives. Our careers may be flourishing, and we may actually believe that it is because of our own greatness and not the will of God (that pride issue again). More so, not realizing it may be the answered prayers of our wives, who pray diligently on our behalf. Our good fortunes may well be results of the thousands of prayers said by our faithful, godly women in our lives. A very humbling moment to have when this comes to mind. Yes, "A wife of noble character who can find?" Love you all.

DAY 67

So you are no longer a slave, but God's child; and since you are his child, God has made you also an heir.

GALATIANS 4

HELLO FAMILY: Yet again, we see another reference to adoption in God's family and heir to His Kingdom. No matter who we were in the past or who we are now, God is waiting for His children to come home. It does not have to be complicated. God is calling His children to His house. We are His children, bottom line. Hold that promise as an heir to God's Kingdom in Heaven. We are not slaves to our career, drugs, alcohol, or other situations that keep us away from our Lord. Our greatest imaginations cannot fathom the majesty of what we are in store for in God's grace. Love you all.

DAY 68

He holds success in store for the upright, he is a shield to those whose walk is blameless.

PROVERBS 2:7

HELLO FAMILY: "A shield to those whose walk is blameless." Blameless of what? Blameless from not having a relationship with Christ? Blameless for not praying or reading God's word? Perhaps blameless for not participating in worship with other Christians. By the way, can we recite the Ten Commandments without looking them up on our phone? Bottom line is that God has standards. A great sacrifice was made on our behalf, and the goal is for each of us to be blameless and to live each day glorifying Him. Rest assured, we are not blameless. But that does not give any of us who are informed an excuse to not make the effort to learn more, do more, and be more. God knows your heart. Make the effort and your life will change for the better. This is a promise from God. Love you all.

DAY 69

> *And God is able to bless you abundantly, so that in all things at all times, having all that you need, you will abound in every good work.*
>
> 2 CORINTHIANS 9:8

HELLO FAMILY: Being blessed abundantly. As parents, we don't want to be stressed out or overwhelmed with the basic needs of providing for our loved ones. Being a successful provider is a parent's dream. Every godly mother and father want to provide for their children. When we look in our kitchens and the food is abundant, our closets overflowing, do we not recognize how abundantly blessed we are? I recognize this is not the case across the world. But in regard to much of America, it takes some folks a good bit of time trying to figure out just what shoes to wear, especially when there are 50 pairs of shoes to choose from! Many of our homes are adequately heated and cooled with plenty of room to fit multiple beds that provide a warm place to rest. Some are very fortunate to have lived in great neighborhoods with peaceful, friendly, and calm neighbors. This is what "abundantly" looks like. God has blessed many of us abundantly to be free and able to perform good works for those around us. Positive, jubilant energy bringing joy to those around us. Which in turn, gives us a means to share and praise the Lord's abundance to others. Do look around. Love you all.

DAY 70

> *Come, let us sing for joy to the LORD; let us shout aloud to the Rock of our salvation.*
>
> PSALM 95:1

HELLO FAMILY: Quite a contrast from yesterday. Here we have singing and shouting on behalf of our Lord and Savior Jesus Christ! Joy! Note this key word. The quest of God for His children is to experience a joyful life in a relationship with Christ, our Rock. Joy is the single emotion every parent feeds off of when they observe their children. No joy means no happiness, perhaps even misery. The outward emotions of our children can make or break our day. God loves it when we are filled with joy, singing praises to Him. It makes His day, too. Love you all.

DAY 71

Whoever has ears, let them hear what the Spirit says to the churches. The one who is victorious will not be hurt at all by the second death.

REVELATION 2:11

HELLO FAMILY: This scripture calls for study. As we read on, we read about the second death, which is referring to the "Judgment." The first death is when our bodies break down and our hearts stop beating. Then, with the second coming of Christ comes the potential second death, our final judgment. Recognize that by accepting Jesus Christ as our Lord and Savior, we are covered by His blood. The blood that Jesus shed on the cross. When we are "saved," we are willfully born again into a new and everlasting life with Jesus as our "lawyer" for that final judgment. You will have no worries with Jesus defending you in person. Love you all.

DAY 72

Your righteousness is like the highest mountains, your justice like the great deep. You, LORD, preserve both people and animals.

PSALM 36:6

HELLO FAMILY: Here, we have another reference to the greatness of our God—the only God, the Creator of all we know, see, hear, taste, smell, and feel. Oh, the textures of it all! It is quite astounding to stop and recognize all of our senses and to think about how it all came to be. It speaks to our soul. Where is our soul, our spirit, our faith, and our relationship with the Creator of us all and the world around us? This scripture calls upon us to pause and seek these answers in our hearts. Love you all.

DAY 73

> *For all those who exalt themselves will be humbled, and those who humble themselves will be exalted.*
>
> LUKE 14:11

HELLO FAMILY: I recall being a Perry Yellow Jacket basketball player in high school. I was number #33. Seeing my stats in the local paper with the highest points scored and most rebounds recovered was a dream! I thought of myself as a basketball king. It all went straight to my head. I had the biggest strut anyone could imagine walking the halls. Then BOOM! It was over. From hero to just another guy in school after that last championship game—which we lost! I was in the dumps. My dad always told me, "Be the best you can be. Even if it's the worst job you can imagine, just humble yourself and be the best at it." The rest is history. As a private in the Army, I was humbled by cleaning toilets, mopping floors, and having kitchen duty, all with no headlines in the Perry Herald, our local newspaper growing up. But humility did me wonders. It did wonders for my sons and daughters, too. It's all part of being humbled and continuing the march with the best of attitudes, never losing faith. God never gives up on us, so we should never give up on ourselves. We are all God's children, to be faithful and to be exalted. Look at us now! Stay humble in all of your blessings y'all. Love you.

DAY 74

> *Listen, my son, to your father's instruction and do not forsake your mother's teaching. [9] They are a garland to grace your head and a chain to adorn your neck.*
>
> PROVERBS 1:8–9

HELLO FAMILY: Many families, children, and parents come from broken homes. Yet, here we have a scripture directing otherwise. Our families here in America have been spared from war-ravaged destruction. Our plates are full. Our homes are warm, and we have phones with all kinds of friends on them to share our "tough" daily walk. Much of the time it is only when we face tragedy, relationship defeats, and financial despair that we call on God. Does God know our voice? When we stay focused on God's Word it guides all of us, no matter what chapter of life we are in. It keeps our tongues, words, and actions focused on pleasing God. God is love. We are experiencing love with each other through Christ's teachings. This is pleasing to God, and we are blessed with joy daily. See how this scripture can resound in a family. "As for me and my household, we will serve the LORD" (Joshua 24:15). Love you all.

DAY 75

The blameless spend their days under the Lord's care,
and their inheritance will endure forever.

PSALM (37:18 NIV)

HELLO FAMILY: "Under the Lord's care." It is a choice. Do we humble ourselves before God and stay loyal to our Shepherd? Or, do we toss aside pride and allow Jesus our Shepherd to take on the wolves that lurk at every corner? We don't have to look far to see what people get into, all by themselves. Jesus is referred to many times in the Bible as the Shepherd and we are the sheep. Sheep are not able to defend themselves. They must have a shepherd or die. Travel around the world and you will see sheep with their shepherds. It is a warming sight to see a shepherd caring for and defending every single sheep in his flock. In this world we humans deal with depression, drugs, alcohol, and lies that sometimes get us deep into situations that can spiral out of control. We can quickly find ourselves in situations where we feel we are not in control at all. So we ask ourselves, "why live like this?" Come home to the flock and rest with our Shepherd. Love you all.

DAY 76

"The time has come," he said. "The kingdom of God
has come near. Repent and believe the good news!"

MARK 1:15

HELLO FAMILY: We have a PowerPoint slide at the end of our sermon in church, it says. "It doesn't matter when you start a relationship with Christ, it matters that you do." Another slide used during the altar calls reads, "The time has come," and never too soon. The angels in Heaven stand ready to celebrate with singing and praises to the Lord when someone makes the decision to accept and receive Jesus Christ as their Lord and Savior. This is the great and good news celebrated across the heavens above when a soul is saved. So, take action to get control of the good news awaiting in your life. Love you all!

DAY 77

> *"I myself said, 'How gladly would I treat you like my children and give you a pleasant land, the most beautiful inheritance of any nation.' I thought you would call me 'Father' and not turn away from following me."*
>
> JEREMIAH 3:1

HELLO FAMILY: "And not turn away from following me." We all have memory problems. We forget all too well how we got to where we are now. It's a defense mechanism, the doctors say, so we don't relive painful occurrences in our lives. The problem is that we don't remember much of anything and are so focused on the hours ahead that we struggle to reflect on our blessings received in the past. Yes, all from God. It does well for our character to humble ourselves. Stop the race and reflect on the blessings God has given us. We shouldn't give ourselves the chance to turn away from following our Lord. With Him, the hours ahead can be handled with grace. Love you all.

DAY 78

> *Therefore, since the promise of entering his rest still stands, let us be careful that none of you be found to have fallen short of it. [2] For we also have had the good news proclaimed to us, just as they did; but the message they heard was of no value to them, because they did not share the faith of those who obeyed.*
>
> HEBREWS 4:1-2

HELLO FAMILY: "No value to them...they did not share the faith of those who obeyed." What message is not being shared? We don't want to be found to have fallen short, do we? Short of exactly what? When we are made aware of the good news, the Gospel, we need to share this joyous information with others. Not doing so is falling short in our faith. Sharing our faith is our proclamation that our blessings in life are from God. Our Joy in life is from our relationship with Christ and Christ alone. Our joy can be spoiled with most any mortal relationship out there, but not with Jesus. Our self-control, our confidence, our choices rely on the Gospel of Christ. Share this news as coming from the peace of the Holy Spirit in our hearts. Go tell it on the mountain. Let everyone know the source of your joy. Love you all.

DAY 79

You turned my wailing into dancing; you removed my sackcloth and clothed me with joy, [12] that my heart may sing your praises and not be silent. LORD my God, I will praise you forever.

PSALM 30:11-12

HELLO FAMILY: The possibilities are endless when there is joy found in Christ daily. What great warmth to experience throughout the family, even though there are miles between us. We praise the Lord for each one of us and our families as they experience the joy and peace that this scripture speaks of. Even when our world is shaking and trembling all around us with the gloom and doom we hear on the news, our praise for the Lord continues with dancing and song. Love you all.

DAY 80

He who did not spare his own Son, but gave him up for us all—how will he not also, along with him, graciously give us all things?

ROMANS 8:32

HELLO FAMILY: "Graciously." That is the key word here. By our faith in Christ we are saved from eternal death. Live in peace knowing that our Father gives us all things. God is gracious with all of us and He expects us to be gracious also, looking out for the others around us. Grace from God is not paid for or earned. It is just given to those who believe and receive Jesus Christ as Lord and Savior. Love you all.

My grandchildren *(left to right)* Leonie, Philipp, and Hannah. Sweetest children ever and such a blessing to be with, here we are watching cartoons before bedtime.

DAY 81

Your word is a lamp for my feet, a light on my path. [106] I have taken an oath and confirmed it, that I will follow your righteous laws.

PSALM 119:105–106

HELLO FAMILY: "Your word is a lamp for my feet." Why is that? So we don't stumble. So we won't fall. Setbacks in life are not the end-all be-all. We always have the opportunity to repent and turn to God. Why stumble, fumble, and trip your way thru life without Christ? Divine intervention is real. We need to be sure Christ knows our voice when we call. The light is our guide to joy each day on the path to salvation. Love you all.

DAY 82

Let the heavens rejoice, let the earth be glad; let the sea resound, and all that is in it. [12] Let the field be jubilant and everything in them; let all the trees of the forest sing for joy.

PSALM 96:11–12

HELLO FAMILY: This scripture rings of spring, of a post COVID-19 pandemic! Spend some time outdoors, do some weed eating, cut the grass, tend to your gardens and feel the nourishing ground in your hands. Listen to the breeze move the trees, feel the gleaming warmth of the sun on your face. Watch the hummingbirds search for the perfect flower from a hanging basket of colorful blooms. Yes, my family, my brothers and sisters in Christ. You know this. Love you all.

DAY 83

Let the peace of Christ rule in your hearts, since as members of one body you were called to peace. And be thankful.

COLOSSIANS 3:15

HELLO FAMILY: In a world of absolute chaos, wars, and rumors of more wars, we need to stay close as a family in Christ. We are called to peace. Instead of making violence, let's make memories. Capture those little moments of our children building sandcastles on the beach, playing tag with cousins at a family picnic, and enjoying a friendly game of Battleship. We all know there is plenty to be miserable about in this world—the politics, trade wars, and insecurities that plague societies are always in the headlines. But **we** are in Christ! Now, I challenge all to time travel. Explore your family history, revisit the smiles in photos from family reunions, and most of all, remember the faith your family had as they survived with peace in their hearts while the world raged on. Love you all.

DAY 84

You care for the land and water it; you enrich it abundantly. The streams of God are filled with water to provide the people with grain, for so you have ordained it.

PSALM 65:9

HELLO FAMILY: "You care for the land and water it...you have ordained it." The more you put into your faith, the more you get out of it. The more Christ recognizes your voice, the calmer you are in a crisis. A life with Christ, prayer, scripture, and worship brings divine intervention. Everything is in His control—every traffic jam making you late, every delay in an adoption process, every day with a breathing treatment, and every day of a vacation with family (happy times). Bottom line: every second of every day, God is in control. Our perception of good days and bad days is only our small speck view. Our best day could have been our worst day if it wasn't for that delay in traffic that saved us from a major accident, and we didn't even know it. Love you all.

DAY 85

And this is love: that we walk in obedience to his commands. As you have heard from the beginning, his command is that you walk in love.

2 JOHN 1:6

HELLO FAMILY: "Walk in love." For us soldiers, it is the word "march." March in love. That just doesn't sound right unless you belong to the Army of God. Why is that? Because the ways of Jesus conflict with the ways of the world. Our culture is in constant competition. We get up and go, go, go, especially today with information moving so fast. Just think of the popularity contests we get into by watching how many "likes" we are getting on social media platforms. Know the languages of real love and get marching. Love you all.

50-CENT BONUS

Hello Family. I pray that everyone has been able to pause and thank our Creator for our Lord and Savior Jesus. Our life on earth would be "hopeless" without salvation, without Christ. Our family is currently spread across the entire globe—Dad in Guam Kim and Lynn and their families in Germany; and family in South Carolina, New York, Tennessee, and Kentucky. Yet we are together in Christ forever! We have accepted Jesus as our Savior and we will be together for eternity. We know and deal with our own temptations as well as witness the evil this world delivers. Jesus Christ defeated death on that cross. He no longer hangs on that cross. He is alive! He lives! Death defeated! With that, a glorious reunion is at hand with God at His table. Our family will be seated together. Blessings to you all this Easter and throughout your days, until we meet again. With all of that being said, be sure to share this joy with your friends. God has put in our paths a spiritual family to be with us wherever we are, to celebrate Christ on all occasions. This family is found in our churches. I want to take this time to mention another godly man that I met at Fort Polk, LA, while I was stationed there. His name is Tom Rea. A fine Special Forces soldier who has been very close to our family ever since we met while fishing along Alligator Pond. We have a little joke with my mom and dad. They have adopted Tom Rea into the family and he has qualified to make it into the family will. Tom is one of those "friends" I wrote about earlier (Day 60) that God puts into your life to guide you along the way, to take care of you in ways a big brother does. So be sure to reach out to these godly friends when we celebrate this day. I know Tom is with my mom and dad at their church celebrating Easter together. Love you all.

DAY 86

> *Good will come to those who are generous and lend freely, who conduct their affairs with justice.*
>
> PSALM 112:5

HELLO FAMILY: "Conduct their affairs with justice." Good will come, so the good book says. Doing good things and being fair garner a great reputation, and that's when people around you want you in positions of authority. We just had some big storms come through our neighborhood. This is a godly neighborhood. We have meetings that start with prayer followed by the Pledge of Allegiance. When the trees come crashing down and the ice and snow covers the roads, we are all out there together getting things cleaned up. On the downside, we have dealt with cancer treatments and even the deaths of spouses. On the upside, we celebrate the best ever Fourth of Julys and fall bashes around big fires. That's what a society that focuses on being generous with each other is all about. Our neighborhood feels very secure, and we are led by the teachings of our Bible. We conduct affairs with justice and good works with joy and cheer. Even though we are not all going to the same local church or even practicing the same religion, our Christian values are the same. So, when those promotions or leadership opportunities come our way, give thanks to Christ for teaching us how to treat others. Love you all.

DAY 87

> *And if the Spirit of him who raised Jesus from the dead is living in you, he who raised Christ from the dead will also give life to your mortal bodies because of his Spirit who lives in you.*
>
> ROMANS 8:11

HELLO FAMILY: "And if." The "if" being whether we have accepted and received Jesus Christ as our Lord and Savior. Have we accepted the Spirit of **Him** who raised Jesus? This is not about our parents doing it for us when we were infants. This is you (very personal), looking in the mirror and getting real with your soul in sincerely accepting and receiving the Son of God. Yes, there will be a celebration in Heaven as well as in your church when that day comes. A baptism will be in the near future to publicly celebrate. I encourage all of you to watch the scene in *O Brother Where Art Thou* where many are being baptized in the river. Love you all.

DAY 88

> *Keep on loving one another as brothers and sisters.*
> *[2] Do not forget to show hospitality to strangers,*
> *for by so doing some people have shown hospitality*
> *to angels without knowing it.*
>
> HEBREWS 13:1–2

HELLO FAMILY: "Hospitality to strangers"? What? Heck, some may have issues with particular family members coming into their homes, let alone strangers. We live in a society where many of the headlines are about "strangers" shooting each other in the streets. We are raised as children to scream "stranger danger" and run for our lives if approached by adults we don't know. Now we have this scripture advising us to show hospitality. All that comes to my mind are pictures of homeless people stretching out for miles in the streets of some of our major cities. Yes, there are great challenges to discipleship. The transformation process found in prayer, scripture reading, and worship works on our hearts. These homeless challenges are a call to leadership to be hospitable, for us Christians to find that leadership so policies to resolve this crisis can be implemented in accordance with God's will. We pray to elect those who will utilize the great resources of our nation to their greatest potentials. Love you all.

DAY 89

> *My Father, who has given them to me, is greater than all;*
> *no one can snatch them out of my Father's hand.*
>
> JOHN 10:29

HELLO FAMILY: "No one can snatch them out of my Father's hand." "Who has given them to me." Know this promise. Understand what is happening here when you sincerely surrender to Christ. God has you in His grip. You may squirm, wiggle, and hang off the edge at times (makes me think of holding my cat when she tries to get away). You will not get away. God loves you more and if you keep squirming, you may get squeezed a little harder. Worse yet, even tied down with a super bear hug until you regain your senses. Either way, you have been given to Jesus and He is now your Shepherd. As we grow in understanding, we will find that having a real relationship with the Lord is as simple as being with your very best friend. Very powerful scripture here. Study this sincerely. Love you all.

DAY 90

Honor the LORD with your wealth, with the first fruits of all your crops; [10] then your barns will be filled to overflowing, and your vats will brim over with new wine.

PROVERBS 3:9-10

HELLO FAMILY: What we are reading here is having the "faith" that blessings are to come when you give your money or donate your time and talents on behalf of building up God's Kingdom here on earth. Now, the decision is where to do that. Who or what gets our money? There are so many religions out there and even more charities. Let us stick with church for this two cents' worth. Many Christian churches refer to this as a "tithe" and the number assigned is ten percent of our income. Putting ten percent of our paycheck into a church can add up huge over time. It really is a leap of faith. It is an investment in your faith on a very personal level. You end up being vested in the work of the church you choose to serve. In this act, we take a real interest in how our tithes are being spent to really further the Kingdom of God. Our faith is a calling to be generous, loving, and forgiving. The blessings will come, and our cups will overflow. I am a witness. Love you all.

DAY 91

Dear friends, since God so loved us, we also ought to love one another. [12] No one has ever seen God; but if we love one another, God lives in us and his love is made complete in us.

1 JOHN 4:11-12

HELLO FAMILY: "If we love one another." Y'all, as I reflect on this past week, we surely are experiencing love in our What's App group as well with each other in traveling range. Our visit with Shane and Katie, my mom and dad, texting with my niece Sami, and Kim and Lynn's video calls. Big joy and excitement! And even Blake! Blake, much like his dad, stays very busy. Plus, he just loves my two cents of advice with these scriptures. None of us are spared the tribulations and stresses of this world, the good times and the bad. With the love of Christ in us, we are experiencing the love of Christ among us every time we communicate. We shop for each other (my Germany box is packed). We make plans for each other. We share our challenges and joys of the day with each other. As the body of Christ grows in our spiritual family and in our churches, this joy spreads throughout the entire body of Christ. As a family in Christ, we gain strength and goodness, which in turn pleases God. As our unique spiritual gifts are shared, they bring joy into the lives of those we interact with. We have come a very long way to have this in our family. The challenge comes when we love one another outside of our family. I know you already do! Love you all.

DAY 92

Let love and faithfulness never leave you; bind them around your neck, write them on the tablet of your heart. [4] Then you will win favor and a good name in the sight of God and man.

PROVERBS 3:3-4

HELLO FAMILY: "Love and faithfulness...win favor and a good name in the sight of God and man." You wonder why some folks get all the blessings—super jobs, great wife or husband, kids, place to live, and so forth. Yes, these are blessings. I have no answer for why one person wins the lottery and millions of others do not. I am writing as a witness to blessings that are priceless. When in the favor of God, the blessings just come. Healing occurs in ways that are unexplainable. Forgiveness happens and doors open. We here in America have access to so much freedom, so many choices and decisions to make. Never choose to quit on God. Never decide to doubt your faith or your relationship with Christ. It is the practice of our faith that others see and trust our intentions. So, I pray for the faithful that faithfulness never leaves you, fully knowing that everything happens in God's time and according to His will. Love you all.

DAY 93

You see that his faith and his actions were working together, and his faith was made complete by what he did. [23] And the scripture was fulfilled that says, "Abraham believed God, and it was credited to him as righteousness," and he was called God's friend.

JAMES 2:22-23

HELLO FAMILY: What would it take to be called God's friend? Now think of **your** closest friend. Think about everything they know about you. How they support you, listen to you, and strengthen and encourage you. We are warned in other scriptures about the "friends" you keep that could be your defeat. Choose your friends wisely. Stay away from ungodly, spiritually stubborn so-called friends who only bring you down. Remember that misery loves company, but **God** is the ultimate friend. Keep your faith in Him, and He will never harm you. His promises will lift you up, and you will always find peace in Him. Love you all!

DAY 94

He says, "Be still, and know that I am God; I will be exalted among the nations, I will be exalted in the earth."

PSALM 46:10

HELLO FAMILY: "**He says**, 'Be still.'" I just told Carol this morning that I feel all this pressure from being gone a good bit, having a big list of things to do, people to chat with (small town, church, neighbors, work folks), and meetings to set up and attend. And that's just a glimpse! Did I mention jet lag? In times like these, she often tells me, "Take a deep breath, Dan." Many of us would find ourselves muttering, "Easy for you to say," under our breaths. Well, this is when God says, "Be still." We need to be still and catch our breath. Amazing how this scripture is short and to the point, yet extremely powerful. It provides us a pause from the race. We all deal with the stresses of life and anxieties of all kinds. What a blessing to know our faith leads us to these scriptures, reminding us to exalt God. So, we can relax. God is in control. Love you all.

DAY 95

Husbands, love your wives, just as Christ loved the church and gave himself up for her [26] to make her holy, cleansing her by the washing with water through the word, [27] and to present her to himself as a radiant church, without stain or wrinkle or any other blemish, but holy and blameless.

EPHESIANS 5:25-27

HELLO FAMILY: What does it mean to be chosen among millions by a person to be your spouse? Why do we ask? Because we as Christians are the "church," the Bride of Christ who He will return for. The Bride (we Christians) must exercise self-control, discipline, strength, and love, for we are chosen to be "married" with Christ upon His return. This scripture really explains our self-worth. We are so worthy, to be chosen by Christ just as a man chooses a woman to be his bride. Remember the old fashioned proposal, the man getting on his knee and asking the classic question, "Will you marry me?" That still gets the crowd cheering. So, think about that for a moment when you look at the word "church." We as men and women belonging to a church represent the Bride of Christ, who Christ has chosen to return to, much like a soldier who returns from a battle to reunite with his bride. There is fire in the sky! Love you all.

DAY 96

> *In him and through faith in him we may approach God with freedom and confidence.*
>
> EPHESIANS 3:12

HELLO FAMILY: "Approach God"? And "with freedom and confidence"? This is a big one! You may be wondering, "Can I approach Him?" Guess what. **We can!** Just like children do with their earthly loving fathers and mothers. Through our faith, God knows our voices. He knows our thoughts, and He knows how we have grown (reading His scriptures). We celebrate and praise Him with our brothers and sisters in Christ (serving in church). You are God's child. Go and run to Him for a big hug. Love you all.

DAY 97

> *The Lord detests lying lips, but he delights in people who are trustworthy.*
>
> PROVERBS 12:22

HELLO FAMILY: "Detests" versus "delights." Our culture likes to flounder in their ways, but our Lord makes it very clear what He delights in and what He detests! I would much rather have my behavior pleasing God than not. And God is in the best place to provide blessings to whom He delights in. Our culture is a mess of detestable twists of truths that wolves put together. We must watch ourselves carefully. Check our motives and the temptations we encounter. Do not twist the truth. Being truthful will not only be delightful to our Lord, but to everyone who gets to know you. Love you all.

My girls are the picture of forgiveness that I write about in this book. Without forgiveness in our hearts, so much will be missed. My girls taught me this and what a blessing, for the promises of God are real.

DAY 98

Let your eyes look straight ahead; fix your gaze directly before you. [26] Give careful thought to the paths for your feet and be steadfast in all your ways. [27] Do not turn to the right or the left; keep your foot from evil.

PROVERBS 4:25-27

HELLO FAMILY: "Let your eyes look straight ahead; fix your gaze directly before you." Ok folks, allow this advice to sink in and focus on the cross ahead. Behind us we may have made poor choices, bad decisions, and sins that mark a trail of moldy bread crumbs. These bad choices may have set us back financially, resulted in broken relationships, and maybe even ended us up in the jailhouse. Hopefully, we are wise and learn from our mistakes, making note of what happens when we don't heed to God's Word. We are wiser today than we were back then. Now hear this! Much all of the alcoholism that I have encountered comes from people dwelling on the past—past mistakes, past battles, past failed relationship issues, etc. We ask ourselves why we are so focused on the past. This scripture is **wisdom**! Don't look back. We must never look back and have a pity party. God's Word helps to direct our focus forward. We are to use the wisdom we have learned to love more effectively, which brings great **joy** to our future. This is our Father's goal for His children. Love you all.

DAY 99

A new command I give you: Love one another. As I have loved you, so you must love one another.

JOHN 13:34

HELLO FAMILY: The "love" word again. Let me think. All five love languages (words of affirmation, receiving gifts, acts of service, **quality time**, and physical touch) are what come to mind. If I may go out on a limb here, I will share that the men folk of our daily bible study like to poke jabs in regards to our wives when scripture takes us out of our comfort zone, especially in regards to love. Sometimes word gets out that "Johnny said," and it shakes the earth with rapid responses from all of our wives to whatever the subject may be, generally all in fun. Yet, we all know and perhaps have experienced tough love, so I have learned over the years. So, application is in order by all of us. Let's focus on loving our spouses today. Call it the "Spouse Appreciation Challenge." Perhaps us menfolk can share the results at our next get together; or better yet, we will all see the results in person. Share an application of one or more of the love languages for you and your honey. Do it today. **With a smile**. Love you all.

DAY 100

He upholds the cause of the oppressed and gives food to the hungry. The LORD sets prisoners free,

PSALM 146:7

HELLO FAMILY: "The LORD sets prisoners free." What great chains of sin hold us down? What in our hearts, or in our thoughts, need to go away? Whatever is in our past, let go and let God take care of it. These are the chains that keep us prisoner and make us unable to experience real joy. These undertones of guilt, failure, and unmet expectations can make us believe that we are not worthy of joy. We must hunger for the Lord to set us free. Pray to our Creator to take charge of our lives and bring that smile back all day long. Love you all.

50-CENT BONUS

Scripture has a way of advising who to hang around with and who to avoid. Far too many times in my efforts to outdrink, fight, and outwit the competition—in some cases, even the ladies—I would end up in situations or using language not fitting of a Christian book writer. God does have His plans and He will provide other godly people to help us along or perhaps help each other along a path of righteousness. I mentioned my person by name earlier: Thomas Rea. We met at Fort Polk. He was just assigned to the unit and I learned quickly that this intense Irishmen was a prior member of the 5th Special Forces Group (Airborne) also. He was short but solid as a rock. From 2nd Battalion, too. Before long, our interests in fishing and hunting brought us closer together. Carol and I even got to see a picture of his future wife Staci on a "cell phone." Yes, this was a big deal back in 1995. Cell phone pictures and Tom even mentioning the thought of getting serious with a woman were magical. Yes, this was a big day.

Having that relationship with Tom led to Carol and I settling in Cadiz, KY. This is where we have raised our family. It is a very faith-based community. This is where we started going to a local Methodist church consistently. We became serving members, and Carol and I continue to serve there today. Tom helped us find a home to live in and helped get our young boys into a classroom with loving teachers for their first and third grade years. Tom was born and raised in Cadiz. He basically became my true brother. God knew we needed each other—God knew I needed a big brother figure in my life. It's just that simple. My youngest brother Rick had died several years earlier in a car accident, and my other brother Ken left the family requesting that we leave him alone. God knew I had no brother relationships at all.

Tom and I immediately had a spiritual bond but didn't even know it. He is a devout Catholic, and his guidance and knowledge led to my spiritual growth in ways he will never know. As brothers do, we butted heads then and we still do on occasion today.

Tom and his wife, Staci, continue to serve the Lord at their church here in Cadiz. When my parents moved here about ten years ago, he took amazing care of them in this new church and community. Just as he did with me and my family when we moved into his hometown in 1998. Tom knew everyone in Trigg County, and he made sure Carol and I never made any bad decisions over the years as we were getting established. I was never a big fan of the Catholic Church. I had my reasons. My parents and I would get in upsetting discussions many times, which I am ashamed to say. Tom filled that love for Catholicism with my parents, and I needed to see that happen in order to learn how to honor all godly religions and the people that served in them. Yes, that statement about Tom being in the will has brought many laughs and joy to our friends and family everywhere. It's quite the shock when first heard, which follows with plenty of stories that true brothers and parents can appreciate. Tom and Staci have been and will continue to be graciously in our lives until death do us part. This is what God does. He knows and He provides. We need to ask ourselves this: Who else has God sent our way?

Standing in the back are Christian, Kim, me, Lynn, and Damian. In front are Hannah, Philipp, and Leonie.

DAILY DEVOTIONALS | 63

DAY 101

As Jesus went on from there, two blind men followed him, calling out, "Have mercy on us, Son of David!" [28] When he had gone indoors, the blind men came to him, and he asked them, "Do you believe that I am able to do this?" "Yes, Lord," they replied. [29] Then he touched their eyes and said, "According to your faith let it be done to you";

MATTHEW 9:27-29

HELLO FAMILY: "According to your faith let it be done to you." Sometimes in life we deal with disappoint after disappointment. Take heart: we have someone to turn to for help. You can be confident in a favorable response from Jesus in His timing, not ours. When you are in God's hands, there is a purpose for the experience you are having. Recognize that God knows you can handle it with Him! Love you all.

DAY 102

When Jesus came down from the mountainside, large crowds followed him. [2] A man with leprosy came and knelt before him and said, "Lord, if you are willing, you can make me clean." [3] Jesus reached out his hand and touched the man. "I am willing," he said. "Be clean!" Immediately he was cleansed of his leprosy.

MATTHEW 8:1-3

HELLO FAMILY: "I am willing." Are we willing to take that total leap of faith? I want to share two huge moments in my life. First, the time I prayed the sinner's prayer in front of that wooden cross, choosing to receive Jesus as my Lord and Savior. The second huge moment is when I went on the Tres Dias Weekend. Going on this weekend retreat, I had no idea what I was getting myself into (as can be the case on many ventures). I sincerely prayed, "Lord, I am taking this experience as a total leap of faith. I open my heart to you. Let the Holy Spirit lead the way." Jesus declares this and He heals! Many of us, our children, and our friends struggle with all kinds of medical and mental conditions that doctors have no easy fix for. No other alternatives are fixing the situation. Is it time to stop and search your heart and put your faith into action? "Lord, if you are willing...heal my child, heal my body, and heal my mind." In the silence of your prayers, make your requests, be still, and listen. "I am willing." J esus will respond. Love you all.

DAY 103

Not only so, but we also glory in our sufferings, because we know that suffering produces perseverance; [4] perseverance, character; and character, hope. [5] And hope does not put us to shame, because God's love has been poured out into our hearts through the Holy Spirit, who has been given to us.

ROMANS 5:3-5

HELLO FAMILY: God's love, the Holy Spirit, and "suffering"? I remember sermons where the preacher was advocating that suffering was part of being a Christian. Part of this sanctification thing to be a disciple of Christ. The thought rang in my head, "I deal with enough suffering, I don't need any more." And what about Lent, when we are to deprive ourselves of "something"? I get a big kick out of listening to folks talk about what they'll choose to give up. My own thoughts on what I will deny myself are the most entertaining, and I am keeping them secret. So, we pick snacks after dinner (so now we seem to be finishing dinner at 8 p.m.). I did hear another one, "I am giving up drinking beer for lent." When asked if they meant alcohol, the reply was, "I switched to vodka!" Either way, as we grow in our relationship with Christ (love), we may find ourselves challenged (suffering) in our daily walk. We are in constant consultation with the Holy Spirit to help us do what is right, speak what is right, to be nice, and to love. Our spirit is troubled when we struggle with decisions that are outside the path of righteousness. This is part of the suffering process that develops our character and transforms our behavior to be even better Christians as we grow, hope, and live. Love you all.

DAY 104

"I will make an everlasting covenant with them: I will never stop doing good to them, and I will inspire them to fear me, so that they will never turn away from me."

JEREMIAH 32:40

HELLO FAMILY: Well, this sounds just like a dad-in-action scripture. "Doing good to them, they will fear me, never turn away from me." I recall my friends and I when I was young saying, "If our dads find out, they will kill us." Now I hear my friends (old dads now) say, "If my kids don't respond to my texts, I will turn their phones off. They will fear me then!" Now, **that's** called a generational gap! This scripture is declaring the respect our Lord demands, just like earthly fathers do. Love you all.

DAY 105

What causes fights and quarrels among you? Don't they come from your desires that battle within you? [2] You desire but do not have, so you kill. You covet but you cannot get what you want, so you quarrel and fight. You do not have because you do not ask God.

JAMES 4:1-2

HELLO FAMILY: This scripture is about being content in your heart with what God has provided for you in His great wisdom. A relationship with Christ fills that void of frustrations over what we don't have. Our flesh always wants more, bigger, newer, and greater satisfactions faster. Having a real walk and talk relationship with Christ brings a peace of mind that relieves that quest of the flesh. Our path will be lit so clearly. Our mind will be engaged in ways our wildest dreams could never have imagined! A purpose-driven life will lead to contentment. Talking directly to Jesus and working out what we really need will bring happiness to our lives. Living within or even under our means to provide for ourselves and our families will come with peace and freedom from debt in due time. Just to focus on the cross and not what everyone else has is a great start. Love you all.

DAY 106

How good and pleasant it is when God's people live together in unity!

PSALM 133:1

HELLO FAMILY: "When God's people live together in unity." Hmmm? Church? One thing I can attest to is that church is a place where everyone recognizes the authority, reverence, and teachings of God and the acceptance of Jesus Christ as their Savior. As we attend church longer, we really get to know each other as brothers and sisters in Christ. We work, serve, cry, and celebrate together. This is much like an actual family, yet unique because you may not really know everyone involved in a worship or prayer service. Being in a church family is a very powerful and supportive experience. Everyone has their spiritual qualities (and faults too) to serve the Lord. In regard to the faults comment, we all learn and practice forgiveness when our toes get stepped on. I pray everyone reading this gets to share that same experience in their local church. With careers having us all over the world, a church family is a blessing to come home to. Love you all.

DAY 107

And even the very hairs of your head are all numbered.

MATTHEW 10:30

HELLO FAMILY: Sorry, kids. I know you, but not well enough and thorough enough to know how many hairs you have. But **God** does! By our faith and acceptance of Jesus Christ, we have inherited God's grace and adoption into God's eternal family. So, when our travel plans falter, our family plans take longer, and our health isn't as healthy as it was hoped for, know that **God** is in charge. To think that our Creator has that detail of knowledge into every single human being whom He has created, in His likeness, is beyond what we can fathom in our minds. Some would say "unbelievable." Have faith, my family and friends. Believe that God knows **you** and every hair you have. Be at peace and enjoy your faith. Love you all.

DAY 108

Be shepherds of God's flock that is under your care, watching over them—not because you must, but because you are willing, as God wants you to be; not pursuing dishonest gain, but eager to serve; [3] not lording it over those entrusted to you, but being examples to the flock. [4] And when the Chief Shepherd appears, you will receive the crown of glory that will never fade away.

1 PETER 5:2-4

HELLO FAMILY: When we commit to Christ, the Holy Spirit will come over us to guide us the rest of our lives. If we listen, we will gain wisdom and with that wisdom, the influence to share with others the joy of a relationship with Christ. We all will be called upon to use our skills "willingly" to stop the wolves from preying upon the sheep of Christ. I am aware of the professions in our family and take note of all the influence we have on the lives of others, "the flock." Serving others brings great joy in our lives. This truly is the best example of love that we can do in our faith. Love you all.

DAY 109

The generous will themselves be blessed,
for they share their food with the poor.

PROVERBS 22:9

HELLO FAMILY: Being "generous" is the key to allowing God's blessings to flow through us. It is not just about "food." It is also our gifts or talents that we can be generous with. Have you ever seen a stagnant pond or noted the name of the Dead Sea? Nothing is moving at all—the water has stopped flowing and may even smell and look like death. This also can demonstrate the lack of God's blessings flowing through a person. Fresh, refreshing waters come to a halt and sit there. Ever see a child hoarding his or her toys sitting all alone, other kids looking on? It's an awkward experience to say the least. Being of a sharing spirit and experiencing the joy of bringing smiles to others is what this scripture speaks of. Allow God's blessings to flow through you to others. Love you all.

50-CENT BONUS

What, then, shall we say in response to these things? If God is for us, who can be against us? [32] He who did not spare his own Son, but gave him up for us all—how will he not also, along with him, graciously give us all things? [33] Who will bring any charge against those whom God has chosen? It is God who justifies. [34] Who then is the one who condemns? No one. Christ Jesus who died—more than that, who was raised to life—is at the right hand of God and is also interceding for us.

ROMANS 8:31-34

What you have said in the dark will be heard in the daylight,
and what you have whispered in the ear in the inner rooms will
be proclaimed from the roofs.

LUKE 12:3

HELLO FAMILY: My pastor proclaimed from the pulpit, "Law reveals. Grace heals." As we read these scriptures, they paint a picture of a courtroom layout. It is the final judgment proceeding for each and every one of us. God is at the throne, and every single sin we have ever committed is about to be "revealed." It is to be brought to "light" and "proclaimed" for all to witness and hear the charges against us before the **Judge** (Luke 12:3). This is far beyond embarrassment. This is the true exposure of selfishness, greed, hate, and other horrible acts. Very frightening to imagine for sure. Perhaps even a reason many proclaim, "Church is not for me, I am too far gone." I assure you this is spot on in regard to the chains of guilt that totally pin a person's life down.

Everyone blames themselves for something. Everyone has a secret they would never want revealed, and everyone knows that God knows it all. So, therein lies Romans 8:31–34. "God who did not spare his own **Son**, but gave him up for us all." Jesus Christ, for those who have accepted Him as their Lord and Savior, "is also interceding for us." While you are on trial you are not alone. Your personal lawyer is Jesus Christ! When the charges are proclaimed, Jesus intercedes and advises the Judge, this person belongs to me—**I have paid** for their sins. Jesus will show the Judge His scars, the holes in His hands and feet, and the hole in His side. The Judge announces that these "charges" against you are dropped, done, paid for! Who can condemn us now? It's never too late. No one is too far gone to start a relationship with Jesus Christ. What matters most is that you do. Love you all.

August 2021: Me with my granddaughters Hannah and Leonie.

DAILY DEVOTIONALS | 69

DAY 110

When you were dead in your sins and in the uncircumcision of your flesh, God made you alive with Christ. He forgave us all our sins, [14] having canceled the charge of our legal indebtedness, which stood against us and condemned us; he has taken it away, nailing it to the cross.

COLOSSIANS 2:13-14

HELLO FAMILY: A good time ago, I went on a weekend Christian event. Part of the program was writing on a piece of paper your deepest regrets ("sins"). Then a wooden cross was carried in and each man nailed that paper to the cross. A very emotional representation of this scripture, you and your sins written on a piece of paper, physically nailing it into the wood. In our flesh, we have fallen out of God's grace with our sin. The longer we put off coming home to our Father and our Lord Jesus, the more we falter. The repentance enables us to turn back towards our Lord, our Shepherd, with a clean slate. When our focus is our Lord, we hear the Holy Spirit tugging at us to be righteous. In turn, we transform into a new character, born again, coming to be in God's grace. Love you all.

DAY 111

For the eyes of the LORD range throughout the earth to strengthen those whose hearts are fully committed to him. You have done a foolish thing, and from now on you will be at war.

2 CHRONICLES 16:9

HELLO FAMILY: "Strengthen [the heart]...fully committed to him...from now on you will be at war." A whole bunch is going on here in this scripture for sure. In the flesh we are sinners by nature. Our only saving grace is surrendering and committing our livelihoods to Christ. Our daily lives are at war with all the temptations to battle. We mourn for those who have fallen because of the bad choices made, choices that bring sorrow into our lives and the lives of those we know. Our Father in Heaven does not want anyone being miserable in sin. "For the eyes of the LORD" are upon you. This scripture speaks truth for those who wander. The truth being we will be devoured by sin and misery in the end without our Shepherd Jesus Christ. Keep Christ close in our thoughts throughout the day and night. Talk to Him. He knows our voice when we call out His name. Love you all.

DAY 112

"'If you can'?" said Jesus. "Everything is possible for one who believes."

MARK 9:23

HELLO FAMILY: "One who believes" should exercise their faith and experience their possibilities. Relationships are fruitful when Jesus is at the top of our favorite contacts list. Birds of a feather flock together. So, fly with the believers. Make Jesus our daily go-to and He will always be there for us. 1 Corinthians 15:33 reads, "Do not be misled: 'Bad company corrupts good character.'" The key of this verse is that we must believe and establish relationships with other believers. This effort to exercise our beliefs will unleash our potential. The possibilities have no limits. Love you all.

DAY 113

Therefore, rid yourselves of all malice and all deceit, hypocrisy, envy, and slander of every kind. [2] Like newborn babies, crave pure spiritual milk, so that by it you may grow up in your salvation, [3] now that you have tasted that the Lord is good.

1 PETER 2:1-3

HELLO FAMILY: As you all know, the travels of this father have kept me far away from home for most of our lives. This scripture is of nurturing. I was not there to do that with you, but God was and still is. That's why I love this scripture. It reminds me of when Jesus had kids running around him. The disciples tried to chase them off and Jesus told them that you have to enter the Kingdom with the heart of a child. While traveling, I watched children experiencing flight for first time. They were listening and hanging on to every word of their parents, totally paying attention to every movement and body language displayed by their parents. Their innocence was pure, joyful, and excited, pure like a "newborn baby." Recognize the purity and innocence of our inner child. If the environment we are in is not healthy to a child's growth, then it's not healthy for our growth, either. Be aware of what we feed every part of ourselves, including our eyes (beware of pornography, greedy wants and desires), our ears (avoid graphic, unwholesome music and talk shows), and touch (physical touch is a language in itself, so do it with genuine sincere care, being sure we are receiving it that way also). Love you all.

DAY 114

The Sovereign LORD is my strength; he makes my feet like the feet of a deer, he enables me to tread on the heights. For the director of music. On my stringed instruments.

HABAKKUK 3:19

HELLO FAMILY: My goodness, this scripture reflects just plain fun, joy, and happiness! Running like deer, "director of music...on stringed instruments." Hey! God our Father wants you happy! Watch the young children around us play tag and hear the joyful laughs and giggles. Freeze tag was always a favorite of mine as a child. To see children today running like deer in excitement to stay free or free others from being frozen is a burst of joy and laughter for all to see. Add some music in the background and you may see the grandparents getting into that game as well. The strength of Christ is filled with freedom to love in all our relationships, spreading joy wherever we may be. Love you all.

DAY 115

Set your minds on things above, not on earthly things.

COLOSSIANS 3:2

HELLO FAMILY: What an early morning it has been. What a blessing it is to be able to relax in the midst of the hustle and bustle of life. Our faith in Christ and our focus on things above allows us to handle the delays, the upsetting news, and even the drama of politics. God is in charge. As our faith and our desire to comfort others in their times of need grow, we draw even closer to God. God does not shout across the mountains and valleys. God whispers, and the closer we are to God, the better we hear His voice. Absolutely Heaven on earth. Love you all.

DAY 116

For this God is our God forever and ever;
he will be our guide even to the end.

PSALM 48:14

HELLO FAMILY: Our Sunday school class has been studying the book, *When Christ Comes Again*. One of the chapters we recently covered was about those who are never churched and never hear the Gospel or even read the scriptures. This got many of us thinking...what happens to them? Reading through the Bible, we discovered that God speaks to many people through nature: in the sounds of raindrops and songs of the birds, the scents of wildflowers and saltwater beaches, and even the graceful movements of His animals. He speaks to all who seek Him. We mortal sheep are not the judge of what happens to us when we die. What is important is that we recognize who God is. All anyone has to do is sit quietly in the woods, on a balcony, or in a yard to recognize God's creation and might. On a spring morning, sit and listen to God's creation. Find that "place" in a park, the woods, or along a stream and look at the life around us. We have a responsibility to be fruitful with our knowledge of God and His Son Jesus Christ. We all need a Shepherd to guide us through life. Love you all.

DAY 117

People of Zion, who live in Jerusalem, you will weep no more.
How gracious he will be when you cry for help! As soon as
he hears, he will answer you.

ISAIAH 30:19

HELLO FAMILY: Yes, early morning here in Guam, having special time with the Lord. Guam has magnificent views with incredible history to match. Many thousands of Christians perished here during World War II. The mountains and jungles overwatching the valleys know the sounds of weeping. "As soon as He hears, He will answer you." Let us find comfort in realizing that when we weep, God hears us. There is no reason to wait until we are in distress (when bullets and bombs are flying) to start screaming for help to the One we know has been by our side our entire lives (God). I know that sounds harsh, but think about it. "You will weep no more." Encourage each other to get that communication line open with our Lord and Savior every day. He knows our thoughts and our dreams before we do. He knows what we are trying to pray about even when we are too scrambled to gather our thoughts. He guides our ways through the maze called life. Love you all.

DAY 118

What good will it be for someone to gain the whole world, yet forfeit their soul? Or what can anyone give in exchange for their soul? [27] For the Son of Man is going to come in his Father's glory with his angels, and then he will reward each person according to what they have done.

MATTHEW 16:26–27

HELLO FAMILY: "Reward each person [for] what they have done." Or for what they have not done. No rewards for you, mister! Can we imagine, talk about self-esteem issues. Many schools have changed their rewards programs so that every kid gets a trophy, whether they earned it or not. This cheapens the award itself and sets the standards to no standards at all. Now what about "once saved always saved" and that man on the cross? The man next to Jesus after he acknowledged Christ and asked for forgiveness? Christ basically told him, "You are coming with me to Heaven!" What "work" did he do as a criminal? To summarize passages Matthew 27:38, Luke 23:32–43, and Mark 15:27, we recognize for ourselves that Jesus is Lord. In our hearts we sincerely work by reading Gods Word, praying, and talking to Jesus. We worship with other biblically grounded Christians. As we work in this way, our hearts transform. Our emotions experience joy as we experience the Holy Spirit upon us in this service. We employ God's talents given to us and God's blessings flow through us to others. We are given more responsibility (rewards) in our godly transformations. In Heaven, our rewards may be very similar. For many are saved by the grace of God, not by the physical labor we do. It's all about our hearts. That is where it is at. It is far too tempting to score points in the church pew and check the box as a "working" Christian. Our hearts and motives have to stay true to the purpose of God's Kingdom here on earth. That must be our final motive when the day is done. Love you all.

DAY 119

Your hands made me and formed me; give me understanding to learn your commands.

PSALM 119:73

HELLO FAMILY: "Give me understanding." We call out to the potter who molded our very being. Help us to figure ourselves out, enable us to make the choices that are in compliance with, "what would Jesus do." The more we learn about ourselves, the better our relationships with everyone around us will be. Case in point: I am a hard nut to crack. It has taken almost 25 years to understand why I would be such a "sour pickle" just prior to deployments. My apologies to Carol and my entire family. I would go through a period of disconnecting or of un-interest to what would be going on in the family business. I was not being responsive to the emotional needs of my loved ones. I was putting up walls, getting silent, and dis-engaging myself in preparation for the tour of duty ahead of me, which could last a lifetime. Emotionally disconnecting from loved ones is not a good place to be. Some may say it is a survival response. Yes, I have my excuses. Coming to a place of understanding and fixing is the action I had to take. My prayer for understanding has been answered! Recognizing and understanding this mental process allowed me to watch my tongue and harness the stress of getting things done and genuinely make the most of the time I had to spend with my family. Controlling these emotions opened the doors to a lasting relationship with my wife, children, and parents. What a blessing! What a relief to have this understanding about **self**. Love you all.

DAY 120

So do not fear, for I am with you; do not be dismayed, for I am your God. I will strengthen you and help you; I will uphold you with my righteous right hand.

ISAIAH 41:10

HELLO FAMILY: "Do not fear." On many occasions we may witness people dealing with anxiety issues. Perhaps some have seen me having an anxiety issue with my kids. The drug industry thrives on us all having to deal with mental calamities, but this promise from God advises us to be calm, think patiently through the issue at hand, and trust God. **You** are in God's right hand. **You** are strengthened in Christ. When the pressure is building, the trips to the hospital are taking their toll, and the stresses at work are wearing us down, take a deep breath and hold it for ten seconds. Call on the Holy Spirit to light that path to success and work through life's challenges with grace, joy, and calmness. Love you all.

DAY 121

> *"If anyone causes one of these little ones—those who believe in me—to stumble, it would be better for them if a large millstone were hung around their neck and they were thrown into the sea."*
>
> MARK 9:42

HELLO FAMILY: During one Sunday school class Carol and I were running, one of the ladies said, "You are held more accountable Dan. You are a Sunday school teacher." If only I had remembered this scripture in that moment! Parents place their children in Sunday school class believing that the teachers in that class will do their very best to guide them as they learn about Jesus. They will guide them and dare not cause them to stumble. Our culture today is so abstract with concepts and teachings that are not in compliance with the biblical scriptures at all. We are warned here to not deviate from God's Word. Do not cause anyone to question or doubt what God's Word has declared, even when God's guidance is not politically or culturally "correct." As teachers, we must call upon the Holy Spirit to guide our thoughts, words, and actions. We are human and God knows our hearts, like He knows the hairs on our bodies. God created this world. He breathed life into it and us. Nothing is an accident. Keep your communication lines open always. Talk to Jesus. Listen for the guidance of the Holy Spirit and live. Love you all.

DAY 122

> *Why, my soul, are you downcast? Why so disturbed within me? Put your hope in God, for I will yet praise him, my Savior and my God. [6] My soul is downcast within me; therefore I will remember you from the land of the Jordan, the heights of Hermon—from Mount Mizar.*
>
> PSALM 42:5-6

HELLO FAMILY: "Put your hope in God." There are and will be times in our lives where we will break down. We will be driven to our knees in fear, disgust, misery, letdowns beyond words in relationships, and other life situations. This scripture is for those moments. This scripture calls out to us when we have been rejected, our loved ones have failed us (they are human too), or we have failed a huge task and the fallout is upon us. This scripture calls to **us all**! To have hope for better days ahead through Jesus Christ. It is God's plan for us to endure these tests. It is **promised** to us that we will come through these challenges much better people (think of the Bible story of Joseph). And because we are in God's hands and He is in control, there is a greater purpose for our troubles in service to His Kingdom. So don't panic! Pray and allow "what would Jesus do" to ring in our thoughts. Jesus would get up, just as He did with that cross on His back. Love you all.

DAY 123

But in your hearts revere Christ as Lord. Always be prepared to give an answer to everyone who asks you to give the reason for the hope that you have. But do this with gentleness and respect, [16] keeping a clear conscience, so that those who speak maliciously against your good behavior in Christ may be ashamed of their slander.

1 PETER 3:15-16

HELLO FAMILY: "Be prepared to give an answer" with "gentleness and respect." These are very wise words that are applicable to all our communications. Scripture always directs our thoughts, actions, and walks with Christ in a manner that "transforms" our characters. We become people who God can use to further His Kingdom here on earth. My pastor said it best from the pulpit one fine Sunday morning, "Don't throw a Bible to a drowning person. It won't help one bit!" How true. Most people that are drowning away in their lives take absolute offense to "Bible talk." With gentleness and respect, we can avoid offending those who take offense to any discussion of Christ. So don't discuss it, just do it. The Holy Spirit will at some point open our discussions at just the right time we may be able to share the Gospel. When those experiences enter our lives, we will know it for sure. Love you all.

DAY 124

"I make known the end from the beginning, from ancient times, what is still to come. I say, 'My purpose will stand, and I will do all that I please.'"

ISAIAH 46:10

HELLO FAMILY: When we are able to pause and enjoy the colors, smells, and sounds of nature, we know of God. We may ask ourselves how all of this came to be. Read and study the Bible to understand that there is a beginning and an end. That everything in between "is still to come." Yes, there are many religions, but there is only one God. One God that has the whole world in His hands and controls time. What is really important is that we accept this before our time comes to an end. God sent His Son Jesus to be recognized, accepted, and received by each of us. Then do "as you please," in Christ. Love you all.

DAY 125

One who has unreliable friends soon comes to ruin,
but there is a friend who sticks closer than a brother.

PROVERBS 18:24

HELLO FAMILY: More words of wisdom here. If your "friends" are not lifting you up, then they are bringing you down, perhaps even ruining you (that can apply to our marriages too). Take the prayer time to get it all figured out and if it walks like a duck and quacks like a duck, it is probably a duck. So, take action. True friends complement us and we complement them, we bring ourselves to perfection in Christ. Together, our words of encouragement and guidance allow us to grow joyfully. This scripture proclaims and promises that there is a "friend" out there for us who will build us up. He will not tempt us into situations that are not healthy and wise for a future or present Christian in the Kingdom of God. We pray that everyone can find that special friend, the one we can always call and converse with at the drop of a dime. Love you all.

DAY 126

Therefore encourage one another and build each other up,
just as in fact you are doing.

1 THESSALONIANS 5:11

HELLO FAMILY: Words of affirmation, family — a big love language that flows with yesterday's two cents' worth. Building joy and hope in one another gives excitement for the future and crushes depression. When we are in the midst of getting up from a fall, the last thing we need is someone making fun of us. What we need to hear is that voice of encouragement and motivation that gives us the energy to stand and fight. Surrounding ourselves in a church of Christians that openly encourage one another is a blessing beyond words. Wounds are healed and smiles are to be had by all who witness the miracles. The glass is **always** half full! Y'all have a super day! Love you all.

DAY 127

Yet you, LORD, are our Father. We are the clay, you are the potter; we are all the work of your hand.

ISAIAH 64:8

HELLO FAMILY: "We are the clay." Clay can be molded in many ways. We see this in all the personalities we experience in our lives, all of which serve a purpose. That purpose is to serve God. Everyone knows that when clay hardens it becomes very fragile and can shatter when a fall happens. Trust God. We don't want to give up. We don't want to stress out and we don't want to lash out at others. Most of all, we don't want to be a hardened spirit. We want to stay close to our Shepherd Jesus and enjoy the green grass He leads us to when it is time. Love you all.

50-CENT BONUS

I mentioned being saved in Germany and reading the Bible in secret. God has you in His hands, and there are actions that we must take in order to follow through on His promises. It is so important to find a church that stays out of politics and focuses on the cross. In regard to testimony, my first attempt failed because I chose to go it alone. I was destined to learn the hard way. In Germany I was without the support of other Christians in a world of beer and ladies, and I had a badge. I was a military policeman, 18 years age and full of pride and attitude. My squad leader would get very frustrated with me and I would get counseled on many occasions, reminded repeatedly that I was not the greatest thing since sliced bread. My squad leader was a golden glove boxer and I was advised that if I didn't straighten up, I was going to be on the receiving end of those gloves. Well, not all that much changed as my career in the military continued. Clearly in God's hands I was surviving; my German wife and I had two young daughters in a world without a church family to help guide us along. The military career had taken us to a Special Operations unit at Fort Campbell in Kentucky, and I had just received the great honor of competing with other Special Operations NCOs across the Special Operations Command. These men were comprised of Rangers, Green Berets, and other Operators in the Command. I was assigned to the Night Stalkers, Task Force 160th. It was 1987, and with God's grace, I completed and won the NCO of the Year competition at Fort Bragg, NC. Immediately after receiving this prestigious award I was led to the office of General Sudduth, by Command Sergeant Major Holmstock. I was a "support" guy, not a "tabber," and I had a packet to sign. This packet was a form that would volunteer me for Special Forces Training in the Qualification Course (SFQC).

This action was the final breaking point for my marriage with my now former wife, Dawn. She departed with our daughters back to Germany.

Continued on next page.

DAY 127, *continued from page 79.*

During my SFQC training on a free weekend at Fort Sam in Houston, TX, was when I met Carol. It was in a night club where I asked her to dance. Yes, God had it all under control. Time was moving very fast. Training was extremely intense and demanding. Carol and I maintained our relationship with phone calls and the occasional weekend visit. Upon graduation at Fort Bragg, we went back to Texas to be married in a small historical chapel in Tomball. Then, we took a fast trip to Clarksville, TN, where I was assigned to the 5th Special Forces Group at Fort Campbell, KY. All in matter of two weeks. Within the next month, I was already on my first deployment to Somalia. It was time to grow up fast for both Carol and me. Deployments led to more training upon arriving home. I was assigned to a SCUBA team, ODA 525 — the Sharkmen. My poor wife Carol was just hanging on the best she could with immense support from parents and the wives group of the unit. I would be home for a week or so only to leave again. In between here and there, our first son Shane was born on July 13, 1990. A month later was the invasion of Kuwait, and I departed with my team to Saudi Arabia. The Gulf War had begun.

Many letters were written and read between me and my wife. Our entire families came together in support. Before long, my team and I were given the mission to operate behind enemy lines in **Iraq**. During that mission we were compromised and had to be rescued. Several books have been written about this along with military documentaries on television. What are not in these books and movies are the deals I was making to and with God while being in this quest to survive. Everything from apologies and excuses to asking for a second chance to do it right this time. I was making more promises to get us out alive than anyone could ever have imagined.

Upon arriving back home with all the celebrations and thanking everyone I could for their support, Carol and I immediately joined a little Methodist Church in Pembroke, KY. During the war, Carol and I both turned to the cross for forgiveness and support, and now we had the support and love of a little country church. We became new members of a much larger family that stretched beyond any borders of any state or country. The family of God.

DAY 128

> *"My eyes will watch over them for their good, and I will bring them back to this land. I will build them up and not tear them down; I will plant them and not uproot them."*
>
> JEREMIAH 24:6

HELLO FAMILY: Growing up, we had "our bed." We had "our room" and other family factors where we felt very secure. We had a mom and a dad. We always had clothes to wear and food to eat. Life as kids was pretty cool. Sure, we had our moments of shakeups in the family, but for the most part, we were "watched over." Our Lord declares in this scripture, no more fear. No more panic. No more doubt. Enough is enough! When we pray for guidance and make wise decisions with Christ, we can rest easy in our homes. Home is where we just happen to be, and that's ok when you are there with Christ. Our real home is with Christ Himself, loved, fed, and healthy. Love you all.

DAY 129

Therefore we do not lose heart. Though outwardly we are wasting away, yet inwardly we are being renewed day by day. [17] For our light and momentary troubles are achieving for us an eternal glory that far outweighs them all. [18] So we fix our eyes not on what is seen, but on what is unseen, since what is seen is temporary, but what is unseen is eternal.

2 CORINTHIANS 4:16-18

HELLO FAMILY: Wow! This scripture today really hits my heart for us all. "**Do not lose heart.**" All of us around the world have experienced disappointments. Disappointments about the past and present and worries about the immediate future. Where does it all end? Read "outwardly we are wasting away." Looking at my dad wasting away recovering from open heart surgery and having all the complications possible, one after another, was as painful for the family to watch as it was for him to live through. Dad lost so much weight and had to deal with so much pain. But he knew he had to get up! Dad never lost heart. He never gave up. That was five years ago! I share with everyone that my parents are prayer warriors big time. They always have an ear for God's voice, managing their lives with service in their church. Imagine what our eyes do not see. Our bodies are always aging. Imagine your spirit growing stronger. The stronger our relationship with Christ is, it brings a better understanding of this scripture. Seek out how to love, then experience pure joy as a child does, no matter how old we get. There is great comfort, security, and warmth being in God's hands eternally. Love you all.

DAY 130

I waited patiently for the LORD; he turned to me and heard my cry. [2] He lifted me out of the slimy pit, out of the mud and mire; he set my feet on a rock and gave me a firm place to stand. [3] He put a new song in my mouth, a hymn of praise to our God. Many will see and fear the LORD and put their trust in him.

PSALM 40:1-3

HELLO FAMILY: "A firm place to stand." We sing "Standing on the Promises of God" in church, praising our Lord. For we have the confidence of our Lord in us. No matter the challenge, in Christ we shall prosper. Notice that "I waited patiently for the LORD." For those who know me well, I am not patient at all. It is a virtue that must be worked on and prayer is required for me as perhaps it is for many of us. Especially when Google always has an immediate answer and I get to pick which answer suits me best. Well, godly patience has a great deal of moving pieces involved—we may not be ready for that new car just yet. Love you all.

DAY 131

Have no fear of sudden disaster or of the ruin that overtakes the wicked, [26] for the LORD will be at your side and will keep your foot from being snared.

PROVERBS 3:25-26

HELLO FAMILY: "Have no fear." I remember as a boy, waiting for Friday, sitting there in a classroom with no worries in the world. When can we get on the school bus! Oh, the days of dreaming what mischief was to be had on the weekend! I had no worries, no fear climbing the deep cliffs of the Genesee River in Letchworth Park. Running with the cows at the farms, playing in the creeks (with snakes), climbing the trees, and playing paratrooper with my friends. Mom and Dad took care of the bills, the food, and providing a warm place to sleep. There was no fear. As I grew older, those weekends included longer overnight hikes along those cliffs, camping, and eating the fish that I caught (frogs, too). I even prepared and cooked frog legs for my mom on one of the adventure hikes (she is very brave). Even riding bikes all the way to town was such a joy for a boy with no fear. The Lord promises to protect us from the ruins that overtake the wicked. Yes, the wicked—we are aware of these people. They cross our paths in life from time to time. When we watch the news, numerous gangs are depicted as wicked. Terrorist organizations, ISIS, and others are shown doing horrible things to people and places on our TV screen and in YouTube videos. Everyone can surely understand the viciousness of the wicked that roam our streets. Our Lord keeps us from the snares of their misery. Listen for the Holy Spirit always, even as other people are talking. Listen when you feel the Holy Spirit warning you to stay away from drugs and alcohol and avoid staying out alone after dark. There is a reason to beware. A snare awaits along these paths that are set by the wicked, and we must choose another way. Being free of the "snares" out there keeps us from addictions and dependence on others who just want to use us. Stay close to the Shepherd and live free to experience true joy in the love of Christ, just as a child does under the protection and care of their mom and dad. Love you all.

DAY 132

Let us not become weary in doing good, for at the proper time we will reap a harvest if we do not give up.

GALATIANS 6:9

HELLO FAMILY: "Doing good"? "Harvest" what? Getting weary is what our pastor referred to as "getting burned out." We can get burned out on church just like anything else that consumes us. When the same core group of churchgoers gets tasked with "doing it all, year after year," it can get exhausting. This scripture proclaims, "do not give up." Carol and I used to provide workbooks for our Sunday school classes, and most of the time we found we were the only ones doing the homework. Well, look at us now! We learned—and now we all do the homework and questions together in the class. Our biblical study over the years has borne a harvest that is still coming at us and our church. Dedication and keeping the faith with a positive attitude is the key to a fulfilling harvest. If we are doing good things for others, chances are our church is growing and souls are being saved. Baptisms in the river to be celebrated come often when joyous hearts are serving the Lord. **Joy** is the key to a happy life. The Lord only knows what harvest is yet to come. Love you all.

DAY 133

For the word of the LORD is right and true; he is faithful in all he does.

PSALM 33:4

HELLO FAMILY: "Is right and true." Those are words of encouragement for all of us in the many promises God shares with us throughout the Bible. There are thousands of promises and our Lord is and will be faithful in every single one of them. Can anyone prove anything "false" in the Bible? Also, this is an encouragement for us to act "right and true" with each other and in everything that we do. When we do our absolute best at work, church, and play, we experience great adventures. Love you all.

DAY 134

> *But store up for yourselves treasures in heaven, where moths and vermin do not destroy, and where thieves do not break in and steal.*
>
> MATTHEW 6:20

HELLO FAMILY: So how do we store up "treasures in Heaven"? We have a hard enough time doing that here on earth, and this scripture wants us to do it in Heaven, too? Treasures in Heaven start with a relationship with Jesus Christ Himself. We must read about Him, talk to Him, and praise Him for what He is teaching us. We must ask Him to help us get through those tough things that frustrate us. What is your toughest thing to do when it comes to being godlike? I will share mine. Loving someone who is hard to love. They may be offensive to your spouse, they may have disrespected your very logical requests, and they may be grumpy and aggressive in nature. It is easy to stay away from these people who don't care a lick about me. So why should I waste a moment of time caring about them? Seems pretty simple—until we are in the spotlight to "store up" those treasures and set an example of love to all of God's children. The task is anything but simple. Know this: we can't work for the treasures we receive from God. We can't earn them either. God's grace is there so we can be graceful and generous with others. In Christ, all things are possible. Love you all.

DAY 135

> *He told them still another parable: "The kingdom of heaven is like yeast that a woman took and mixed into about sixty pounds of flour until it worked all through the dough."*
>
> MATTHEW 13:33

HELLO FAMILY: When flour is ground, it forms starches (sugars) and proteins. When water is added and the flour is kneaded, the tough elastic substance that is formed is called gluten. Gluten can stretch and trap the gas bubbles it gets from the added yeast. The gas is formed when enzymes from the yeast transforms the glucose in the sugar into carbon dioxide, which bubbles up throughout the mixture and causes the dough to "rise." "The Kingdom of Heaven" is like yeast. What does the yeast do? It transforms the glucose in the dough, allowing the dough to rise. So, Heaven is comprised of those who have transformed, like yeast does to dough. Their lives have risen to the occasion, so to speak. Their characters, hearts, and thoughts have become godly. A transformation in our lives and in our faith in our Lord Jesus Christ occurs as it does with yeast worked through dough. Love you all.

DAY 136

Let everything that has breath praise the LORD. Praise the LORD.

PSALM 150:6

HELLO FAMILY: "Everything" owes its joy in life to our Lord. Have you ever gotten the flu with major sinus congestion? Or perhaps you have experienced asthma attacks or Chronic Obstructive Pulmonary Disease? These conditions are horrible. When we witness a person dealing with the struggle to breathe, it causes great concern and the need for immediate prayer. Sometimes a trip to the hospital to recover. This scripture, Psalm 150:6, takes breathing to a whole new level of thought. Life is all about "breathing" and until you struggle getting a breath, you may never really appreciate it. For those blessed with great lungs get to enjoy all kinds of activities. Please stop and really thank God for your health. Use that health when the Holy Spirit calls on you to serve others who need a hand. Praise our Lord for all the days we are blessed with the ability to breathe fresh air freely. Love you all.

DAY 137

Humble yourselves, therefore, under God's mighty hand, that he may lift you up in due time.

1 PETER 5:6

HELLO FAMILY: "Humble yourselves." Oh yes, with all the blessings that God pours out gracefully among His children, one could get a little lazy and not give credit where credit is due. It is far too easy to fall into a prideful rant when our lives are just hunky dory in every way we can think of. We are warned to humble ourselves in greatness and even in despair. When our times are at their worst, this is when we must humbly return to our Father and pray for relief. When I think of being a young boy, full of pride and realizing there is no way I am getting this tractor out of the ditch by myself, I would humbly go to my father for help. Staying humble and in God's favor will aid in our relief in due time. Love you all.

DAY 138

There will be no more night. They will not need the light of a lamp or the light of the sun, for the Lord God will give them light. And they will reign for ever and ever.

REVELATION 22:5

HELLO FAMILY: A relationship in Christ grants our adoption into God's family—eternal life in God's presence with Jesus. A bright light it will be and to think there will be no more night. Death and the darkness that is thought of at that end of our lives is totally defeated. We do not need to think of death as darkness at all because it would not exist for us. I must grin a good bit when I think of my wife Carol turning on all the "night lights" in the house before we settle into bed. It is a security thing for her, to have that light on when our eyes open in the middle of the night. Light is security. God is security. He is always with us and will always be a light in both the metaphorical and physical darkness here on earth. We can rest assured we will be secure in the light of God. Love you all.

DAY 139

Surely your goodness and love will follow me all the days of my life, and I will dwell in the house of the LORD forever.

PSALM 23:6

HELLO FAMILY: "Goodness and love." With that daily in our lives, we should have big time smiles of joy always. That's what a father wants for his children. That's what our Father wants for us. Don't waste our thoughts on things we have no control of. Instead, focus on making future plans of action that bring joyous occasions to our lives, through "goodness and love." Joy fills my heart when making plans for our families to get together, which does not happen often. I get to watch my dad light up with joy when we discuss the details of upcoming events. Mom puts these special dates on a big calendar, and then everyone gets involved and the plans begin to flow. The joy of anticipation fills our hearts daily as the date gets closer. Take that goodness and love to work and bring big cheer there too. Love you all.

DAY 140

For in Scripture it says: "See, I lay a stone in Zion, a chosen and precious cornerstone, and the one who trusts in him will never be put to shame."

1 PETER 2:6

HELLO FAMILY: The "cornerstone" is the "stone" that sets the placement and sturdiness of an entire structure. The structure is you! We must have our minds locked in and know what to stand for, like every building that was ever built had a plan from the beginning of its construction. Structures that do not have a solid cornerstone to build upon will be offset, off balance, and uneven. Gravity will take its toll in a short amount of time. The structure will crumble, crack, and eventually crash down. Just like us when we don't build our lives upon the "rock" of faith. We are created with a purpose and must stand firm on the cornerstone, so we don't fall for all of the myths and temptations out there. You will suffer no "shame" standing firm in your relationship with Jesus. Love you all.

DAY 141

"Praise be to the LORD, who has given rest to his people Israel just as he promised. Not one word has failed of all the good promises he gave through his servant Moses."

1 KINGS 8:56

HELLO FAMILY: "Good Promises." Remember being a kid and one of your parents made you a "promise" and perhaps didn't keep it exactly like you wanted? I know I never did that as a parent with my kids, but I sure remember such occurrences growing up. Perhaps we may recall, "but, but Mom, you said we could stay up till 11 p.m. if we were good in the store." We later learn as parents, telling our kids anything to get them "moving along" or to prevent a "fit" in public is well worth a little light-handed promise. Our Father in Heaven is not breaking any promises. It is not who He is. This is why we read scripture daily. Focusing on the promises when they come up and there are thousands. There are so many that it gives us strength, hope, and joy for our future. We read "daily" because we forget easily, as the race of each day roles into weeks and months. When a "crisis" comes we aren't in a panic. Read daily! Faith must be practiced daily. Praise the Lord always and be confident in the paths set for us all. Love you all.

DAY 142

> *Once you were alienated from God and were enemies in your minds because of your evil behavior. [22] But now he has reconciled you by Christ's physical body through death to present you holy in his sight, without blemish and free from accusation— [23] if you continue in your faith, established and firm, and do not move from the hope held out in the gospel. This is the gospel that you heard and that has been proclaimed to every creature under heaven, and of which I, Paul, have become a servant.*
>
> COLOSSIANS 1:21-23

HELLO FAMILY: This is the **Gospel**, so please read this scripture again and again. "Established and firm." Because of the "original sin" that we all have had from the very start (reference the story of Adam and Eve in the book of Genesis), we were all alienated from God. We could not be in the presence of God stained by the original sin of Adam and Eve. Of course, we have sinned many times over to boot (our flesh being what it is) in addition to this original sin. Jesus is the only way for us to be free of the blemish of sin and accusations that this scripture is saying. "**If** you continue in your faith, established and firm." Know what you stand for, so you don't fall for anything. Love you all.

DAY 143

> *Let them praise his name with dancing and make music to him with timbrel and harp. [4] For the LORD takes delight in his people; he crowns the humble with victory.*
>
> PSALM 149:3-4

HELLO FAMILY: So great to spend time with Shane, Katie, and Bruce the German Shepherd too. And oh yes, the cat named Sherbet. I call him Garfield because he is Garfield made over (cartoon). We take delight in spending time with our family members. I am "humbled" to see God working in our lives, and I fully recognize the humble beginnings of our family growing up in a double wide trailer, in the back woods of Linton, KY. So many memories of laughter and love in those woods and fields. Our family is growing, just as the family of God grows. Dancing and music are heard in the heavens each time a member of the human race accepts Jesus Christ as their Lord and Savior. God is so good to all of us. Our lives are filled with singing and dancing. Love you all.

DAY 144

Love is patient, love is kind. It does not envy, it does not boast, it is not proud. [5] It does not dishonor others, it is not self-seeking, it is not easily angered, it keeps no record of wrongs. [6] Love does not delight in evil but rejoices with the truth. [7] It always protects, always trusts, always hopes, always perseveres.

1 CORINTHIANS 13:4-7

HELLO FAMILY: This would be a perfect scripture for Valentine's Day! Look at the "love" definitions here to ponder and take note. The biggest take away is its emphasis on what love is. "It keeps no record of wrongs"—that's the big one! How many times in our lives do we hear of relationships crashing because one of the parties involved will not forgive the other? What price is paid by children, parents, and other family members when spouses cannot forgive? When a son or daughter will not forgive a parent or a sibling? That is the big take away on this scripture. Rejoice for patience and kindness when dealing with our families. Truth, honesty, and forgiveness are pillars of godly character when starting, staying, and keeping a relationship healthy and growing. Yes, at times the truth can be hurtful, embarrassing, and humbling to disclose. Rest assured, it is the best path in the end. Love you all.

DAY 145

Those the LORD has rescued will return. They will enter Zion with singing; everlasting joy will crown their heads. Gladness and joy will overtake them, and sorrow and sighing will flee away.

ISAIAH 51:11

HELLO FAMILY: I was a little shocked that nobody asked, "Hey, where is our scripture devotional today Dad?" Every now and then we get caught up in these situations that take up our every waking moment. So to those waiting, patience was the call of this morning. Isaiah was a prophet around 700 years before the birth of Christ! 700 years these writings were written, reviewed, and read to the Jewish people by the great Jewish religious leaders in the places of worship throughout the land of Israel. So, when our patience is wearing thin, just imagine waiting for generations for the coming of Jesus. Are we not waiting now for the second coming of our Lord Jesus today? Every one of us is a "child" of God, needy of patience in our hearts. What an everlasting joy awaits those who are faithful. We await our inheritance of gladness and joy to come in God's time. Love you all.

DAY 146

*The Lord appeared to us in the past, saying:
"I have loved you with an everlasting love; I have
drawn you with unfailing kindness."*

JEREMIAH 31:3

HELLO FAMILY: "Unfailing kindness"! Can you just imagine applying that with the relationships we are in today, just starting with family? Whether it's our spouse, kids, parents, work mates, or neighbors, we have to ask ourselves, "Do we pass the test of unfailing kindness?" By accepting Jesus as Lord, we recognize that our God is the only true God that actually walked the earth with us and is still alive. No other faith can claim that. Our Lord Jesus Christ walked among us mere mortals and loved us with kindness. The body of Jesus Christ has never been found, because He has risen. Jesus lives at the right hand of God today. This scripture reminds us we serve a living God that was tempted in every such way as we are still today and did not sin. Love you all.

DAY 147

*"Again, truly I tell you that if two of you on earth agree
about anything they ask for, it will be done for them by
my Father in heaven. [20] For where two or three gather
in my name, there am I with them."*

MATTHEW 18:19-20

HELLO FAMILY: Carol and I pray together, holding hands at least once a day when I am home. Carol informs me of needed prayers to be said on whose behalf when I am on the road, so we can at least be on the same subject. Then at noon, Carol and I stop what we are doing and say the Lord's Prayer. Our family and church family are also saying the Lord's Prayer together at that time. Our Pastor Kenny Rogers started this over a year ago, and it brings great peace knowing our spiritual family is praying each and every day together at noon. Praying works, as I and countless others are witnesses to. Much of the answered prayers are reflected in the relationships our families enjoy together. I encourage all families to commit to family prayer. If you can hold hands with your family members and pray each day, that is awesome. If you are all separated, as our family is much of the time, pick that special time when everyone stops and prays together. Love you all.

DAY 148

Know that the LORD is God. It is he who made us,
and we are his; we are his people, the sheep of his pasture.

PSALM 100:3

HELLO FAMILY: Note the reference to sheep. Sheep are nothing but victims without their shepherd. Sheep need a shepherd for protection, guidance, and every bit of care. Sheep have the DNA to know their shepherd's voice. Ever wonder how multiple herds of sheep grazing in a massive pasture get separated in the evening when it is time to go to their shelters and follow their shepherd? The sheep actually know the voice of their shepherd and follow him. Some sheep are referred to as "bell sheep." These sheep have a very tight relationship with their shepherd. They stay on the shepherd's actual heels. They follow his or her every move. So, the shepherd will put a bell around their necks to assist the other sheep on where the shepherd actually is. Jesus is our Shepherd. Stay close to Him and know He will guide you to water, green grass, shade, and secure shelter. Perhaps someday you will get a bell put around your neck and find yourself on the heels of Jesus in the ministry of God among us mortal sheep. Love you all.

DAY 149

Trust in the LORD with all your heart and lean not on
your own understanding; [6] in all your ways submit to him,
and he will make your paths straight.

PROVERBS 3:5-6

HELLO FAMILY: It does not matter when you start your new year with Christ. For that matter, how about right now? Straight paths. Do we know what that means? No wasted time making mistakes, bending into peer pressures, or getting into situations where you need to clear your bank account to make things right. No need in being depressed over outcomes you had no control over. Because God is in control and we understand that. The drama of life will be limited when we trust in the Lord. A straight path gets us to the purpose of our lives the fastest and smoothest way! We have examples of those who have suffered greatly by getting on the crocked path. It is not for us to understand as it is written above. It is for us to trust the Lord and His teachings for our lives to remain on a straight path. As many great parents have said and our Lord is saying now, "Trust me, just do what I say, and everything will be fine." Love you all.

DAY 150

> *The LORD will rescue his servants; no one who takes refuge in him will be condemned.*
>
> PSALM 34:22

HELLO FAMILY: We had a situation at church where the daughter of one of our church attendees was in a car accident. Late for softball practice, she was speeding back to school and lost control of her car. She crashed over an embankment out of view from the road into a group of trees, trapping her inside her totaled car. She began to cry and pray feverishly. Her phone was out of reach with no cell coverage anyway, and it was starting to get dark. A young man saw a tree limb in the road. He stopped his truck to pick up the limb and remove it from the road by tossing it over the edge of the embankment. He did this to protect other drivers so they wouldn't hit the limb as he almost did. He heard crying from the trees below and went to investigate, finding our frightened 16-year-old driver. She is totally fine now. She had some bruises from her seatbelt and being banged around a bit, but that was it. Now reread that passage and take heart. Whatever a child of God may get themselves into, God is there. You will be rescued. Even from ourselves and the situations we get into on a day-to-day basis. Love you all.

DAY 151

> *And whatever you do, whether in word or deed, do it all in the name of the Lord Jesus, giving thanks to God the Father through him.*
>
> COLOSSIANS 3:17

HELLO FAMILY: "Giving thanks to God." Whatever situation we are in, always be thankful. Being in a thankful spirit makes our days much happier and filled with much more joy. And everyone who is working around us senses the peace we have, which calms the work environment. As we grow and accept more responsibilities in our careers, managers take note of those who can handle the additional tasks with a peaceful self-controlled spirit. No cursing and no drama body language to speak of. Just peace of heart to think through the tasks ahead and take care of each situation as it comes up. What is the big secret? We recognize that God is not going to task us with anything we cannot handle and we are thankful for the experience and opportunity to challenge ourselves with Christ at our side. Love you all.

DAY 152

> *Listen to your father, who gave you life, and do not despise your mother when she is old. [23] Buy the truth and do not sell it—wisdom, instruction and insight as well. [24] The father of a righteous child has great joy; a man who fathers a wise son rejoices in him.*
>
> PROVERBS 23:22-24

HELLO FAMILY: Wise words here, coming from your Father in Heaven and supported by your father here on earth. As a family grows, we are all accountable to each other. We must be righteous and caring and do our best each day. I recall getting pretty darn upset when my sons were not in compliance with their mother's instructions, especially being away from home and hearing the hurt in Carol's voice that the "boys" were or one of them was not being very kind and obedient. It would just fester in my heart, making me stew in thought on how to handle it all. But then on the flip side of the situation, I would also receive news from Carol that the boys were such a big help—working on the yard together, doing their chores, playing, and being nice with each other. This good news brought amazing joy to my heart. Hearing this news from afar got me thinking of great ideas to share with my boys as a reward upon my return. Think about God and Jesus getting and receiving this information about us! Those good news stories are the best ever for any parent, especially from a teacher or a coach at school! Parents love to "brag" about their children, and why not? We see how this scripture is very truthful still today and will be for eternity. Love you all, and one day I know my dad will read this and feel the same way.

DAY 153

> *The light shines in the darkness, and the darkness has not overcome it.*
>
> JOHN 1:5

HELLO FAMILY: Light is energy. God is the source of all energy! Where there is no energy, there is total darkness. Think about the activities that are dependent on darkness, many of which are criminal. No burglar wants to get caught, especially clearly on camera when they trigger a motion sensor light that illuminates their crime. The "light" shines and exposes truth. All the little secret tales that the hateful come up with to smear one another seem to be the darkness of this day, especially with social media platforms. We need light. We need truth to expose what is really going on these days and always. Our faith teaches us to be honest, to be the light, and to be righteous. What a blessing it is when we have leaders who hold themselves accountable to our Savior Jesus Christ. What a blessing we can be to each other. Be faithful and accountable to our Lord and Savior Jesus Christ. In this, we are morally accountable to the highest authority—God. Love you all.

DAY 154

*In peace I will lie down and sleep, for you alone,
LORD, make me dwell in safety.*

PSALM 4:8

HELLO FAMILY: "Lie down and sleep." Well, we all know how grand it is to get a great night's sleep. In the US Army Ranger School at Fort Benning, you are trained to operate under serious sleep deprivation under some very challenging work environments. You must (or you fail) complete very demanding physical and mental tasks under sleep and food deprivation. You will patrol all night long and be expected to stay awake for days on end. You will be conducting missions utilizing small unit tactics against the enemy. You will be graded on whether or not you got your squad or platoon "killed" in action, and you get big deductions if caught taking a "nap." To lie down and sleep takes on a whole new meaning to those who have been through this training or other similar experiences. This scripture takes an even greater meaning to those who have survived in combat operations. Our Lord is keenly aware of those praying for a peaceful sleep. My memories are absent of plentiful sleep in miserable situations—getting only three or four hours would barely allow me to recharge my body. This scripture has brought many Christians a much-needed peaceful sleep over the thousands of years it has been written and shared. Our faith and being aware of this very scripture have comforted many of us to lead men and women in battle. This scripture has brought astronauts safely back to earth and given peace of mind and rest to presidents during major crises. A deep, peaceful, and safe sleep—how great it is! Trusting in God and staying close to the Shepherd allows our hearts to be well rested for the days and challenges ahead. Love you all.

The story behind this photo is that my wife would get after me when discussions would differ and call me the "Wizard" because she accused me of "knowing everything." When we were teaching Sunday school classes and I would express my thoughts that would not precisely match Carol's, the "Wizard" comment would resurface. Before long, the "Wizard" label was alive and well. After a good bit of fun over the years, a close church friend was out and about and saw this car—got behind it and took this picture for a good laugh. Ironically enough, it was their daughter who had the car crash, stranded in a ravine. I wrote about this on Day 150 *(page 93)*.

DAY 155

You are my hiding place; you will protect me from trouble and surround me with songs of deliverance.

PSALM 32:7

HELLO FAMILY: A hiding place, a time out, a place to reflect, and a place to pray. Every Christian has this place to go to and get real with our Lord. It's a must. For many years, my "place" was in the wilderness wherever I was. Whether on patrol on a field exercise or even in a combat situation, I found a place. Generally, it was next to a stream, under a tree, a shaded place in the desert, or even an empty bombed out building with a view. There are troubles around every corner, and our mind needs to quickly "hide" and regain the edge, to solicit the Holy Spirit to the fight. This scripture reminds us of the songs of deliverance to call upon and celebrate each challenge as a way to grow in Christ. We will be victorious! This is a means to calmly deal with all of the decisions at hand and be able to articulate a direction to those in our influence when chaos and troubles lurk along our paths. Love you all.

DAY 156

May our Lord Jesus Christ himself and God our Father, who loved us and by his grace gave us eternal encouragement and good hope, [17] encourage your hearts and strengthen you in every good deed and word.

2 THESSALONIANS 2:16-17

HELLO FAMILY: "Eternal encouragement and good hope." Note eternal—that's forever and ever. We are afforded encouragement and hope in our faith. Never give up on prayer, on God's Word (scripture), and gathering together for worship with others in faith, praising our Lord. Know that this practice draws you closer to God! You will hear God's voice and even the whispers. The blessings will flow. These pillars of Christianity will surely strengthen you in every way the human body can be strengthened. Love you all.

DAY 157

> *Dishonest money dwindles away, but whoever gathers money little by little makes it grow.*
>
> PROVERBS 13:11

HELLO FAMILY: Money earned is money respected. Example: fast money won at a casino disappears about as fast as it's won. Who can resist the chance at fast money? Look at the lotteries and casinos all around us. Huge enterprises with billions of dollars tempting us all at every turn on the billboards across our nation. I can remember as a young boy getting my first savings account book. Every few dollars I would earn on the farms around us, I would make a special trip to the bank. It was a super big deal! I felt so important and official going into the bank building, walking up to the teller with maybe $14 or so. I would pass the teller my money and then have to update that little book of mine. My secret plan was to earn enough to buy a motorcycle. A green Kawasaki 125 dirt bike. I had all the marketing books from Kawasaki featuring this bike hidden under my bed. The numbers slowly grew, and I earned interest too! After a good many years, I was old enough and had enough money to buy that motorcycle. It cost $728! That "dirt" bike was the cleanest dirt bike in the world! Yes, it was ridden hard across the farm fields and woods in all kinds of weather, but it was cared for meticulously. This dirt bike was earned, "little by little." It took years to save up for, to ponder over the magazines, to look in the window of the Kawasaki dealership, and to dream on. Proverbs 13:11 is clearly a word of wisdom. Consistent savings from our efforts will be fruitful for the years ahead. Love you all.

DAY 158

> *"And whoever wants to be first must be slave of all. [45] For even the Son of Man did not come to be served, but to serve, and to give his life as a ransom for many."*
>
> MARK 10:44-45

HELLO FAMILY: This scripture directly challenges our worldly rule, "What's in it for me." Many times as a child of God, you will feel the tug of the Holy Spirit to "stop and pick up that stick in the road." You saw the stick, you could go around it, you could get hit by another car out there picking it up, but you stop so somebody else doesn't hit it. As a child of God, trust the serving tugs of the Holy Spirit, even when nothing is in it for you. God is leading the way, and we never know where that path will lead us until we make the turn. Love you all.

DAY 159

I pray that out of his glorious riches he may strengthen you with power through his Spirit in your inner being, [17] so that Christ may dwell in your hearts through faith. And I pray that you, being rooted and established in love, [18] may have power, together with all the Lord's holy people, to grasp how wide and long and high and deep is the love of Christ, [19] and to know this love that surpasses knowledge—that you may be filled to the measure of all the fullness of God.

EPHESIANS 3:16-19

HELLO FAMILY: "May have power, together with all the Lord's holy people, to grasp how wide and long and high and deep is the love of Christ." Huge love! There is a reason worship is a key to pleasing God. He wishes for us to witness to each other, to hear each other's prayers and blessings that we all experience as God's children. Our worship services are filled with the "Lord's holy people" and are a means to be "filled to the measure of all the fullness of God." I for one had a big stumbling block to climb in order to go to church with a serving heart. I was in a spiritual ditch, evaluating each sermon with a "what did I get out of that" attitude. That ditch was hard to get out of, but when it happened, my life was totally changed for the good. Love you all.

DAY 160

He will swallow up death forever. The Sovereign LORD will wipe away the tears from all faces; he will remove his people's disgrace from all the earth. The LORD has spoken.

ISAIAH 25:8

HELLO FAMILY: "Swallow up death forever"! This was written about 700 years before Christ was even around! Christ "He" defeats death. He is the final sacrifice, affording us to obtain eternal life, therefore, defeating death once and for **all**. Amazing how God's timeline works. It is not our impatient timeline, that's for sure. As we all are aging each and every day, we experience and witness the numerous funerals, lives gone in a breath. Take the time to remember these scriptures that proclaim victory over death through our Lord Jesus Christ. It is a celebration, knowing that our brother and sisters in Christ will be in their eternal resting place where we all will soon be. Wipe away your tears. The Lord has spoken. Love you all.

DAY 161

> But we have this treasure in jars of clay to show that this all-surpassing power is from God and not from us. [8] We are hard pressed on every side, but not crushed; perplexed, but not in despair; [9] persecuted, but not abandoned; struck down, but not destroyed.
>
> 2 CORINTHIANS 4:7-9

HELLO FAMILY: Ah yes, the clay mentioned again in scripture, this time in reference to the challenges of life, of our faith, and our relationships. What do we mean about relationships? We persecute, crush, perplex, create, and cause despair with others via our relationship skills or lack thereof. It's 2021! The age of social media. The age of critical thinking and reading between the hashtags. The age of smear campaigns. See if it sticks and watch them crumble in dismay. It is time to set some goals and write them down so we can post them on our phones' home screens. This way, it is the first thing we see in the morning when we reach for our phones. First, be positive, employ words of encouragement with every sentence we speak and every text and post on social media. Second, be keen to catch ourselves and correct ourselves before we hit the send button. Third, let us go a step further and make **time** to make voice calls to our family members who may struggle texting, hashtagging, or finding Facebook posts. There are those out there who love us dearly and would love to hear our voices. There is a great deal of power out there in our communications systems, many of which are too high speed to keep up with. Take care to not leave out our loved ones who are getting as fragile as clay jars. Love you all.

DAY 162

> "Consider carefully what you hear," he continued. "With the measure you use, it will be measured to you— and even more. [25] Whoever has will be given more; whoever does not have, even what they have will be taken from them."
>
> MARK 4:24-25

HELLO FAMILY: "Consider carefully what you hear." Ever hear the saying, "Believe nothing you hear and only half of what you see"? This is a direct reference to gossip, or fake news as we call it in America these days (thank you, President Trump). What all this means is that we should cherish our credibility and not destroy it by being the naysayer or embellishing the truth. Which can be very entertaining at times. (I know from some fishing stories shared.) We must put ourselves in check by asking what our motives are for repeating what we hear from others. That "motive" will clearly identify if there is going to be any good that comes from spreading hearsay news. We need to ask ourselves, "Are we adding to the story?" Because then we must deal with the consequences of the actual truth coming out in the future. It can be "measured onto me" as the source of the false preaching, and we don't want to be that source. Be honest with our words and the news we share. Gossip can cut like a sword. Love you all.

DAY 163

> "What should we do then?" the crowd asked. [11] John answered, "Anyone who has two shirts should share with the one who has none, and anyone who has food should do the same."
>
> LUKE 3:10-11

HELLO FAMILY: Here we are encouraged to be "generous" with our belongings. I used to get perturbed when writing checks to the church in my younger days. Honestly, there are moments I still do. Growing up and listening to my parents, friends, and family members, I learned that money was never easy to come. There were times we kids would even have to pitch in with our money earned from working on other farms to help out with the bills. But when it is all said and done, this isn't about the money. It is about our faith. Do we have faith to be as generous with others as we are to ourselves? God is going to bless us generously. It is one of the many promises written in the Bible. There are many ways to be generous with our blessings and spiritual gifts as a Christian. It is not just about the cash flow. "What should we do, then?" Pray and the answer will come upon you. There will be peace in your heart when the right decision is made. Love you all.

DAY 164

From birth I have relied on you; you brought me forth from my mother's womb. I will ever praise you.

PSALM 71:6

HELLO FAMILY: "I will ever praise you." Rely on our Lord and Savior in all that we do. Read those Bible stories to our children and be sure they hear the Word of God. It is just plain critical for children to hear the Word of God! Each of us has been brought forth from birth to where we are today with the means to provide support and love to each other in Christ. We all so graciously do. Know in our hearts where that comes from. Teach our children where that comes from. Praise God for our families and loved ones. Pass it on to our good friends and neighbors that make our lives a joy to live. Live with a thankful heart. Praise God each and every morning. Love you all.

DAY 165

My dear children, I write this to you so that you will not sin. But if anybody does sin, we have an advocate with the Father—Jesus Christ, the Righteous One. [2] He is the atoning sacrifice for our sins, and not only for ours but also for the sins of the whole world.

1 JOHN 2:1-2

HELLO FAMILY: Yikes, there is that word again, "**sin**." As sheep, we can't help ourselves from getting into dangerous situations (sin). Notice "and not only for ours but also for the sins of the whole world." Sometimes we can catch ourselves being very judgmental, making excuses to not love the folks out there who are hard to love. These folks may even be members of our families or our so-called friends. It is not for us to be worried about it nor judge why a relationship exists in this way; they just do. **And** we are not expected to endure harm to ourselves or our loved ones because of sin. Our calling is to be generous and to love one another–be safe doing so! We have an advocate with the Father–Jesus Christ–bring it to Him. Stand for Christ and recognize what He has done for all of us. Love you all.

DAY 166

> I love the LORD, for he heard my voice; he heard my cry for mercy. [2] Because he turned his ear to me, I will call on him as long as I live.
>
> PSALM 116:1–2

HELLO FAMILY: This exact scripture happened with me in Iraq, in that ditch, which explains why there is a deep passion to write all of this down and create a book. Our Special Forces Team ODA 525 was completely surrounded many miles behind enemy lines. We were overwhelmed by the number of men hunting us down and shooting at us. When the bombs started dropping dangerously close, I cried out for **mercy**! "He turned his ear to me." **And**, we all survived. Regretfully, my stubborn heart took years to go all in with trusting God. How quickly we can forget the troubles that we have survived in the past. These dire situations—we call out to Jesus for help and miracles actually happen on our behalf—cannot be forgotten. Having daily prayer and time with God is a precious reminder of the grace that has been bestowed upon us all. Love you all.

DAY 167

> For it is God who works in you to will and to act in order to fulfill his good purpose.
>
> PHILIPPIANS 2:13

HELLO FAMILY: "To fulfill His good purpose." Just look at how the world turns. Look at how our aspirations and our motives have changed over the years. God works in each of us differently on different timelines. We are in different seasons of spiritual maturity, and God's wisdom is keenly aware of what we can handle and at what time in our lives we can handle it, much like an infant growing and able to eat different foods as he or she develops. Getting God involved in our daily activities is our conscious effort to please **Him**. This will open up more opportunities to learn more about God, which will lead us to becoming better people to serve our families and our communities. This process fulfills God's good purpose in our world in ways we may never understand. One time I asked my pastor, "What should I do?" He simply stated, "Just do what you do." Call out to God and request guidance. Request the presence of the Holy Spirit in your daily walk and let the good times roll. Love you all.

DAY 168

Now listen, you who say, "Today or tomorrow we will go to this or that city, spend a year there, carry on business and make money." [14] Why, you do not even know what will happen tomorrow. What is your life? You are a mist that appears for a little while and then vanishes.

JAMES 4:13-14

HELLO FAMILY: This is one of those scriptures where we really have to think hard. Why wouldn't we make plans to go and make money for the next year? This scripture implies that we don't even have a clue of what tomorrow will bring. So why make plans? The takeaway is, "What is your life?" There is the possibility that we will not make it to next year, and I agree. The scripture states that "we" are going to focus on making money and that's it. But then it warns that each day is a gift and we should live it being present, being in the moment. Not worried about tomorrow or the day after. Love you all.

DAY 169

Defend the weak and the fatherless; uphold the cause of the poor and the oppressed. [4] Rescue the weak and the needy; deliver them from the hand of the wicked.

PSALM 82:3-4

HELLO FAMILY: This scripture reflects the title of this book and recognizes how vulnerable we are without a father. We are called as Christians to be defenders. Serving in the military has opened the eyes of many veterans, to witnessing firsthand an oppressed people. One reason I was attracted to the Special Forces was my hope to live among an oppressed people and see them liberated, much like, what we saw in the streets of Kuwait when liberated from Iraq many years ago. Evil forces of greed and wickedness seemed too great to overcome, which I saw firsthand in Somalia. Orphanages were the saddest sights while on such deployments. Innocent children foraging through garbage dumps and begging in the streets. Only the very strong survived. Not everyone is able to serve the Lord in the military, but there are always opportunities right here at home to contribute and make a difference. Ministries serve throughout the world with assistance from other international organizations on every continent. Ask the Lord where you can assist in these efforts and answer your calling. The fatherless, elderly, sick, and widows with kids needing a helping hand may even be as close as a neighbor. Love you all.

DAY 170

If we confess our sins, he is faithful and just and will forgive us our sins and purify us from all unrighteousness.

1 JOHN 1:9

HELLO FAMILY: Stay firm and exercise your faith. What? This scripture is saying we have to confess to being "bad," and who are we confessing to? Growing up in a loyal Catholic family, I recall the many trips to the confessional booth to "tell" my bad behavior to the secret voice behind the darkened window with the little holes in it. I was pretty sure it was the priest of the parish. But every once in a while, I wondered what would happen if someone else was in there. So, when I was a little older and braver, I dared my friend to sneak in there and "be the priest." Now you know why I had to go confession each and every weekend! As we grow older, reaching our teens, chances are we know everything, right? Of course not. We have to deal with our new freedoms and keep an open line of communication with our Lord even more! This is why it is so important to share the word of God with our children when they are young and still listen to us parents. They grow up very fast and we want them to always know that God loves them and wants the best for them, just like our earthly moms and dads do. Love you all.

DAY 171

You have searched me, LORD, and you know me. [2] You know when I sit and when I rise; you perceive my thoughts from afar. [3] You discern my going out and my lying down; you are familiar with all my ways.

PSALM 139:1–3

HELLO FAMILY: No secrets! Just think back of all the "tall tales" we have told. How about all the bold-faced lies we told our parents to get away with our secret agendas. Telling these lies just gets easier and easier the more we get away with them. Far too many times, my boys would be into something and I would question the situation. When a pause in the answer occurred (they were creating a storyline in their head), I knew I wasn't getting the facts. We all inherently twist the truth just enough to survive and go about our business, maybe even to help a friend or sibling. Scripture challenges each of us to be honest with ourselves, our family, and everyone we meet. Our faith and our Lord call for it for our own good, and for the good of our character. Love you all.

DAY 172

> *But when the set time had fully come, God sent his Son, born of a woman, born under the law, [5] to redeem those under the law, that we might receive adoption to sonship.*
>
> GALATIANS 4:4–5

HELLO FAMILY: "Adoption to sonship"! Eternal family of God! "Adoption"! Jesus as our Lord and Brother! Just pause and think about that. It's here now at our fingertips. Engage in that relationship. Harness the communications and guidance in decisions we make from our family in Heaven. God, Jesus, and the Holy Spirit. We had a wonderful example of faith and trust today in church. The scene is during a children's sermon and the teacher asked for a volunteer. One of the 8-year-old girls raised her hand. The teacher advised her that she was going to demonstrate faith by being blindfolded and in the dark. She was to trust her teacher and obey her commands as she was led around with the teacher holding her hand. Then came the moment of truth. The teacher let her hand go free and said, "Do you still trust me?" "Yes," the girl replied. The teacher then commanded her to take three long steps forward then turn around (remember the 8-year-old girl is still blindfolded). A chair was quietly put behind her after she turned around. The teacher then commanded her to sit down. But the girl did not sit down until she felt for the chair behind her. Then she sat down on it. After the blindfold was removed, the teacher asked the girl, "Did you not trust that a chair was there for you to sit on?" Everyone smiled a huge grin as this little girl blushed and hugged her teacher. This example of trust, blind faith, is exactly what we are doing as siblings of Christ. We just need to trust our Brother. Love you all.

DAY 173

Enter his gates with thanksgiving and his courts with praise; give thanks to him and praise his name.

PSALM 100:4

HELLO FAMILY: We have "entered" a new day, a new "gate." Bring blessings of joy and praises to everyone we meet. Blessings to us from God are to be passed to others and to bring them joy, too. I had an 8-month-old baby in my arms today at church. That was not planned at all. To be honest, I was feeling a bit in the slumps, just exhausted from a super-hot and humid week of activities, work issues, and internal struggles. I even complained about the 40-minute drive to church that morning. Yep, just one of those Sunday mornings where I was the one in great need of spiritual encouragement. Our pastor's wife was helping one of the moms, and this little boy wanted no part of it. The little rascal wanted to come to me! My pastor's wife just simply asked, "Can you hold him?" So I did. What followed during that church sermon was the best of times for me and that baby boy, while he was playing with my eyeglasses holder, rocking with the gospel music, singing, and trying to figure out how to remove my wedding ring from my thick finger. We even got a game of toe pincher in there between the music. This little boy was not fighting me at all. He was quiet and content with big smiles and soft giggles. God knows our hearts and our internal issues. His gates are always open, just like the church doors are always open on a Sunday morning. Let us all be thankful for a God who responds to our hearts in ways only He knows will make a difference. Love you all.

DAY 174

Finally, be strong in the Lord and in his mighty power. [11] Put on the full armor of God, so that you can take your stand against the devil's schemes.

EPHESIANS 6:10-11

HELLO FAMILY: Full body armor. Thinking of the time when I served in the military and most recently visiting my son at Fort Benning brings back awful memories about body armor. It's always heavy. When wet, it gets even heavier and absolutely cumbersome, restricting our movements in every way imaginable. As soldiers, we are not "asked" if we would like to wear body armor. It is a direct order — "Put on that Kevlar helmet now." One of my friends who had recently returned from the war in Iraq explained to me that he was shot in the head while wearing the dreaded Kevlar® helmet. He made it very clear that the Kevlar helmet saved his life. The impact of the bullet about broke his neck. He totally accredited this helmet of armor for saving his life. Faith in our Lord, His commands and directives are there to "save" our lives as well from miserable times here on earth. Listening keenly to the guidance of our Lord will bring us joy while on earth and eternal salvation when we pass. Love you all.

DAY 175

Whoever is patient has great understanding, but one who is quick-tempered displays folly.

PROVERBS 14:29

HELLO FAMILY: Ah yes! A day for memories. I do recall a time in my younger years where patience was absent. Follies were plentiful, and many around me closed their eyes and ears. My foul words and body language could be deplorable. Regretfully, my sons have referred to these moments with Dad as being on death row. They knew it was coming, they just didn't know when ("quick-tempered"). What my sons were referencing were my explosive outbursts, being impatient with the boys when there was a job to get done. For me, hearing them say that was a kick in the gut, knowing that my sons didn't value the time with their dad out in the work fields and woods at our little farm. I am extremely thankful that now my sons and I can be "freely" open in our conversations without getting too fired up. They are both much bigger than I am now, too. I do take that into consideration before I return my jabs. It takes hard truths to become more understanding in our quest to be better fathers, husbands, and sons. Being a godly person takes great understanding about ourselves more than anything else. Whoever has patience has great understanding, just as this scripture proclaims. Love you all.

DAY 176

> *"'But I will restore you to health and heal your wounds,' declares the Lord, 'because you are called an outcast, Zion for whom no one cares.'"*
>
> JEREMIAH 30:17

HELLO FAMILY: Restored health and wounds **healed**! Where do I sign up? Wounds are not always physical, that is for sure. As we age with grace (some are laughing), many occasions arise with our fellow friends and families that bring into discussion matters dealing with depression. The actual word "depression" may never come up because that word can be taken as a meaning of weakness. The signs are all there. The longing to find a place to live alone. The drunken discussions of past memories, some good and some not so good. The bitter references to marriages gone bad and current ones to complain about. Going to a place and having it "my way" is a big one. Not too long ago, a close veteran friend was dealing with immense anxiety issues and was sent to be evaluated. He was receiving treatment after his diagnoses and pretty much had all of us fooled into believing he was well, up until one evening when a phone call came to me from a detective. My good friend had taken his own life. As I sat there in disbelief, recalling every conversion we had had over the years, and some very recently, I came to realize that he just needed and wanted to be left alone. We may find ourselves needing to be left alone at times. God has blessed us with places to retreat and be in "His" creation. We can use these places to heal and recharge ourselves. God is there to help us organize our thoughts and pick up the pieces so we can rebuild. One of these places is church. So declares the Lord, "I will restore you to health and heal your wounds." This is a **major** promise that we all can be a witness to. Love you all.

DAY 177

Jesus answered, "It is written: 'Man shall not live on bread alone, but on every word that comes from the mouth of God.'"

MATTHEW 4:4

HELLO FAMILY: Eat up every word in the Bible and stand by it, totally. We must be confident in our faith and put into practice the study of scripture to allow the Holy Spirit to speak to us. For us to hear the voice of God, we must be close enough to hear Him whisper. Truly interpreting what a particular scripture means in our daily walk is a gift that will feed us always. There are too many accounts to reflect upon in which my old self would anchor in and not go to church, not read the Bible, and for sure not pray with any sincerity. It took some hard knocks to shake me up and get level with God, to put into practice what all the promises from God meant to a man who thought he had it all figured out. It is still a challenge to just "do it" sometimes. We will still struggle with our old ways and backslide from time to time. Our Lord truly does have us all in His hands and will show us very quickly how love conquers all. We just need to stay the course and trust God. I pray for us all that His Love will conquer our daily walk. Love you all.

DAY 178

Sing to him, sing praise to him;
tell of all his wonderful acts.

PSALM 105:2

HELLO FAMILY: Wow! What timing. "Tell of all his wonderful acts" is what this book is all about. Like I stated earlier, I want my children to read these scriptures to their children every day. I want everyone to be aware of God's promises and how they have been offered to us all. I especially pray that every child gets to hear the Word of God. God's grace on their families. Every single person has tribulations of their very own and if they are reading this, they have survived. We live with constant reminders of the struggles that humanity has—they're in every news story and headline in the paper and on the television. It is so very important to provide hope to humanity around us of how God's Word has moved our hearts with hope and strength to carry us on in this life. It brings great joy to our Lord when we recognize Him as the source of our resounding joy. Our Creator deserves all the credit and we are called upon to "sing to Him." As many may know, singing is not my day job. However, in church I have on rare occasions been called upon to be the "Song Leader." It does take a good bit of time for me to be called upon for that duty. Good thing for short memories. That's worship, folks! Sing with joy on Sundays and every opportunity we get. Love you all.

50-CENT BONUS

Enter Monty Flanigan from Day 60's 50-Cent Bonus. We were both working behind the scenes in our units in support of operational teams deploying to forward operating bases (FOBs). As time permitted, Monty and I would pray and talk about the biblical times we were living in. It was not long before news of casualties, and then fatalities, of our brothers on the ground in Afghanistan came in. The days and nights that followed were prioritized to support the families of the fallen in every way conceivable. I still carry those very emotional and heart-wrenching memories of pain in the loved ones faces. I watched as "Brother" Monty, still MSG Flanigan, found the composure and words of the Bible to calm and give peace to rooms filled with broken hearts. Brother Monty provided countless prayers for so many during this time. Monty prayed at the memorial services. The Holy Spirit was present in his speech and voice, bringing peace to so many. As time passed, I was eventually allowed to retire from the military. I had a "job" as an air marshal with big plans in Chicago. With the realization of the devastation it would have on my family, leaving such a godly community in Cadiz, KY, I resigned. Thankful for the relationships in Cadiz, I was immediately granted a position in the Trigg County Sheriff's Department. My mentor and yes, another big brother from God was Kenneth Butts. He was tasked to train me.

Ken was a devout Baptist with a heart of pure gold. Ken worked till he dropped to serve the community he grew up in and loved. A worn-out Bible was in his patrol car and came out every day for a lesson after every traffic stop or call out. Ken and I really hit it off, and our wives did, too. They were soon to be working together at the elementary school. Carol and I eventually attended the Baptist church Ken and Kathy attended. This was a big change for Carol and me. We had Sunday morning service, Sunday school, then fellowship, and then evening prayer service. Times were changing, moving in the right direction. Yet at times I still felt like I was just checking a box, so to say. Our pastor was moving on and we received news that a new pastor was coming in. His name? Brother Monty Flanigan! Go figure. How God has plans in store for us all! When Monty and Rhonda arrived, there were big hugs and tears of joy. Everyone in the church was like, "Y'all know each other?"

When your war buddy asks for help, you just say yes. So I became the Sunday school teacher for the high school class! What in the world had I agreed to? I was fired up for the challenge and determined to do my best. I had to study, really study. These Baptist kids are sharp as a tack on their Bible verses (I was not). I had to study and enjoyed it! I was sort of figuring things out and had to articulate this with the young adults. I lasted about three years. In the meantime, our old church in Linton had a new pastor. Monty and Rhonda were going to move, as well. Carol and I went back to our old church, far more knowledgeable in God's Word and able to serve honorably at Linton United Methodist Church.

DAY 179

Therefore, as God's chosen people, holy and dearly loved, clothe yourselves with compassion, kindness, humility, gentleness and patience. [13] Bear with each other and forgive one another if any of you has a grievance against someone. Forgive as the Lord forgave you. [14] And over all these virtues put on love, which binds them all together in perfect unity.

COLOSSIANS 3:12–14

HELLO FAMILY: This scripture emphasizes the confidence in living our lives as God's children and how our Father expects us to **behave**. And as my children will recall, when father is happy, so is everyone else. I remember the days of kids running through a small house, two cats dodging the German shepherd, beagle, or maybe it was the dachshund, or Petie (the dog Carol and I rescued from a cornfield where he'd been dumped to die). I recall the utter chaos of getting to t-ball, football, or dealing with a snake that ended up in our bedroom because the back door was left open by "something." Even the "police" at the front door because our kids ran out the front door and into the street / driveway unsupervised makes the list. On many occasions it was very rare to put this scripture into practice. The chaos of the family didn't lend itself to being gentle and patient much of the time. Hence, maturity in God's grace comes to fruition when making the time to go to church and be at peace spiritually. As the pages of life roll onward, we see children become parents, parents become grandparents, and even now, great-grandparents. So, witness the love that this scripture speaks of as a miracle in and of itself. A promise to hold onto and understand that in Christ, all things are possible, no matter how crazy life can get. Love you all.

DAY 180

What other nation is so great as to have their gods near them the way the LORD our God is near us whenever we pray to him?

DEUTERONOMY 4:7

HELLO FAMILY: How great thou art! Very early in my relationship with Carol, we would visit her grandmother and grandfather, Nanny and Papa. The gospel song, "How Great Thou Art" was their very favorite. When Nanny was moved to a nursing home after Papa passed away, she could be heard from the hallway singing this song softly in her room alone. To this day, I remember her and the smile she had every time we walked into that room. Early on, God was working on my soul to witness and remember these moments of joy, perhaps to write about in this book. Finding joy in being near the Lord our God, no matter what the situation before us was unfolding. This witness later provided me great comfort during the challenges ahead in my training and later in combat, being in lonely situations surrounded by those who would bring me harm. Our God provides the Holy Spirit to give you moment-to-moment guidance, comfort, and protection. A lit path to take when darkness appears to be all around you and panic is at the doorstep to make things even worse. Jesus Christ is Lord! Talk to **Him** every day! Love you all.

DAY 181

Is it not to share your food with the hungry and to provide the poor wanderer with shelter—when you see the naked, to clothe them, and not to turn away from your own flesh and blood? [8] Then your light will break forth like the dawn, and your healing will quickly appear; then your righteousness will go before you, and the glory of the LORD will be your rear guard.

ISAIAH 58:7–8

HELLO FAMILY: It's all about being generous and helping others to have a better day. Churches are credited for being very generous to the needy. Our tithe monies pay for these functions. I struggle a good bit when the pulpit is turned into a political soapbox in order to promote a culture that is directly forbidden in the scriptures. Churches need to stay focused on reading scriptures like these and many others rather than promoting behaviors that I will not even mention. I pray that church leaders stay out of politics and focus on this scripture firsthand. We are directed to focus our efforts on the physical needs of the people before us. We have tens of thousands of people in our streets who are homeless. They need food, shelter, and clothing. If we are to encourage each other to tithe for the purpose of this scripture and God's will, then make that a priority on which the money is spent. Love you all.

DAY 182

Join with me in suffering, like a good soldier of Christ Jesus. [4] No one serving as a soldier gets entangled in civilian affairs, but rather tries to please his commanding officer.

2 TIMOTHY 2:3-4

HELLO FAMILY: This scripture goes well with yesterday's two cents also. "Join me in suffering"? To anyone who has not served in the military and "suffered" through the long training events, being homesick, being deprived of food and water, or even the "Dear John" letters of a sweetheart saying good-bye, knowing that serving a commander and keeping him pleased involves sacrifice. Many people have to wonder, "Who would choose to suffer?" Our service members, first responders, and law enforcement—just to name a few in our communities—choose to "suffer" and serve their commanders on behalf of their communities, just as Jesus chose to suffer and die on the cross in order to please the Almighty Commander God on behalf of humanity. Did I mention teachers and social workers? Their duties of service expose them to the horrors of humanity, and they are held to the highest of standards at times, trying to help judgmental, demanding parents. Yet, they are expected to get up every morning and be perfect. We need these selfless patriots in the Army of God. Be thankful for them all! Hang in there, folks. Keep in prayer and worship with other faithful people and seek God for guidance. God our Commander in Chief is pleased. Love you all.

DAY 183

You who fear him, trust in the LORD—
he is their help and shield.

PSALM 115:11

HELLO FAMILY: "Help and shield." What is there to fear? When I recall my childhood, there were times I messed up and would fear the moment my dad would get home from work. I feared my dad big time. The biggest fear came when I knew I messed up. I knew I was guilty as charged and every one of my siblings knew that their big brother was going to pay the price when Dad got home. We had standards of behavior in our home, rules to follow, and chores that had to be done. Not much tolerance for "maybe" or "perhaps" or grey mystical thoughts of elves coming to feed the cows or clean hog pens. We all knew the expectations at hand each waking morning. Why? Because my dad cared enough to put it all on the line when molding his children to survive the realities of life. It started every Sunday morning in church. No snow days. No cancellations of any kind. We were in church on Sunday mornings. My dad ran the risk of his children not understanding his firmness. My dad was not my friend. He was my father. Dad was the one who made sure food was on the table, clothes were on our backs, and a warm roof provided cover and security while we slept. God did it with Jesus, His own Son, fully knowing that we may not understand the cruelty of crucifixion, or the mystery such a sacrifice for the sake of eternal salvation was. We may never understand the "shield" Jesus provides for our eternal life in Heaven or of the Holy Spirit always there like a shield in our daily walk. Trust and accept Jesus as your almighty helper and shield. Love you all.

DAY 184

But God demonstrates his own love for us in this:
While we were still sinners, Christ died for us.

ROMANS 5:8

HELLO FAMILY: "Still sinners." This is what really amazes me with the love of our Lord. Do we tolerate people that are messing everything up in our lives, let alone go out of our way to "love" them and help them out? Much of our reasoning for cutting people off in our "friends" and "contacts" lists are because they offend us in some way. The most common reason is that they become "bad choice makers" and their lives are going down, not up. Not a very godly attitude is it? Repeatedly we must remind ourselves that we are still sinners each and every day, even though we try to do all the right things. Our Lord, fully knowing our lack of self-discipline and wayward ways, took death head on. Christ never gives up on us at any moment. He came here on the earth to be with us and is as alive today as He was when He returned to offer "doubting" Thomas assurance that He **lives**. Love you all.

DAY 185

My brothers and sisters, believers in our glorious Lord Jesus Christ must not show favoritism.

JAMES 2:1

HELLO FAMILY: I had to think about this because everyone shows favoritism. Being parents, Carol and I would **always** make sure we treated our kids equally. Whether it was in gifts, encouragement, privileges, and punishments, it was always equal pay. And so it goes on even to this day! Why? Jealousy is an easy temptation to fall into. **And** even though we try our best as parents to not show favoritism, those kids still try to get our goat by saying things like, "You like 'xxxx' more than me." That's when I would tell the one complaining that he was adopted and to get over it. On the other hand, my daughters have shown great patience and forgiveness beyond any measure I can think of. They have seen the photos of my boys growing up with a dad. For sure favoritism can create a major wedge in family communications, so be aware of it. It must be addressed and dealt with when it comes up. Jesus did not have favorites (even though it seems like John refers to himself as "the disciple whom Jesus loved" in the book of John). Keep the air clear and breathe easy. Love you all.

DAY 186

Commit your way to the LORD; trust in him and he will do this: [6] He will make your righteous reward shine like the dawn, your vindication like the noonday sun.

PSALM 37:5-6

HELLO FAMILY: "Righteous reward." Committing to Christ is a commitment to living "right": treating ourselves like a temple to house the Holy Spirit and doing good things at work just because. Helping in our communities is a witness to others of our commitment to our faith. Allow others to recognize your character as a Christian without putting stickers on your car. Just a few of the priorities we should keep high on our list include being the best fathers we know how to be, the best husbands (loyal and honorable), and taking care of our health so we are around to take care of others in need. Let's also not forget to take care of our careers and the workmates we are surrounded by. Show them all we care as a witness to the teachings of Jesus Christ our Lord. Our rewards will "shine like the morning dawn." Love you all.

DAY 187

This calls for patient endurance on the part of the people of God who keep his commands and remain faithful to Jesus.

REVELATION 14:12

HELLO FAMILY: "Patient endurance." Sounds like marriage, waiting for a baby to be adopted or born, or waiting to get over the flu. However put, it is going to be for the long haul. I can't help but think of my long deployments and wondering what was going on back home. One day I saw the home videos of Carol and Shane having Christmas without me during the first Gulf War (Carol always had tears in her eyes). Then there were the home videos seeing Shane asking where Daddy was while I was in Somalia. I could go on. How about those families left behind while their loved ones deployed into harm's way? We should have immense respect and admiration to the parents who kept the family light on for those troops deployed for months on end, and multiple tours at that. This, my friends, is a wonderful example of patient endurance. The thought of the children listening to the news and hearing a "report" of something happening in the country of where a parent may be, everyone's heart just stops. Just today, another Green Beret was killed in Afghanistan. They don't announce the name right away. The family needs to be notified. I assure you every family of every Green Beret is sitting on pins and needles right now. Surviving the patient endurance will lead to love flowing in and through you, much like a fountain of fresh water for all who have suffered and survived under patient endurance having their faith in Jesus. Surviving this type of endurance requires great divine strength that only comes from true love, the love of God. For I am a weathered witness of God's Word shared today, surrounded by a loving family, and I am thankful. Love you all.

DAY 188

"However, do not rejoice that the spirits submit to you, but rejoice that your names are written in heaven."

LUKE 10:20

HELLO FAMILY: Big one here, folks! When we mere mortals were created by God, God declared our value greater than angels! Spirits submitting to mere mortals is what this scripture proclaims. This scripture from Luke reminds us of what great value we are to God. When we accept Jesus and have our names "written" in the Book of Life, the angels rejoice. What great love God has for us, with Christ His Son as our Lord. Rejoice that we have accepted Jesus as our Lord and Savior and that our names have been added to the Book of Life. Love you all.

DAY 189

> *I hold fast to your statutes, LORD; do not let me be put to shame. [32] I run in the path of your commands, for you have broadened my understanding.*
>
> PSALM 119:31-32

HELLO FAMILY: This scripture praises God's Word for the "statutes" featured to manage our behavior and, therefore, our lives. We understand why we behave as we do, to honor God. We hold ourselves not to manmade laws and regulations. We are held accountable to a higher authority. We hold ourselves accountable to God even when no one is watching us. We behave our best in order to be godly. This behavior is one without cursing, being generous to others, patient with others, and so on. This behavior displays sound confident character and calmness about us. There is no panic or distress. This behavior is a blessing to others and puts us in a position of leadership, to do the right things for who we serve. Show no fear for we have learned, understand, and have faith that God is in control. Our righteous decisions will not be put to shame. Love you all.

DAY 190

> *This is good, and pleases God our Savior, [4] who wants all people to be saved and to come to a knowledge of the truth.*
>
> 1 TIMOTHY 2:3-4

HELLO FAMILY: "Pleases God our Savior." Now this is a scripture to really pay close attention to. Everyone generally wants to please their father. We learn that as children, you get more of the stuff you ask for when Dad is in a great mood. I am teaching my granddaughters to say, "Pretty please, Daddy," in English. It is so cute with their German accents. It sounds so sweet and it melts their dads when they do it. Too funny to say the least. I just heard that my granddaughter Hannah and grandson Philipp are getting a puppy Labrador retriever. I have to wonder if the "pretty please" tactic was used. God wants all people "saved," and with great "knowledge of the truth," and why not? Where does this truth come from? This truth comes from reading the scriptures, our relationship in prayer, and listening to the Holy Spirit as our guiding light along the path of life. Enjoy the journey! Love you all.

DAY 191

Do not forsake wisdom, and she will protect you; love her, and she will watch over you. [7] The beginning of wisdom is this: Get wisdom. Though it cost all you have, get understanding.

PROVERBS 4:6-7

HELLO FAMILY: When you pray and are lost in thoughts, pray for wisdom and discernment (knowing right from wrong). These qualities prevent us from making poor choices—those hasty and costly mistakes that we regret. We also learn the value of using proper words to communicate. Our communication skills are paramount when getting through the day in our relationships at work, with family, and with friends. With wisdom, we will grow with God's grace and communicate wisely. Peace and joy will follow our footsteps. Do ask for wisdom specifically in each of your morning prayers. Love you all.

DAY 192

But because of his great love for us, God, who is rich in mercy, [5] made us alive with Christ even when we were dead in transgressions—it is by grace you have been saved.

EPHESIANS 2:4-5

HELLO FAMILY: Yesterday here in Germany we experienced the great beauty of God's creation. We went hiking along trails that took us into the high mountains. Our senses become keenly aware of God's creation when we grow in our faith and get closer to Him. We witness His creation on a whole different level as we learn more through reading the scriptures. Accepting and receiving Jesus Christ as our Lord (being saved) brings an immense learning experience that will joyfully guide us the rest of our days. We are moved by the grandeur of God's creation wherever we may be. He is calling out to us. When we listen, we learn to be the light of Christ to all we meet wherever we are. Love you all.

DAY 193

You, LORD, will keep the needy safe and will protect us forever from the wicked,

PSALM 12:7

HELLO FAMILY: Another one of the many promises from God. Guess what? We are "the needy." We need protection from all the hackers, the burglars, the pedophiles, the robbers...we could fill this page with all the threats out in this world. But safety and security are vital to experiencing true joy. We learn here that wickedness really exists! Unfortunately, we see that firsthand every day in the morning news. To think that this scripture knew that thousands of years ago when it was written is remarkable. I believe we must embrace the security offered by God, because there may be a time when we fall short and find ourselves in a world of hurt, whether of our choice or as a victim. A child of God, one who has inherited the Kingdom through accepting Christ, shares a place at the family table. A place of everlasting life, joy, and peace with God. Love you all.

50-CENT BONUS

HELLO FAMILY: It's 3:30 a.m. in Germany. Sami (my niece) and I have been wined, dined, and cared for with hugs and kisses our entire stay with my daughters and their families in Germany. My grandchildren have expressed without any coaching that "these days are the best adventures of my life." My children Kim and Lynn are strong and loving mothers (did I mention great boat and car drivers too?) with precious skills to manage the lives of their families with grace (their husbands too, really). Know this my family: God is blessing us all! Our cups overflow with great joy! Many years ago, these prayers were said and all of them have been answered and then some. Now we may understand why Carol and I have proclaimed, as we pray all of those reading this book do, "For me and my house; we will serve the Lord" (Joshua 24:15b). Yes, our bags are packed and will be on the road with Lynn to the Frankfort airport in an hour or so. Love you all.

DAY 194

So then, dear friends, since you are looking forward to this, make every effort to be found spotless, blameless and at peace with him. [15] Bear in mind that our Lord's patience means salvation, just as our dear brother Paul also wrote you with the wisdom that God gave him.

2 PETER 3:14-15

HELLO FAMILY: "Our Lord's patience" is an example once again for us to follow. It leads to salvation. As we grow in wisdom, we are called upon to be patient with each other. We must prepare ourselves for the baby steps involved in spiritual maturity and understanding. It is not "get saved" and everything just comes together like a magic show. Our understanding of ourselves is a big part of our spiritual growth and for me, that spiritual growth took the longest. Getting prepared for the long haul up front keeps expectations of our faith realistic. Fact is, we will never be perfect. We just need to stay in the fight. Being "spotless, blameless, and at peace" will come in God's time. We are called to keep the faith and to not ever give up. Our families are depending on us to take on this greatest of challenges: being faithful. Spotless and blameless wisdom will groom each of us at our own pace to live godly lives. It's a promise! Love you all.

DAY 195

"You will seek me and find me when you seek me with all your heart."

JEREMIAH 29:13

HELLO FAMILY: Do you recall the Bible stories played on TV? A favorite of mine is the movie *The Ten Commandments* starring Charlton Heston as Moses. Moses would get in these horrible situations. Then he would "seek" God for advice. Moses would just call out to God in the middle of the desert and there they were talking with each other. Moses was seeking God with all of his heart, the ultimate example of what this scripture tells us. These moments depicted brilliantly in scenes are something we can expect also in our intense communications back and forth with God. Moses had his whole heart into his relationship with God. He was able to deliver Israel right up to the doorstep of the Promised Land. Moses had to be all in it with God for protection from the Pharaoh and others in his own Jewish circles. The miracles performed spoke for themselves—God was with Moses! Freeing the nation of Israel was not an easy task. The movie features the great brutalities and hardships endured by all. Much can be said of our own meditation, prayer time, and scripture study with no distractions. Seek and you will find God. Listen and you will hear God. Love you all.

DAY 196

Cast all your anxiety on him because he cares for you.

1 PETER 5:7

HELLO FAMILY: Who knows something about anxiety? Every single one of us! Moms, mothers-to-be, dads, dads-to-be, grandparents, and grandparents-to-be. Get the picture? Life without Christ is nothing but anxiety. Ever spend any time with a person who complains every minute of every day about something? It will break us down and wear us out fast. It takes five positive comments to make up for one negative one, so try to reduce those negative comments and add some light to that dark tunnel of negativity. It is so sad to see people all upset about things that they really have no control over and get so worked up. So much of their day is ruined because they are angry about politics, who the President is, their water bill, or the neighbor's cat and dog, not to mention anxiety about finances and taxes. Okay, I will stop mentioning things to stress about and lose more sleep over. This scripture says enough of it! God is in control. Trust in Him. He cares for you. Love you all.

DAY 197

Clap your hands, all you nations; shout to God with cries of joy.

PSALM 47:1

HELLO FAMILY: Where can we go to clap our hands and "shout to God with cries of joy"? It is **church**! Surprise for some. Worship services include "joy and celebration," like children do at parties. Far too many times I have visited churches and just about left depressed. Fellowship with other Christians who get excited about God is a blessing and wakes up our soul and our spirit. It gets you motivated! Being celebratory wake us up. It gets our blood flowing and our hearts racing. It's fun! We all clap and get excited about football and baseball games; well, it applies to our Lord too. Love you all.

DAY 198

May we shout for joy over your victory and lift up our banners in the name of our God. May the LORD grant all your requests.

PSALM 20:5

HELLO FAMILY: When we pray that our children will live with joy and happiness and it becomes a reality, we celebrate in "victory." I am a witness to this answered prayer. As I review the pictures we share over the internet, there are big smiles all around. I see no stress over relationship issues, and everyone appears to be happy with each other. I truly believe that this is what we will experience in Heaven also but on an even grander scale. God and I spent the night camping by the pond last night. We had a full moon, clear skies with stars so bright, a small campfire (Ranger TV), and lots of crickets singing loud with the cicada bugs. No camper. No tent. Just eyes to the starlit skies above, God and me. Then recognizing the acknowledgement and detailed memories of every requested prayer answered. I am a witness to God's promises, and I pray that you can be to. Love you all.

DAY 199

Before they call I will answer; while they are still speaking I will hear.

ISAIAH 65:24

HELLO FAMILY: God is well aware of our sincere hearts. He will listen as long as we seek to speak with Him. Those who have accepted His Son as their Lord and Savior and who dedicate their time in sincere faith to communicate with God have His divine attention. Great blessings come to those who put their trust in the Lord. Before the crisis even arises, God is standing by to answer the call for assistance. Trust that God hears our desires. Follow the guidance of the Bible and go ahead and take that rest on Sunday. All the work will get done in due time. Love you all.

DAY 200

> *Honor your father and your mother, as the LORD your God has commanded you, so that you may live long and that it may go well with you in the land the LORD your God is giving you.*
>
> DEUTERONOMY 5:16

HELLO FAMILY: So there you have it, kids. I will refrain from the joyous temptation to take some digs at you all this fine morning. God's blessings are bestowed on those who honor His Word. In God's grace we live very well, blessed by a family filled with wonderful memories. My parents have a great deal to smile about when they sit in church on Sunday mornings after a week of enjoying the pictures they see in our WhatsApp family group. I have such fond childhood memories of the visits by my grandmother and great aunt. They always brought fresh donuts and other candies that we just didn't have around much. It was a huge treat. We would all wait eagerly for their arrival. Watching the window, then the clock, then back to the window again. When they finally arrived, it got really noisy because all of us kids would swarm them with hugs and kisses. The best part was listening to them tell stories of the old farm—of how they raised chickens, cows, pigs, geese, you name it. The farm had it all and they had the stories to share. My dad would sit his mother at the head of the table so she could watch and listen to all of her five grandchildren. You could just see the glow on her face while each one of us smothered her with attention. These are the honorable memories and examples I remember dearly. I pray that I have done and will continue to do the same with my parents. Heads up kids: it is my turn to sit at the head of the table to visit with grandchildren too! Love you all.

DAY 201

A thousand may fall at your side, ten thousand at your right hand, but it will not come near you.

PSALM 91:7

HELLO FAMILY: What will "not come near you"? Bad news, bad health, or bad accidents? May we never know? Back when this scripture was written, it was common to have nations battle with shields, swords, and spears. Thousands would lie dead or wounded on the battleground in horrific scenes due to hand-to-hand combat. Recognize that disasters happen all around us. Really bad ones and even evil ones. We just heard of a horrible incident of a drowning not too far from home — a father of two young children drowned while attempting to recover a boat that broke loose from the dock. There is the possibility of something terrible occurring in the wake of every dawn, thousands of them. In God's hands we are to be patient, remembering that it is in His timing always. Be thankful and remain joyful in all circumstances. We may have been spared from a horrible accident while waiting in that traffic jam. Don't ever panic or get down. Everything happens for a reason. Know that our delays, like forgetting the phone at the house, all happen for a reason, for reasons we may never know. What we must remember is that it happened for a reason and God is in control. Love you all.

DAY 202

And what more shall I say? I do not have time to tell about Gideon, Barak, Samson and Jephthah, about David and Samuel and the prophets, [33] who through faith conquered kingdoms, administered justice, and gained what was promised; who shut the mouths of lions, [34] quenched the fury of the flames, and escaped the edge of the sword; whose weakness was turned to strength; and who became powerful in battle and routed foreign armies.

HEBREWS 11:32–34

HELLO FAMILY: All the names mentioned in this scripture are in the Old Testament. All are graphically illustrated in our children's Bible stories as great heroes of our faith. These stories have been shared for thousands of years and we need to think about that for a good bit. Now referred to as the Dead Sea Scrolls, these stories were found in the 1940s documented on animal skins and had been preserved for thousands of years in jars of clay. How does that happen? They are a testament to who is in control. God Almighty is in control. He is the greatest hero of them all. Our Bible has survived, and its stories serve as a beacon of assurance in our Almighty God. Live in Christ and fear not! Love you all.

DAY 203

The Lord will guide you always; he will satisfy your needs in a sun-scorched land and will strengthen your frame. You will be like a well-watered garden, like a spring whose waters never fail.

ISAIAH 58:11

HELLO FAMILY: Accepting God and His guidance leads to a very joyful and productive life. You are never thirsty. Spring water flows throughout your day giving you unlimited energy to do the wise things. Look around and note the sun scorched lives of misery around us. Watching the news these days, we may wonder if we are we living in the land of a "sun-scorched" earth. Commentators feature men and women of great leadership who pit themselves against each other as if in civil war. This is where this scripture comes into play. Why not be a person who lives as a "well-watered garden"? We do not have to get dragged into this sun-scorched earth and bogged down into daily hate. Accepting Christ as your Savior provides you a personal mentor, the Holy Spirit, who lights your righteous path each step of the way, leading you to a spring-fed pond. Our minds and bodies become refreshed in the word of God. Love you all.

DAY 204

I pray that the eyes of your heart may be enlightened in order that you may know the hope to which he has called you, the riches of his glorious inheritance in his holy people,

EPHESIANS 1:18

HELLO FAMILY: "The eyes of your heart." My son-in-law Damian looks people directly in the eyes when we clink our glasses of soda pop together to lift a cheer. I have been told that the eyes are the window to our souls and our hearts. All those who conduct interviews of any kind are advised to stay focused on the eyes of the one being questioned. Shifting eyes can mean that the answers to the questions asked are not entirely true. Look into those eyes to see truth, to see the character of the beholder. This scripture recognizes our souls and our hearts as they are to be enlightened with great hope, never darkened by loss of joy. Never bare a broken heart, and most of all, be positive in our prayers. A positive attitude is contagious to everyone. Be that light of hope in Christ to all those around you. Love you all.

DAY 205

From the ends of the earth I call to you, I call as my heart grows faint; lead me to the rock that is higher than I.

PSALM 61:2

HELLO FAMILY: When you grasp the concept of God looking down on the entire earth with people that are calling for mercy in their situations, it can be overwhelming to say the least. People are in pain, in horrible situations that are far worse than what we see in our local news. Entire countries are at war and have been at war for decades. It never ends. There are factions and cultures in other countries that enslave thousands into real slavery and bondage situations today! We hear about the human trafficking of children and other abuses that we rarely dare think about in our daily walk. Yet God sees all of this and rest assured, He hears their calls. "Lead me to the rock that is higher than I," for strength. America has been very blessed. To those that inhabit her land, I pray they will show reverence for her. America came to be the only Christian nation on this earth and has been spared from the horrors that create faint hearts. God bless the USA. Love you all.

DAY 206

Give thanks in all circumstances; for this is God's will for you in Christ Jesus.

1 THESSALONIANS 5:18

HELLO FAMILY: Here we go. "All circumstances." Every time our Aunt Laura visits, we have something to remember. Well, on this trip it was going to be the tornado with downed trees, no power, and big excitement on the drive back to the airport. With all that said, we are thankful that nobody was hurt and that there was no serious damage to any buildings or cars. All the neighbors grew closer by doing the big cleanup together. Our neighborhood really enjoyed that big cleanup, too. Every single resident was in the mix with chain saws, picking up limbs, dragging big trees with their Gators, and making huge piles to burn on another day. One for our community history book for sure. Always look for the blessings in any circumstance. They are always there, along with God's grace. Love you all.

DAY 207

> *Hope deferred makes the heart sick,*
> *but a longing fulfilled is a tree of life.*
>
> PROVERBS 13:12

HELLO FAMILY: No hope, no life. What are we hoping for? Can you imagine being so beaten down that you don't even bother to "hope"? When I see the statistics of suicide and after having a very close friend pass that way, I ponder to think that maybe hope ran out. What I do know is that faith brings an understanding of patience, persistence, and perseverance. We never give up. We never quit and we stay positive. Always find joy in the challenges ahead. That is what hope is all about. Remember this scripture when doubt drags you down so much that it makes your heart sick. Love you all.

DAY 208

> *If you are insulted because of the name of Christ,*
> *you are blessed, for the Spirit of glory and*
> *of God rests on you.*
>
> 1 PETER 4:14

HELLO FAMILY: What challenges we have in the quest to be faithful, consistent, and loyal to our Lord. All the standard temptations, distractions, and business we get ourselves into make it hard enough. Now this scripture warns of being insulted? Are we insulted when we hear the words of our Lord used in a curse? Are we offended when we see people degrade the cross? In many countries and places on this earth it is forbidden to openly display the cross. Some countries forbid the practice of Christianity in any form. This means going to prison or even being executed for mentioning "Jesus Christ." And here we are as Americans, so blessed to openly choose the living God to worship. The God that became human, born of a virgin. The God who performed numerous miracles, who defeated death in front of many witnesses and was even written about in Roman government files as well our Bible scriptures. God's Word became flesh in Jesus Christ. He was tempted in every way possible and defeated them all with the Word. As you walk down the path of life and encounter a fork in the road, choose wisely. Choose the path of the living God. Love you all.

DAY 209

My comfort in my suffering is this:
Your promise preserves my life.

PSALM 119:50

HELLO FAMILY: Suffering comes in many packages. It can be straight up pain. It can be a bad memory. It can be a temptation eating at us. It may even be a selfish demon creating jealousy in our hearts. Suffering of any kind is real, and we all have to figure out a way to rope it in or there is no joy to be had. Preserve our lives in Christ and stay focused on the cross. Blow off all the other garbage and rise above your worries. Comfort will follow for sure. Then find that lucky person out there who needs a big hug! Love you all.

DAY 210

Listen to advice and accept discipline, and
at the end you will be counted among the wise.

PROVERBS 19:20

HELLO FAMILY: Some of us who are receiving advice from our family, peers, neighbors, and friends may be receiving this advice as an insult or degradation. Some may not really listen to any such advice because they interpret it as negative feedback for their actions. Then again, some may get really agitated after receiving so-called "advice." Truth be told, only time will tell if we can overcome those painful moments of truth. We can either improve or dig our heels in and show those rascals who is right after all. Stop that madness! These are the voices of loved ones getting our attention, so we can get our lives back on tract or just be better versions of ourselves. Yes, some are better at giving advice than others. It is how we receive that advice that will make the bold difference. Blessings your way. Love you all.

DAY 211

Get rid of all bitterness, rage and anger, brawling and slander, along with every form of malice. [32] Be kind and compassionate to one another, forgiving each other, just as in Christ God forgave you.

EPHESIANS 4:31–32

HELLO FAMILY: This scripture says to get rid of it all! All the years of squabble and unrest! It is far easier to be bitter, to snap at situations, to write people off, or to not even bother communicating with them (so glad Jesus didn't do that to us). Holding grudges is not healthy and it is not a joyful place to be. It can be just darn stressful and cause immense physical issues like heart palpitations, high blood pressure, and major painful headaches, as well. We need to be comfortable with ourselves and our relationship with Christ. When we are comfortable, we can articulate our issues with Christ Himself and come to some understanding of why we are so bothered. When we picture ourselves talking directly with Christ, we begin to realize the situation at hand and how to resolve it. So be still and know that Christ is there in forgiveness, kindness, and compassion. Let Christ deal with all of the "brothers and sisters" who upset you. Love you all.

DAY 212

No, in all these things we are more than conquerors through him who loved us.

ROMANS 8:37

HELLO FAMILY: "More than conquerors." I read this and it says to me, "More responsibilities." As we conquer more skills, navigate through relationships and politics, and grow in our communities, the more responsibilities come our way. In Christ we have become teachers, managers, administrators, facilitators, mentors, parents, and grandparents. All carrying a responsibility to be compassionate, generous, and selfless in our duties in order to reflect the love of Christ. That is the "more than" in this scripture. Love you all.

DAY 213

Create in me a pure heart, O God,
and renew a steadfast spirit within me.

PSALM 51:10

HELLO FAMILY: "A pure heart" and "steadfast spirit." "Create in me." Sounds like consistent, steady, and patient character with a righteous spirit as the goal. I just received an update about some of our relatives in Texas who have chosen to pursue the missionary life in Africa. When asked when they would return, their answer was, "When the Lord sends us home." When I read about missionaries, this scripture comes to mind. It is totally giving up one's life to perhaps live in very uncomfortable places, exposed to diseases and numerous security issues. The missionary life requires the steadfast spirit. As we read the news of certain cities in America, we too see the need for a steadfast spirit in caring for the homelessness and seeking an end to the relentless killings. Those of us with an enormous calling for service are the people who are always representing godliness—we live it. Everything else comes before us. No selfish motives. That's a big task, all possible through Christ. Love you all.

DAY 214

"The God who made the world and everything in it is the Lord of heaven and earth and does not live in temples built by human hands. [25] And he is not served by human hands, as if he needed anything. Rather, he himself gives everyone life and breath and everything else."

ACTS 17:24-25

HELLO FAMILY: Boy, are we in for a surprise in eternity when we meet Jesus and God our Father! Reading this scripture gives us a mere glimpse of who God is. God is not a temple dweller. He is not some "high" priest of any kind. God is life. He is our spirit, our soul. Find that time to be alone and talk to Him. Stop and observe His creation. God is real! This is a reality that can take a good bit of time to sink in. God does not need us. He wants us, and this scripture is proof. "He himself gives everyone life and breath and everything else." He provides for us all, because we are His children and He loves us. He gives to us so we may give to others. Love you all.

DAY 215

Whoever loves discipline loves knowledge,
but whoever hates correction is stupid.

PROVERBS 12:1

HELLO FAMILY: "Discipline" is one of those words that may cause some to cringe. In this scripture, it means getting up in the morning with a purpose, a drive, and a sense of being to get the job done. Some may say that it is being motivated with a self-disciplined character needing little or no guidance. A self-starter. These are great descriptors on a resume. This scripture says if you hate correction, you are stupid. When we are out in this world, we will be corrected in many ways and by many means in the quest to achieve our goals. Do not take these corrections as a defeat. Learn from them. Be open to learning how to become better children of God, understanding and adjusting our lives to live for His purpose. Love you all.

50-CENT BONUS

There are those final nudges everyone needs to get off of the high dive. There is no board that bounces, just an edge we look over and don't think about much because our nerves will get the best of us. Just like jumping out of airplanes. We just do it when the time comes. After returning to our country church, Linton United Methodist Church (LUMC), an older gentleman kept working me over to go on a Tres Dias Walk. This is a "godly man" retreat that I honestly thought was some kind of cult fad. My "little brother" Tom Rea had been on it, along with other men in the community that I was aware of. I told "Moose," the older gentleman, that if work ever had me off an entire weekend that I would go one day. Fair enough, we agreed. I figured there was no way that was going to happen in the police scheduling. I was the new guy and new guys worked nights and weekends. Honestly, I think some backdoor "godly men" work happened behind the scenes, because about four months after that discussion with Moose, I had a three-day weekend coming up on the schedule. Not thinking about that "retreat" weekend, I made plans for my sons and I to disappear in the backwoods. I went to church the Sunday after my schedule came out and Moose walked up to me with a paper. He was going to sponsor me on the upcoming Tres Dias Weekend. I was shocked to say the least! What could I say? I had given my word.

Folks, I can tell you this: I did **not** want to go! My wife did **not** want me to go. I knew I had to go, so I told God specifically this: "This is for you, Lord. I am trusting you, Lord, like jumping out of a plane, like jumping off the high dive. I am leaping off this cliff—do to me as you wish. I surrender all." Ladies and gentlemen, that weekend truly opened my eyes to how God had carried me through life so far—like a father carries a fighting, wrestling child. God spoke to me and showed me everything.

The very first night after meeting everyone, we were told not to speak at all to anyone. Total silence. Only prayers. It was on this night I experienced a vision of my past, parts that you are reading about in this book. On that first night of the Tres Dias Weekend, I witnessed God's hand in various chapters of my life. Dragging me much of the way. I was never to be the same. Now I am relaxed in God's arms. I have stayed very close to Him, willingly and joyfully, as a sheep in the arms of its shepherd, the bell sheep. Love you all.

DAY 216

What, then, shall we say in response to these things? If God is for us, who can be against us?

ROMANS 8:31

HELLO FAMILY: This scripture was covered at church this past Sunday. Here I am looking over the world headlines this morning and the top stories are a heat wave, climate change, a presidential candidate campaigning in Mexico (I guess Russia isn't allowed), a body is found, North Korea fires another missile, riots in Hong Kong, another American dies in Afghanistan, and a big explosion in Kabul. Will it ever stop? The scripture says "What, then, shall we say in response to these things? **If** God is for us, who can be against us?" "US," the United States of America. As we quickly approach Independence Day, our declaration to this world has always been and I pray will always be, "**One nation under God!**" A Christian nation. The only one on this earth! The one nation that has policed up tragic historic episodes everywhere on the globe since its existence practically. Who can be against us, when our faith is in God? Nothing! Love you all.

DAY 217

Teach us to number our days, that we may gain a heart of wisdom.

PSALM 90:12

HELLO FAMILY: The fact is our days are numbered and we don't have a clue as to what that number is! Just having a birthday year after year can make a person complacent. One cannot help but to ponder their past and grab hold of dreams for the future (we still have to make a wish before blowing out the candles on the cake) as the days, months, and years pass on those birthdays. The birthday wishes may change as our wisdom grows and the cake is totally covered in candles. This scripture encourages us to recognize our numbered days on this earth. It encourages us to gain wisdom with each waking day, to do what we must to be aware of the truth. Read the Bible and pray for wisdom and understanding. Learn what is right and wrong and gain discernment. That may be the wisest decision of a lifetime. Love you all.

DAY 218

> *When hard pressed, I cried to the Lord;*
> *he brought me into a spacious place.*
>
> PSALM 118:5

HELLO FAMILY: As my travels take me from city to city, I am amazed at how many people are all crowded together. There are actually times when total strangers are within inches of each other for hours at a time, and there simply isn't any room to get away and get some space. Heaven forbid if something breaks down — subways, trains, buses, planes, hotels, and cruise ships to name a few. We are getting crowded in this world big time! With all of us jammed together, smart phones directing our every second, traffic jams slowing us down…what do we do to recharge our batteries? We cry out and pray for help! Our Lord responds and takes us to a place of freedom. A spacious place of peace, a place to stop and take a deep breath of fresh air. A green lush pasture of freshness and clear waters to bask in. His promises. This place is called the Bible, the Word of God. C'ya there! Love you all.

DAY 219

For in six days the LORD made the heavens and the earth, the sea, and all that is in them, but he rested on the seventh day. Therefore the LORD blessed the Sabbath day and made it holy.

EXODUS 20:11

HELLO FAMILY: I feel another **50-Cent Bonus** coming. This is one of the Ten Commandments—the Fourth Commandment from God. What immediately yanks my chain is that I remember growing up there were no stores open on Sundays. After we would get home from church, we would be looking forward to a visit from our grandparents or aunts and uncles. My parents were both home with us and Dad didn't have a job to report to because his store was closed on Sundays, too. By and large, Sundays were a family affair where we would see our cousins again. The uncles would work on a project together that needed extra hands and power. In today's culture, Sundays are just the same as all of the other days. Time is so full of running here and going there. All the stores are open, the restaurants are open, and the streets are all a hustle and bustle just as they are any other day of the week. We currently live in Trigg County, KY—big time Amish Country (they moved here from PA). I so admire their determination to keep Sundays for worship and family. We see their horse drawn carriages on the roads in the mornings. Everyone is dressed in their finest Sunday clothes. No work is done at all on Sundays in the Amish community. The women have prepared all the food the day prior and the men have completed their chores by sunup. The entire Amish community enjoys a full day of worship in the mornings and then a huge meal with all the family members and friends of their community. Then you have us other churchgoers, racing from our homes all stressed out because we left late for church. We may be fussing and perhaps cussing those slow "dangerous" horse carriages in the way of a high-speed race to make it on time to church and to avoid a stare down from our preacher. Then after church, where we study the Ten Commandments, we may go to a restaurant with our friends and eat a big meal. The poor waitress will be running back and forth with the food, taking requests for more water and the occasional complaint. Then we go to Wal-Mart and pick up a few things for this and that. Kids are staring at their phones, playing games in the shopping carts, and shouting out a request or two for soda or candy as their parents push the carts down the aisle. Then we race home to work on a home project or to watch a football game and stuff our faces with beer and chips all before going to bed, getting little rest before we do it all again on Monday.

My frustrations are many. By going to the restaurants and stores, we are feeding the cause and economy to keep these establishments open on Sundays. Think of all the moms and dads working to keep the money train moving who don't get that quality time with their children because so many have chosen to no longer value that or make allowances to refrain from having to go to the store or restaurants on Sundays. We as Christians are in direct violation of the very commandments of our faith. First off, I am not tooting my horn here of any innocence at all. I am the guy getting frustrated behind the horse drawn carriage and stopping at Wal-Mart to pick up whatever. It's a challenge to really turn Sundays into true days of worship, but we can at least try. And I proclaim that Carol and I are, finally! Our culture has turned its population into a work-till-you-drop machine. It will take some serious reprogramming to just stop this madness. I won't get into the football comments. That may be another ***50-Cent Bonus*** in the future, maybe a whole dollar's worth for that subject. We can do better, and the Amish are a great example to learn how to do it right. Love you all.

DAY 220

For the wages of sin is death, but the gift of God is eternal life in Christ Jesus our Lord.

ROMANS 6:23

HELLO FAMILY: "Wages." We all earn wages of some kind or another. Most of us have all heard the saying, "You reap what you sow." If we are not motivated and "employed" our wages may be pretty sparse. This is my point with this scripture. Standing there late in our lives, perhaps spiritually wage-less, with nothing to show for being a godly person is not the end. It's never over until it's over and you have not a breath to speak with. A recognition and a receiving of Christ as your Lord brings you eternal salvation and a joyous wage as well. An earthly life in Christ brings great wages of delight to all who are in our sphere of influence, and we are exalted and happy. Our wages of delight become contagious in a world of stress and depression. Leave behind the wages of sin and accept Jesus as Lord. Love you all.

DAY 221

Before the mountains were born or you brought forth the whole world, from everlasting to everlasting you are God.

PSALM 90:2

HELLO FAMILY: Our imaginations cannot fathom how God created the world we live in. Part of me believes that our pride is afraid to come to terms with the greatness of God, kind of how Dorothy, the Tin Man, the Scarecrow, and the Lion felt and acted when they met the Wizard of Oz for the first time. I would have been like the Lion, running out of there and smashing into the big window in a panic. With that said, it takes great courage (Lion) to come to terms with the reality that we will all pass away and some form of judgment for our decisions on earth will occur. Eternity is at our doorstep. Thanks be to God! Know that Jesus Christ awaits your call. Love you all.

DAY 222

We have much to say about this, but it is hard to make it clear to you because you no longer try to understand. [12] In fact, though by this time you ought to be teachers, you need someone to teach you the elementary truths of God's word all over again. You need milk, not solid food!

HEBREWS 5:11-12

HELLO FAMILY: Talk about a scolding. The word of God has been documented for thousands of years (ref: Dead Sea Scrolls). As it is written here, humanity insists on taking baby steps in its enthusiasm over the teachings God has prepared for us. As Americans, we are the only Christian nation on earth. It is no secret that Islam controls the vast majority of the world and the United Nations. As mere mortals, we must take time to read and understand the dynamics of the history of Israel and the Jewish Nation. Ask ourselves, "Where does the United States fit in on the global plan of God's work in building His Kingdom on earth?" As babies in our spiritual growth, we are not privileged to the understanding of eating a steak dinner with butter-soaked baked potatoes. Most of us will rarely progress to the level of beholding a "Big Mac" at McDonalds, spiritually speaking of course. We flutter along, making a living, not moving mountains, just climbing them. This scripture screams, "Learn about our Creator!" Love you all.

DAY 223

"Now I am about to go the way of all the earth. You know with all your heart and soul that not one of all the good promises the LORD your God gave you has failed. Every promise has been fulfilled; not one has failed."

JOSHUA 23:14

HELLO FAMILY: I choose joy! All the promises have been fulfilled. Thousands of them that we have read over the years have truly been completed for billions upon billions of believers. Note where we all were just 10 years ago. Are we not witnesses in our own family to this scripture? We can surely see how God keeps His promises with His adopted children—all of us. I encourage all believers who have received Jesus as their Lord to look back at the last 10 years and take note of the promises kept and still coming. We cannot change the past. We cannot change our family. We cannot change the mindset and opinions of anybody. Only God can. What we can do is our homework and pray for righteousness in our lives and others. The promises will be forthcoming. God promises. Love you all.

DAY 224

For though we live in the world, we do not wage war as the world does. [4] The weapons we fight with are not the weapons of the world. On the contrary, they have divine power to demolish strongholds. [5] We demolish arguments and every pretension that sets itself up against the knowledge of God, and we take captive every thought to make it obedient to Christ.

2 CORINTHIANS 10:3-5

HELLO FAMILY: Who controls the decisionmakers in regards to waging war on this earth? Who controls our minds, before we fester up and lash out in anger? What is the point of backing off or backing down from attacking one another? We as Christians are not to "wage war as [this] world does." We are not to use these worldly techniques to change people's minds and force them to believe the truths in God's Word. We are to plant the seed. We are not to push our opinions and motives on others to profit and get even. We are called to be gentle with everyone, to be knowledgeable of God's Word, and to be peacemakers in a selfish and violent culture. We are called to be humble and peaceful, exercising our faith as an example for others to follow. Allow yourself to be led by the Holy Spirit and bring peace before us. Love you all.

DAY 225

The angel of the LORD encamps around those who fear him, and he delivers them.

PSALM 34:7

HELLO FAMILY: Angels are camped "around those who fear him," "him" being God. Do we understand that the angel of God is setting up a secure perimeter around the encampment of those who respect and fear the Lord? A secure perimeter is utter glory to those in the military and those rangers on patrol! What is our greatest fear? Rejection is a great fear to address. Many of us live our lives feeling afraid of rejection in our own families — "watch out for those first impressions" when you meet the parents! (Poor Katie, my daughter-in-law. We have some memories to smile about forever.) Social events can be a challenge, too. Whether it is with work associates, among church members, or even on the school playground. I never really thought about fearing God in a sense of the same fear I would experience meeting a big grizzly bear on a hike. The fear addressed in this scripture is more like the fear of disappointing God by not honoring and obeying Him. All we need to know is this: faith in God secures our daily walk in Christ. We are in good hands. Love you all.

DAY 226

If I have the gift of prophecy and can fathom all mysteries and all knowledge, and if I have a faith that can move mountains, but do not have love, I am nothing.

1 CORINTHIANS 13:2

HELLO FAMILY: Love is what brings joy. Unconditional love is what Jesus demonstrated for us to witness. We hear of this unconditional love coming from moms who, no matter what, will tolerate their kids to no end. Moms will most always protect their rascals from just about anything. Moms will love their children no matter what. There may be some pain to pay later, but moms are usually in the fight till the end. We all have special God-given talents and gifts for the purpose of loving each other. The purpose of our God-given gifts is to further God's Kingdom here on earth with a loving heart. If we search ourselves, we will find these God-given talents. With prayer and asking for God's guidance, these talents will blossom and bring big smiles to many. Just like Mom can bring a smile in any situation. Love you all.

DAY 227

Two are better than one, because they have a good return for their labor: [10] If either of them falls down, one can help the other up. But pity anyone who falls and has no one to help them up.

ECCLESIASTES 4:9-10

HELLO FAMILY: So big time true! Make no bones about it, there is no "I" in "Team." Husband and wife, mother and father, grandma and grandpa! Shane and Blake, Kim and Lynn! Coffee and cream, beer and brats! Do you get the concept? In the military it was the "ranger buddy." In training at the US Army Ranger School you always had your ranger buddy with you. He even stood guard over you when you slept, ate, took a crap, etc., etc. If you were caught without your ranger buddy, you dug a six foot "grave" — 6 feet long, 6 feet deep, and 3 feet wide (we did that for cigarette butts found in the morning too; that's another story) — then the platoon would designate a chaplain to officiate a notional funeral for the "lost" ranger, and the hole would be filled in. Working together joyfully is a marriage made in heaven, y'all remember that! It is a blessing beyond words if you have this same relationship with your coworkers. Building bridges together in Christ is the key. Love you all.

DAY 228

Now to him who is able to do immeasurably more than all we ask or imagine, according to his power that is at work within us.

EPHESIANS 3:20

HELLO FAMILY: Take some time soon and look though our family photos. Every family has their special times to get together. The reunions were always my favorite growing up. Looking at my parents when they were little fascinated me. Photos and videos make for great family moments and memories, especially when we get older, as I am experiencing now. They are priceless! Observe the work that Christ is working within us all as we mature as a family. Observe the planning and the resources that had to come together for the family to cherish those special times, those visits from far away. If you have access to home videos, see if you can find someone praying over food before one of our family meals. I saw one of Carol's grandfather praying blessings for his family prior to our Thanksgiving meal. They all came true. The prayers we pray are immeasurable joy to Christ our Lord. So, if we are looking for something to be thankful for at church, there you have it. Memories of our family. Love you all.

DAY 229

I am laid low in the dust; preserve my life according to your word.

PSALM 119:25

HELLO FAMILY: King David wrote this, the one who killed Goliath. David was loved by God and performed miraculous feats in keeping his country safe. King David wasn't perfect, though. He too was tempted and sinned against God. David at his lowest moments was still wise enough to reflect upon the promises of God, the words of God, and the restoration that comes from God. We may be in situations where "laid low" sounds like a walk in the park. Here in this scripture we are called to review and repent. Give it to God, according to His Word. Whatever may be dragging you through the dust, trust in the Lord always. Love you all.

DAY 230

*"'For in him we live and move and have our being.'
As some of your own poets have said, 'We are his offspring.'"*

ACTS 17:28

HELLO FAMILY: As you know, I always start my daily two cents with "Hello Family." This scripture emphasizes that we are all the offspring of our God. We are all "family." This is a celebratory scripture, something to feel joyous about. We recognize the blessings of belonging to a family with examples of the joy that we share in our families today, with plans for tomorrow. We experience the purpose of belonging to our families, the responsibilities we have to each other and the values that guide our decisions. We know we do not want to disappoint our family by doing things that would embarrass our family name. (My dad made that very clear to us five kids growing up). Now when we measure the moral authority we have as direct children of God, we recognize that we are beholden as Christians in our behavior. What splendor there will be when we experience the joy with our family together in Heaven with God sitting at the head of the table. Love you all.

DAY 231

"Let us acknowledge the LORD; let us press on to acknowledge him. As surely as the sun rises, he will appear; he will come to us like the winter rains, like the spring rains that water the earth."

HOSEA 6:3

HELLO FAMILY: Acknowledgment is something we all like to receive for our efforts. How about at work with a big bonus or even a pat on the back? Maybe it's acknowledgement from our families, like handwritten notes in birthday cards and the thoughtfulness shown by what gifts we receive. All forms of acknowledgement are appreciated greatly. God created us in His likeness. God likes to receive acknowledgment, too. This scripture validates this big time. Let us "press on" to acknowledge all that we are in God's glory. Praises to our Creator for refreshing our daily walk like cool rain showers that bless our earth. Love you all.

DAY 232

"Therefore keep watch, because you do not know on what day your Lord will come. [43] But understand this: If the owner of the house had known at what time of night the thief was coming, he would have kept watch and would not have let his house be broken into."

MATTHEW 24:42-43

HELLO FAMILY: Like a thief in the night. We have no clue when he comes. This, my family, is how death happens, too. When I read this scripture the first time, I was totally focused on the second coming of Jesus Christ. Now as I get some life experiences behind me, the same can be said for death here on earth also. This scripture was written as a clear warning! A truth that we must always be prepared for, the second coming of our Lord, as well as our last breath. We must always do our best to love one another as our Lord God loves each of us. Love each other as if it's our last breath. Hold, hug, and communicate. Be kind and helpful. Use your speech to give words of encouragement. Make plans to have those quality moments that create memories to think back on. Live this way that Jesus says. Love you all.

DAY 233

Cast your cares on the LORD and he will sustain you; he will never let the righteous be shaken.

PSALM 55:22

HELLO FAMILY: "Never...be shaken." Do we understand? Do we understand that we should not get dramatic or emotional about anything? Being able to calmly deal with any calamity or issue that presents itself is a huge quality and a sign of wisdom. There are no "normal" situations in anyone's life. We all have tribulations to deal with. Sometimes being silent, taking a step back to evaluate our options, saying a prayer for divine guidance, and recalling that God is in control can make all the difference in the world. Our confidence in making righteous decisions will bring joy to our day. You will know you did your very best and God was at your side. So says our Lord. Love you all.

DAY 234

Come near to God and he will come near to you. Wash your hands, you sinners, and purify your hearts, you double-minded.

JAMES 4:8

HELLO FAMILY: Do we see how James didn't cut us any slack here, us "double-minded" rascals? James speaks of the voices in our heads, like the Fred Flintstone and Barney Rubble cartoons we used to watch as kids. The demon angel would pop up on the left shoulder and speak into the left ear, then poof, a godly angel would appear on the right shoulder and whisper into the right ear. Double minded we are, I dare say. Each waking moment we are making plans, doing projects, washings our hands from mistakes made, and clapping those same hands for impressive celebrations. James advises us to keep God in our hearts always, so we hear His voice when He speaks. We are never to doubt or feel uncertain about His promises of care, grace, guidance, and love for us all. Love you all.

DAY 235

*Joshua said to them, "Do not be afraid; do not be discouraged. Be strong and courageous. This is what the L*ORD *will do to all the enemies you are going to fight."*

JOSHUA 10:25

HELLO FAMILY: I read this and asked, "What enemies are you and I in battle with?" On a grander scale, we are witnesses in our country of a battle over morale and cultural righteousness. We have generations of people voting now who grew up without God in their daily lives. No church, no Ten Commandments on their school properties, and no mention of prayer or Christ in their school classrooms. We now have generations that have little understanding of the greatest Nation on this earth and the sacrifices it took by the Christians of our past to build this Nation. Our Nation has been spared the horrors of the World Wars within our borders and on our continent. Our Nation hit its knees in prayer not all that long ago. Remember the Cuban missile crisis? Unfortunately, many do not. To survive in the years of the Great Depression, God's Word was all that many had to live on, to trust on, and to build on. Too many people in this generation have sacrificed nothing, built nothing, paid for nothing, and complain about everything. No thankfulness, and worse yet, they seek to destroy the history and foundations that created this one and only Nation that was founded on Christian values. We are called to be strong and courageous. Don't be afraid to challenge those even in our families about what is right about our faith, our country, and our future. Love you all.

DAY 236

"I have told you these things, so that in me you may have peace. In this world you will have trouble. But take heart! I have overcome the world."

JOHN 16:33

HELLO FAMILY: If there is one thing I have learned, it is that the more people you know, the more trouble you hear about. It is a wonder that anyone has enough peace in their daily walk to get a good night's sleep. I heard a speech by a famous coach once. He said something similar to this: "Don't talk about your troubles to others; 95 percent of them don't care and the other 5 percent are glad you have them, except your parents of course, and that is not a guarantee either." Our Lord has overcome this world of troubles. There is no such thing as "normal," and I dare say that word is absent from the Bible. If anyone can explain to me what it means to live a normal life, please post that on Facebook for the world to see. Christ Jesus is standing by to get involved and to help us get through each and every one of those troubles and bring peace to our hearts. Love you all.

DAY 237

He will respond to the prayer of the destitute; he will not despise their plea.

PSALM 102:17

HELLO FAMILY: I truly pray for those who feel destitute. Many feel this way all the time. King David wrote this scripture from his experiences in desperate situations. Until you have been destitute or desperate, you may not grasp the full greatness of this scripture. The promise that God will respond to your calls for help is very powerful in our daily walk. He is already aware of the circumstances and has a plan of action in place to set us free. Love you all.

DAY 238

Blessed is the one who perseveres under trial because, having stood the test, that person will receive the crown of life that the Lord has promised to those who love him. [13] When tempted, no one should say, "God is tempting me." For God cannot be tempted by evil, nor does he tempt anyone; [14] but each person is tempted when they are dragged away by their own evil desire and enticed. [15] Then, after desire has conceived, it gives birth to sin; and sin, when it is full-grown, gives birth to death.

JAMES 1:12–15

HELLO FAMILY: This scripture takes some time to pray about. The "test" was taken and passed by Jesus. Jesus defeated each temptation presented by the devil with God's scriptural words for 40 days and nights. It all starts with a "desire," a motive to do something or get something. Then all of the options flow into our decision making process and we get to make the choice to be righteous or not. So we ask ourselves, "What is the right way to go about meeting the desire at hand?" If we find ourselves twisting stories, making alliances, schmoozing peers to build up our case under peer pressure, and not allowing the truth be forefront, we are probably on the path to sin. It's easy to do. We have examples all around us, and that's why the reward from God is so high for passing these tests in our lifetime. Hang in there. Love you all.

DAY 239

As iron sharpens iron, so one person sharpens another.

PROVERBS 27:17

HELLO FAMILY: This is major! As a family and a church family in our faithful march, we sharpen each other's skills. We give words of encouragement, soft guidance, and lots of hugs and kisses to each other to strengthen each other like this scripture expresses. Think about this when speaking and working with our spouses as we are trying to get through the challenges of life, when the finances are tight and the bills are piling up. Be sure to sharpen and not dull our ironclad marriages for the days, weeks, months, and years ahead. We are blessed in this family to witness the hundreds of years of marriage shared by generations in our family's history. These marriages survived the World Wars, the Great Depression, and many other trials where sharp iron spears were needed to survive. Love you all.

DAY 240

Jesus went throughout Galilee, teaching in their synagogues, proclaiming the good news of the kingdom, and healing every disease and sickness among the people.

MATTHEW 4:23

HELLO FAMILY: When Jesus gets involved, things get taken care of fast. It is so important to start our mornings inviting Jesus into our hearts and asking Him to heal the wounds and worries of our hearts. Many of us and our friends deal with sicknesses their bodies have and stealing the happiness from their lives. Whether mental, physical, and yes, even spiritual, we all have some kind of health issues along with the weight of responsibilities that we have to deal with. Did you catch that I wrote "spiritual" as well? How many times did the disciples do what they were told by Jesus? Jesus was teaching His disciples every waking moment: One time, He told them to leave on a boat without Him only to be driven into a windstorm, and **then** Jesus arrived walking on water (Matthew 14:22–34)! Those disciples were probably wondering, "Why did I listen to this guy? Look at us now! Here we are doing what He told us, and we are going to drown out here in the sea!" But what happened? Not only did Jesus walk across the water, He commanded the seas to be calm. It is written then that the disciples "worshiped" Jesus for the first time after this "education." They witnessed the Son of God calm the seas instantly, on top of the "good news," healing and nurturing the sick. Remember those godly promises. We are in God's hand and Jesus is there for us to tackle the day ahead. Love you all.

DAY 241

The LORD is near to all who call on him, to all who call on him in truth. [19] He fulfills the desires of those who fear him; he hears their cry and saves them.

PSALM 145:18–19

HELLO FAMILY: I read this scripture and immediately was drawn to the part "to all who call on him in truth." In truth, being honest and sincere. Selfless and caring. Righteous in what we are praying for and calling out for God to do. When we pray, do a self-check. Review the motive of what we are asking. Is it for totally selfish reasons? I often catch myself in my discussions with God being a little selfish, and then we laugh about it together. There is no fooling God. So go ahead and have a good laugh with it — "You got me Lord. Sorry!" I like to remind God that He made me this way, then submitting in acknowledgement of what would be righteous to ask for and getting some help with it. Let us all know that God is way ahead of us in our desires and requests. He responds when our heart is in the right place. Love you all.

DAY 242

Dear friend, do not imitate what is evil but what is good. Anyone who does what is good is from God. Anyone who does what is evil has not seen God.

3 JOHN 1:11

HELLO FAMILY: "Has not seen God." I was anticipating it to say "is from the devil." So what does this mean, to not have seen God? I know many good people who do good things and never proclaim to have seen God or of being a Christian for that matter. Once again, what does it mean to "see God" then? God is "love." Someone who grows up without experiencing love may become empty and angry at the world. They may lash out and do evil things. They may not have "seen" God in the relationships they were stuck with as a child. They may not have experienced sincere love from a godly person in their lives. Children just want to be loved. Even as teenagers when we already know everything, we want to be loved. We must be loved in order to "know that God exists." God challenges all of us to love people and to treat them as family, no strings attached. Love you all.

DAY 243

"So do not fear, for I am with you; do not be dismayed, for I am your God. I will strengthen you and help you; I will uphold you with my righteous right hand. [11] "All who rage against you will surely be ashamed and disgraced; those who oppose you will be as nothing and perish. [12] Though you search for your enemies, you will not find them. Those who wage war against you will be as nothing at all. [13] For I am the LORD your God who takes hold of your right hand and says to you, Do not fear; I will help you."

ISAIAH 41:10–13

HELLO FAMILY: Fear is a very powerful tool of the devil himself. It can create situations of panic and dismay in an effort to destroy us. When we live with fear in our hearts, we cannot experience any joy at all. This scripture is addressing fear directly because God wants to take care of us. When our anxiety levels are out of control and all we do is worry, read these words of encouragement. There is no need to make a hasty decision out of fear when you are in God's hands. Sadly, fear can lead to many other negative health conditions like stress, which can really work away at your physical health. But enough of this fear chatter. This scripture is a major promise from God to not live in fear! Stay close to God for protection, and He will erase our enemies no matter what they are. Love you all.

DAY 244

I lift up my eyes to the mountains—where does my help come from? [2] My help comes from the LORD, the Maker of heaven and earth. [3] He will not let your foot slip—he who watches over you will not slumber; [4] indeed, he who watches over Israel will neither slumber nor sleep. [5] The LORD watches over you—the LORD is your shade at your right hand; [6] the sun will not harm you by day, nor the moon by night. [7] The LORD will keep you from all harm—he will watch over your life; [8] the LORD will watch over your coming and going both now and forevermore.

PSALM 121

HELLO FAMILY: A great reading for strength that Carol has read every day since I deployed to the Gulf War in August of 1990. This reading lives in her daily walk. And she is a Texan! Strong, true, and faithful in her relationship with Christ. Read this when uncertainty is in your midst. Love you all.

DAY 245

Praise be to the God and Father of our Lord Jesus Christ, who has blessed us in the heavenly realms with every spiritual blessing in Christ.

EPHESIANS 1:3

HELLO FAMILY: "Every spiritual blessing" has been and continues to be poured upon our family. There was a time in my life when my faith was weak and my body was very strong. I did not call upon God for help in my daily walk or decisions. Truth is, I was in a great struggle always trying to make ends meet. I declare the "I" in that statement was the spiritual stubbornness of a prideful man who just had to do it all by himself. Numerous times God put me through injuries that made time for me to pick up and read the Bible, which I did. Then finally, in God's time, I was shaped and humbled into recognizing who God is. He is alive! Today, our entire family enjoys jubilant communications across the globe. In many lands and cites we live a safe and fruitful life. I encourage everyone reading this to not give up on your faith in Christ. Even in those times when pride is at the forefront. Call on God in your daily walk. Love you all.

DAY 246

Do not be misled: "Bad company corrupts good character." [34] Come back to your senses as you ought, and stop sinning; for there are some who are ignorant of God— I say this to your shame.

1 CORINTHIANS 15:33-34

HELLO FAMILY: I saw this scripture and I remember Carol taping it to my youngest son's headboard on his bed so he would see it multiple times a day. I wish I had this scripture taped to my bed when I was growing up. It would have helped for sure. Yet even as adults, we are surrounded by peers who drift from righteousness and are always inviting others to join them in their exploits. Misery loves company. Sitting for hours on a bar stool is just one example of wasting valuable time and money and for what? I recall even using the excuse to party as a way to reach out to lost souls. To talk about Christ in a drunken mess of dialogues at the local bar. Life is full of choices and many times we will be called upon to be firm in our beliefs as godly people. This does not mean we have to be cold and "nerdish" to the social scene. Just pray and be responsible in our words and actions. Remain in the light and stay out of the darkness where danger is lurking for us all. Love you all.

DAY 247

The LORD has done it this very day; let us rejoice today and be glad.

PSALM 118:24

HELLO FAMILY: I must confess that I am not the one who wakes up in the morning with rejoicing and excitement all the time. When we experience those who are like that, it could expose our lack of spiritual understanding of what has just occurred—the mere fact that we do wake up. Our bodies are vulnerable to many physical, mental, and spiritual influences. It is very important to recognize how our Creator planned that, and it is to be appreciated. Carol is always in a wonderful mood no matter what the day has in store. There is cheer in her voice when she says good morning, which is followed by a hug and, if it's a really good day, a kiss on the cheek. My daughters Kim and Lynn are the same in Germany. Their husbands are the same way too (no kisses from the guys though), always very excited to bring in the day with all who they meet. It is so very refreshing, to say the least. I am like my grandchildren; it takes a little coffee, perhaps some Lucky Charms to figure out where we are going in the world. This scripture is a reminder that we should meet each day with joy. Share it with everyone you meet even in the early mornings. Love you all.

DAY 248

> "For I know the plans I have for you," declares the LORD, "plans to prosper you and not to harm you, plans to give you hope and a future."
>
> JEREMIAH 29:11

HELLO FAMILY: I really enjoy our group app we have. We get to share photos as our families grow even though we are oceans away from each other. We can see the plans unfolding with pictures of puppies, soccer practice, horseback riding, camping, big lush gardens, and goodness all around. We see no harm at all in these pictures. We see plans for a grand future with our children and grandchildren, with lots of good food and drink. These are the "plans" that a godly life brings for those who stay close to the Word of God and the teachings of our Lord and Savior Jesus Christ. Love you all.

DAY 249

> *Rejoice always, [17] pray continually, [18] give thanks in all circumstances; for this is God's will for you in Christ Jesus.*
>
> 1 THESSALONIANS 5:16–18

HELLO FAMILY: There are times and days when we may wonder why we are going through some very tough challenges, whether it is with our health, somebody else's health, finances, children, and perhaps even our marriage! This scripture brings it all into perspective. We are to stay in great spirits no matter what is happening and know that God is in control of the situation. He is using it to further His Kingdom and bring great goodness for us after the storm has passed. No one can imagine or comprehend the plans God has selected for us here on earth. We have been chosen. We just have to do as this scripture says: keep the faith. Stay positive at all costs. Do our best and give thanks in all circumstances, good or bad. Soon we will see the brilliant rainbow of answered prayers. Love you all.

DAY 250

The LORD your God, who is going before you, will fight for you, as he did for you in Egypt, before your very eyes,

DEUTERONOMY 1:30

HELLO FAMILY: What power it takes to control water! As the Red Sea parted for a nation to pass, and another to be destroyed, it was witnessed and documented in great detail. This event has been verified by many archeologists so that many generations can be aware of it for themselves. We are called to believe just as we did as a child in Santa Claus or the Easter Bunny bringing presents and candy on those precious exciting mornings. God knows that we are in a battle every single day as we try to stay focused on His glory. That's why God sent His Son Jesus to experience these battles here on earth. He wanted all of us to witness and learn how to overcome them with the Word of God. Know that God has done battle already and that He continues to battle for us in our daily walks today. Love you all.

DAY 251

"Come to me, all you who are weary and burdened, and I will give you rest. [29] Take my yoke upon you and learn from me, for I am gentle and humble in heart, and you will find rest for your souls. [30] For my yoke is easy and my burden is light."

MATTHEW 11:28-30

HELLO FAMILY: There will be times in our lives when our weary bodies enter a physical battle to survive. We have seen it with my dad's heart and my daughter's tumors. They met, and in some ways exceeded, the descriptions above of how weary their bodies really were. Now think of our spirituality. How weary are we spiritually? The soul of our being makes us who we are. Are we a joyful spirit, or not? Being a witness to my dad's recovery and watching my daughter recover through pictures and also while visiting her were testaments to this scripture big time. My family's spirits, their priorities on life are profoundly godly, surviving what they had been through. They know what is important and they know how to pray with sincere hearts. Our family and friends must recognize the glow they carry when in their presence. They have been rested and healed by God, and they bring joy to us all. What blessings they are! Think about others in our lives who have lived through near death experiences and observe their spirit. Love you all.

DAY 252

You make known to me the path of life; you will fill me with joy in your presence, with eternal pleasures at your right hand.

PSALM 16:11

HELLO FAMILY: The key phrase is this scripture is, "you make known to me." As our relationship strengthens with God, our eyes are opened to those little blessings perhaps not captured in the past. Some examples that come to mind: bald eagles watching over me every time I swim at the pond, a rainbow showing up over Noah's Ark at the Ark Encounter exhibit, a traffic jam keeping you from waiting for an hour in the parking lot. I could go on, as I am sure we all can. There are always signs that God is with us. Stay calm and "recognize the path" that is planned just for you. Love you all.

DAY 253

Many are the plans in a person's heart, but it is the LORD's purpose that prevails.

PROVERBS 19:21

HELLO FAMILY: As many of us know, we are a busy bunch much of the time. Lots of things to do each and every day, from the moment we wake in the early morning. We make all kinds of plans at work, church, community activities, and so on. That is a great trait to have and productivity is to prevail. However, there are things that happen that require a change in plans, like helping others in trouble, comforting a neighbor, and responding to emergencies in our path. Those are the God plans that take priority. The right things to do. Do these things even when you are exhausted, grumpy, and just don't want to get involved. God blesses those carrying out His plans. Love you all.

DAY 254

For the foolishness of God is wiser than human wisdom, and the weakness of God is stronger than human strength.

1 CORINTHIANS 1:25

HELLO FAMILY: What a point blank, "telling it like it really is" scripture to humble a prideful humanity. The greatness of God is something we mere mortals can never imagine, not in our wildest dreams. This is the Easter season when we celebrate life over death through Jesus Christ. Jesus Christ is no longer on the cross. Jesus Christ lives and is there for each and every one of us until the final days of our lives. We must not be foolish in thinking that our mortality has an end here on this earth as we know it. Yet Jesus set the example by being here on earth. He set the record straight. Jesus defeated death so that we may live with Him forever. Love you all.

DAY 255

"Do not be afraid, little flock, for your Father has been pleased to give you the kingdom."

LUKE 12:32

HELLO FAMILY: You just have to wonder, what are the details of this "Kingdom"? We are referred to as a "little flock" (of sheep) because if left alone without our Shepherd, we would be devoured by the ways of this world. I wonder if the Kingdom is a little bit different for each one of us, matching our likes and our favorite things. I hope my room has a jacuzzi to relax in and a great big bed for all my past pets to share with me during naps. Imagine that! It will be way more majestic than that, though. The talk of the Kingdom is throughout the entire Bible. It is that spectacular. It should make us want to please our Father in Heaven even more! One can only imagine what our Lord has in store for us all. Love you all.

DAY 256

The Lord loves righteousness and justice; the earth is full of his unfailing love.

PSALM 33:5

HELLO FAMILY: When the news is full of hate crimes, mass shootings, and just plain evilness, we may wonder where righteousness is. I will tell you where it is. It is everywhere there are Christians being faithful. There are three pillars to live by. First, "Do no harm." Second, "Do good." Third, "Love God." Only forgiveness will set you free from anger, and we know that God is not a fan of anger. We can't go wrong with these three pillars or tasks to follow. These pillars are very pleasing to our Father in Heaven. My pastor, Kenny Rogers, gave a sermon on these pillars many years ago and they really stuck in my head. As a Ranger and Green Beret, I used to tell my kids, "Faith, fitness, and knowledge are pillars of each day." As I have matured as a Christian, our new pillars are now prayer, scripture reading, and worship. Many are very thankful to the millions of Christians who have taken these pillars to heart and set the standard for unfailing love. Love you all.

DAY 257

"For I know the plans I have for you," declares the Lord, "plans to prosper you and not to harm you, plans to give you hope and a future."

JEREMIAH 29:11

HELLO FAMILY: Prosperity! What does prosperity mean to each one of us? Have we ever sat quietly with God and defined prosperity with Him? When Carol and I first moved to where we are now, I would go for walks around and along the roads of the back woods and ponds of our property. On these walks I would open my heart to God. I was revealing my dreams to God. He already had the plans in His hand to prosper us when the time was right. Plans for fellow veterans to bring their grandchildren to camp, fish, and hike along our ponds and woods, experiencing God's creation together. Big plans have very many pieces, twists, and angles. With God, all things are possible. We must have sincere hearts. The plans Carol and I had with God have prospered. We have been able to witness kids learn how to swim, catch their first fish, harvest their first deer, and shoot a shotgun for the very first time, just to name a few. We have even celebrated our son Blake getting the biggest buck ever in the family. Never lose faith in this promise from God. He knows our hearts. It may take a great deal of time, even decades, as it did with our plans. But the wait is well worth it and greatly appreciated. Praise our Lord! We need to keep the prayers flowing. Love you all.

DAY 258

Let us hold unswervingly to the hope we profess, for he who promised is faithful.

HEBREWS 10:23

HELLO FAMILY: I hope we enjoy the descriptors used in this scripture. "Unswervingly" means there is no messing around. The path is straight. No dancing around with this message. Stay on the straight and narrow path and don't worry about our hopes and dreams not coming true because God keeps His promises. We must remember that God knows us best. God knows when the plans we have can be received. We may need some more time to mature and gain some experience before our plans can be received in order to be successful. I believe we are given what we can handle responsibly. Kind of like getting our boys BB guns—they didn't get the high-powered kill-a-rabbit kind at first. Or getting ATVs—my boys got the battery-operated ones first. In both cases, I observed their maturity before they got their first shotgun and gas-powered ATVs. God does the same thing with us. Show responsibility with what you have and remain faithful in keeping your hopes alive. Love you all.

DAY 259

Be strong and take heart, all you who hope in the LORD.

PSALM 31:24

HELLO FAMILY: Being strong calls for our tenacity and persistence. We just keep on going like the Energizer Bunny. Our culture today is instant gratification. Google it. Same day delivery, social media, immediate feedback, dating apps, Uber, and don't forget to fill out the survey. Everything in the service industry is about getting that service the fastest and best way possible. Critiques follow every order we do on the apps. The deliveries are coming to our front doors in hours. Health matters don't work that way, unfortunately. Health issues can take a lifetime to work with and through in many cases. To be strong and take heart in the Lord can give many a happy spirit in the midst of physical misery. This scripture advises us to be strong and take heart. The Lord our God is alive and with us. Love you all.

DAY 260

The one who has knowledge uses words with restraint, and whoever has understanding is even-tempered.

PROVERBS 17:27

HELLO FAMILY: It's all about having that good godly character to move forward in life in a righteous way. Being "even-tempered" was not a strong point for me. A mere perception of anything in my sights could lead to an instant outburst. I have been known to fire off ridiculous words that may not have been appropriate. The fact that we have a Bible that has a chapter dedicated to wise behavior, guiding our daily thoughts and actions, is "dad" action from our Father. Today's guidance is very specific and directly explains what we look like to others around us when we do not use restraint and remain calm. Very specific instructions that are as applicable today as they were hundreds of years ago. Using appropriate words builds trust with everyone in hearing range. Love you all.

DAY 261

In everything set them an example by doing what is good. In your teaching show integrity, seriousness [8] and soundness of speech that cannot be condemned, so that those who oppose you may be ashamed because they have nothing bad to say about us.

TITUS 2:7-8

HELLO FAMILY: Now here is the real challenge in life. Not just with our peers, but with our families as well. Our culture has shifted greatly just in my lifetime. Just imagine what our grandparents are thinking when we show them a dating app. We are called to be gentle and blameless in our daily and nightly walk. We never know who may be closely watching, listening, or reviewing our every word and action. In today's culture, we must consider that everything we do is being recorded! We are called to perform our tasks each day to the very best of our abilities, "doing what is good," whether related to church, school, or jobs. Everything we do is an "example" that others are really watching and even recording. Kids are even watching their parents on the home video security apps on their phones now. Boy, have times changed! Do great things in everything we do, whether we are being watched, recorded, or not. Do it with a joyful heart. Love you all.

DAY 262

By the word of the LORD the heavens were made,
their starry host by the breath of his mouth.

PSALM 33:6

HELLO FAMILY: Families really enjoy their time off with summer trips. Everyone takes pictures to make photo books — a way to remember being together and having fun. Keeping these family trips a tradition with the pictures flowing from year to year is something our future children will love to look at, seeing their moms and dads as little as they are now. I assure you that without a doubt, it lifts the entire family up, seeing the old photos of traditions that have been passed down over the decades and how they have grown, especially for the grandparents. The heavens above are watching also. Our Lord is pleased with the joy and smiles that are shared. Traditions are a way of honoring our family's past. Can we imagine the smiles in Heaven when those old photos are admired? We lift up our praises of joy we witness in our families and especially in that special place called Heaven. When other family members are having a bad day, these pictures bring memories of closeness and warmth. We are part of a huge family under the gleaming heavens of God. Love you all.

DAY 263

For since the creation of the world God's invisible qualities—
his eternal power and divine nature—have been clearly seen,
being understood from what has been made, so that people
are without excuse.

ROMANS 1:20

HELLO FAMILY: See that? "Without excuse." Currently there are shows that depict other planets, moons, and even galaxies in great detail. There is no other that is remotely close to our earth in creativity and life. Now watch some shows that depict ancient cities up to 10,000 years old. This is what really brings our Bible to life. The book of Genesis gets my blood flowing. To think of the times before Noah! Real advanced engineering stuff here, folks. There is so much evidence out there that clearly validates the story in our Bible of the Great Flood and so much more. Carol goes nuts when I watch those shows about ancient times until I show her how they truly are validating the Old Testament. If you take a moment to "see" this scripture come to life, you too can share this reality with others. Love you all.

DAY 264

The LORD is good, a refuge in times of trouble.
He cares for those who trust in him,

NAHUM 1:7

HELLO FAMILY: Well this is perfect for today, especially being late too. I had to put this scripture into practice this past week; hope, praise, trust—all of them. I have been really sick. Bed ridden since Sunday with symptoms of a fever, massive headaches, and body aches. It took a good bit to get figured out. The doctors were giving me different medicines, and the misery was painful and getting depressing. Last night was big time prayer for Carol and me. I really wanted to take my little sister to the airport at 9 a.m. It's a two-hour drive one way. At 10 p.m., I was still in misery. I asked Carol to hold me so we could pray together. At midnight, all of the pain left me. I was able to sleep until 7 a.m., but then the pain returned. Carol questioned, "Could this be a migraine?" I insisted on taking my sister to the airport, so I stopped for Excedrin on the way to pick her up. Wow! It worked! I totally got a break from the pain. I was finally able to recognize a potential solution to my sickness. That's what the Lord granted me—Carol to figure it out. I am not 100 percent, but I am on the right path. Praise God! That drive with Mary to the airport was precious. My sister and I shared memories. We looked back on memories of our parents and stories about Blake in Nashville. We also reflected on Blake's testimony that he had shared with me: how the Lord moved him from a police career in Dallas to a super successful career in Nashville. I also shared precious pictures of my family in Germany. This time was a blessing altogether in and of itself for a brother and sister to share. Answered prayer big time! I encourage us all to reflect on those moments of answered prayer when we needed a refuge in our lives. Love you all.

DAY 265

> But the LORD said to Samuel, "Do not consider his appearance or his height, for I have rejected him. The LORD does not look at the things people look at. People look at the outward appearance, but the LORD looks at the heart."
>
> 1 SAMUEL 16:7

HELLO FAMILY: I seem to recall my parents telling me things like, "God sees everything we do—our thoughts and even things we have yet to do." It would kind of freak me out, because I was that kid sneaking goodies out of my great-grandfather's pantry when no one was looking. We all have our little secrets, even as adults. My wife just told me stories from her childhood of raking up pine needles with her sister Laura and putting dog poop in the piles. It was to get a dig on her older sister who had to pick up the piles, which they considered to be the easier job. God is well aware of our hearts and thoughts, who the rascals are and who the angels are. We are all held accountable by God for our truthful hearts and the motives we carry throughout each day. It's very important to ask God for help in being righteous in our ways, in the treatment of others, and in all that we do. Love you all.

DAY 266

> "You will seek me and find me when you seek me with all your heart."
>
> JEREMIAH 29:13

HELLO FAMILY: There is a great deal to be said for sincerity. Way too many times in my life I would curse. I would call out to God for very selfish reasons, and most of the time I would not even consider calling out to God for the tasks ahead. What I have learned is that when we "seek" God at the very start of each day, inviting Him in to assist us with all that comes our way, there is great peace and profound progress. The flash points of cursing don't seem to occur at all anymore. There is a calm solution to all the problems that occur in my day. I truly encourage each of us to wake up and immediately praise our Lord for the day and to call on the Holy Spirit to fill us with strength and encouragement to share with others. Love you all.

DAY 267

The way of fools seems right to them,
but the wise listen to advice.

PROVERBS 12:15

HELLO FAMILY: Getting advice from the right source is the key to making wise decisions. What is critical is knowing what advice to pray for. What do you want to happen with this advice? Identifying the prayer to pray is half the quest. Remember to ask yourselves what the motive is for the advice you are waiting to receive. This will be a key indicator. Prepare for the Lord to send a wise friend to guide you along the way. Love you all.

DAY 268

Do not conform to the pattern of this world, but be transformed
by the renewing of your mind. Then you will be able to test and
approve what God's will is—his good, pleasing and perfect will.

ROMANS 12:2

HELLO FAMILY: Conforming to the patterns of this world can make us mentally exhausted. There is no humanly way possible to keep up with all of the drama. I have to admit, I have allowed Facebook and politics to get the best of me at times in the past. I am fighting back the temptation to get on Facebook right now just thinking about it as I type along here. Our minds can get so caught up and engulfed in issues of this world that these issues will consume our every thought and desire. Take that a step further and note the many addictions that tempt us, and we can have a real mess on our hands. This is what we must prepare and warn our children about daily. God sees our hearts and not what the world sees. Stay focused on the good pleasing ways of Christ and your state of mind will be much clearer. Our performance at work and at home will be much more appreciated as our relationships grow for the long haul. Love you all.

DAY 269

For we do not have a high priest who is unable to empathize with our weaknesses, but we have one who has been tempted in every way, just as we are—yet he did not sin. [16] Let us then approach God's throne of grace with confidence, so that we may receive mercy and find grace to help us in our time of need.

HEBREWS 4:15-16

HELLO FAMILY: As a young teenager, I recall sitting on a ledge overlooking Letchworth State Park in Western New York. At times I would be alone, unhappy about something or someone at the house and pondering exactly what this scripture is talking about. Did Jesus have to deal with His parents? At that time, I really believed that my ideas were better and brighter than anyone's in the family, especially my parents. So there I would sit and wonder, how did Jesus deal with His parents not being as smart as He was? Even as a young rebel, I had already learned that Jesus was here on earth dealing with the same "issues" and temptations that I was dealing with, that we all deal with. So, seek that wisdom from our Savior Jesus Christ to power through our days. Love you all.

DAY 270

Let the morning bring me word of your unfailing love, for I have put my trust in you. Show me the way I should go, for to you I entrust my life.

PSALM 143:8

HELLO FAMILY: Speaking from experience, every morning is a great morning when it starts with a conversation with our Lord. I kid you not. To just get up and go after the daily grind day after day, we have to start to wonder what the heck is going on. We are just working ourselves to our graves. Seeking Jesus our Lord first thing in the morning guides us where we need to go, where our hearts need to be focused, whether it is another family member, a coworker, a church project, or whatever. The Lord will guide us in that direction, and we will have purpose. "Show me the way I should go," is the foundation of each morning's wakeup call and motivation for the blessings to follow. Love you all.

DAY 271

Be devoted to one another in love.
Honor one another above yourselves.

ROMANS 12:10

HELLO FAMILY: Many times we read or use the word "love" with its many different meanings in our culture. We may bypass the true actual meaning of it when it comes to this scripture. After I read the book *The Five Love Languages* (Chapman, 2001) on a mountain top in Uzbekistan, it all finally came together for me. I was intrigued by these five areas of effort. They were time, words of affirmation, gifts, service, and physical touch, all equaling love. Love is what Jesus demonstrated while He was here on earth. Our Lord actually spent time with humanity, always providing words of hope. He gave us the gift of salvation with His life. He demonstrated service by washing the feet of His disciples the day prior to going to the cross. He healed everyone He touched (or who touched Him). This is the sincerity we are called to represent when we execute our marriage vows, have children, and take care of our elderly parents and others in need. Love is the answer! I love you all.

DAY 272

You have searched me, LORD, and you know me. [2] You know when I sit and when I rise; you perceive my thoughts from afar. [3] You discern my going out and my lying down; you are familiar with all my ways. [4] Before a word is on my tongue you, LORD, know it completely.

PSALM 139:1-4

HELLO FAMILY: We had church today folks, and Brother Kenny was really fired up about our hearts. Everything described within the above scripture was covered in our sermon. God knows our hearts better than we do and He is working on those hearts to further His Kingdom here on earth. Many Christians have checked all the blocks, myself included. I have surrendered to Christ. I have been baptized many times, and on most Sundays, I am in church wherever I may be. On many occasions though, when asked to serve for one reason or another, my mind jumps to twice as many excuses than to what I am being asked to do. **Ugggg!** Why is that? Truth is, the heart. The passion is not all in. Now don't get me wrong in regard to having other commitments. I am talking about the times when we decide it would be better to just take a nap, fish at the pond, cut grass just because, or whatever excuse rather than help out on a church project or issue. Yes family, as the opportunities present themselves for solid self-evaluation when asked to serve, be honest and move out. Love you all.

DAY 273

> *But you are a chosen people, a royal priesthood, a holy nation, God's special possession, that you may declare the praises of him who called you out of darkness into his wonderful light.*
>
> 1 PETER 2:9

HELLO FAMILY: Our family is sitting on pins and needles awaiting word on our son Shane and his wife Katie to get approval to receive their adopted child. This process has taken the entire year, cost tens of thousands of dollars, full of emotions up and down, and we are not even close to the finish line yet. But as I think of this child, AKA #BabyK, I think of this scripture and this child being "chosen" for adoption. I recall, in not too happy moments, the hundreds of kids left orphaned in Somalia and the looks in their eyes for the least bit of acknowledgment for some kind of recognition. They wanted food and clean water. How can you place a value on being chosen from darkness? No one in this family has experienced the darkness that I am speaking of and that this scripture is referencing. Darkness is a horrible place to be, and it brings sadness to think that children are victims in this darkness everywhere. **But!** We are not in darkness! Recognize and give credit to God for sparing our lives and being able to enjoy the great light of love that we do and share daily. We are God's special possession. Praises to our Lord and Savior Jesus Christ for the blessings we live with each and every day. Love you all.

DAY 274

> *Rather, clothe yourselves with the Lord Jesus Christ, and do not think about how to gratify the desires of the flesh.*
>
> ROMANS 13:14

HELLO FAMILY: As the summer family pictures keep coming in, I see a family serving each other. The kids have great big smiles. Eating ice cream, on hikes in the park, parents are holding hands and smiling (at each other), and all my kids are busy and making happy plans for the future. I pray that each day when we awake that we recognize Christ and our focus stays on the cross. Christ came to serve and not to be served. This is what is so important in our daily walk. When we look to care for others above ourselves, all the pieces and the blessings come together. I strongly encourage everyone to always make time for themselves with their spouses. However short and sweet, make it a point at this moment to serve each other and to love. Make sure each of us knows we are number one to each other and that they come first in our thoughts and desires. Yes, as our children watch us grow in our marriages, they learn. Their confidence can grow in the love they witness in their homes. Love you all.

DAY 275

For this is the message you heard from the beginning:
We should love one another.

1 JOHN 3:11

HELLO FAMILY: Reading scripture after scripture about loving one another, I think to myself, *Is God trying to tell us something?* Then I have this little episode of anger in communicating with the love of my life Carol and I am reminded immediately of God's Word consistently encouraging us to love. It is because many of us need to be reminded often. My weakness is pain. When I am in discomfort with my back, headaches, or whatever, I tend to get zippy and tart with my words and attitude. I know I am not the only one. We all have moments of weakness. Sometimes a mere look from another can set us off. Now I was just going to make a comment about women, but my wisdom took over and I will decline (Proverbs kicked in just in time). With all that said, it is important to recognize when we are weak and not in a loving mode. These are the times to reach out to our healer, Jesus Christ, and get some help. Remember, words cut worse than a knife and we can't get them back after the missile launches. Love you all.

DAY 276

The LORD gives strength to his people;
the LORD blesses his people with peace.

PSALM 29:11

HELLO FAMILY: The blessing of "peace." We can understand strength, being strong, healthy, and energetic, but what about peace? Peace is initially thought of as not being at war. War can be described as what is raging in our thoughts and makes for rough days ahead. War is the restlessness in a relationship with a spouse, child, parent, or friend. War is the stress at work or the neighbor next door, the rascal kids at school messing with my kids. War is a bad place to be. Literally, too! Hopefully, most people know that. It rages every day on this earth somewhere. We are promised in this scripture that strength and peace come from God, the One who comforts us in our lives. We have to recognize that if there is war in our thoughts, we can't bring peace. What is the cause of these disturbances in our lives? Seeking guidance from our Creator through prayer is a great start for a grounded self-evaluation. Only then will true peace be given a chance to comfort our lives and our loved ones around us. Praise the Lord daily. Love you all.

DAY 277

"You are worthy, our Lord and God, to receive glory and honor and power, for you created all things, and by your will they were created and have their being."

REVELATION 4:11

HELLO FAMILY: I woke up this morning and thought perhaps I'd pick a scripture from Revelation. Then thought, *Nope, better to stay with the plan so I don't get partial to particular scriptures.* We were created. We have our being, we have our space, our territory, our respect, and our world. It all belongs to the One who created it, just like we take ownership to all we create. I remember when my son Shane started working for Walmart, I told him to "own" it. It's not your job, it is "your" store. Now Shane is a proud store manager for Walmart and, yes, I am seriously proud of my son. The better our attitude, the more creative we are, which can translate into being the best at what we do. God created us to have purpose with passion, excitement to get up and go each morning. That is the message here. As big as we may get, all of the credit goes to God. So don't let your britches stretch too far. Be sure to give credit to where it all began. Love you all.

Me and my adopted grandson Colton. Shane and Katie adopted Colton in 2020.

DAILY DEVOTIONALS

DAY 278

Whoever walks in integrity walks securely, but whoever takes crooked paths will be found out.

PROVERBS 10:9

HELLO FAMILY: Remember when we were little kids, doing something we should not do, having to sweat it out on whether anyone would find out? Well, that's how it was with me anyway. I remember my sweet granddaughter little Hannah during the missing candy mystery just before Christmas. Hannah was the prime suspect and was being investigated. All the "Advent" stocking candy that was in the little pockets for each day was gone! After Aunt Lynn and Mamma Kim did some searching around, candy wrappers and unopened candy were found under Hannah's bed. Hannah was not aware of her mom's discovery. When Hannah was questioned, her little eyes said it all. When specifically questioned about what Santa would think about this, wheels were turning fast. And then it came out: "Philipp did it." Now, little brother Philipp was still in diapers and at two years old, was standing in total astonishment. "Why is everyone looking at me?" It didn't take long for Hannah to realize that the cover story of "Philipp did it" was not working. Hannah took her mom's hand and led her to the crime scene, softly explained that she had done the dirty deed, and merely said, "I don't know why I did it. It just happened." As adults, we get into similar situations and the price to pay is our character. Integrity is a super big deal. Sad part is, nobody is trusted anymore, and we have cameras literally everywhere to keep people honest. Do be true to your heart and know that God sees all. Just like Santa. Love you all.

Uncle Blake is hanging out with Colton Christmas 2020.

DAY 279

Give to the one who asks you, and do not turn away from the one who wants to borrow from you.

MATTHEW 5:42

HELLO FAMILY: When we moved to the city here on Partridge Point in Cadiz, KY, it took a little getting used to our super friendly and loving neighbors. I was not even asking to borrow anything and folks were offering me their golf carts, boats, sprayers, you name it. Our neighborhood is comprised of church-attending United Methodists and Catholics. Our community consists of ten residences, mostly retired couples who love to spoil their grandchildren. We all get together four times a year to celebrate spring, 4th of July, fall, and the New Year. When we get together, we always start out with a fellowship prayer praising our Lord and Savior Jesus Christ. During our meetings, it is always common for someone to voice a need and the offers flow with ease to take care of the situation. Throughout the year, neighbors check on each other, work together cleaning up after storms, and being there when tragedy strikes. This is what God intended when He called (and still calls) His children to fellowship together, to be there for each other in all situations. Like family away from home. Love you all.

DAY 280

Do everything without grumbling or arguing, [15] so that you may become blameless and pure, "children of God without fault in a warped and crooked generation." Then you will shine among them like stars in the sky

PHILIPPIANS 2:14-15

HELLO FAMILY: When I was growing up on the farm, cleaning calves' pens, hog pens, and other fine locations where animals live, it was hard at times to keep a good attitude. Spending your days in school and being taunted for not joining the football team or other after school activities can really wear on you. My dad was pretty firm on the priorities of the family and playing high school sports was not one of them. I did get to play basketball, though. I put my every ounce of energy into it. Basketball consumed my thoughts throughout the year leading up to the season. I did very well and at times my dad would have to reel me back in with some counseling on the other areas of responsibilities that I had. He would emphasize "attitude." Whether you are washing dishes for your mother or cleaning the garage for your father, there is no tolerance for grumbling or arguing about it. Well, I don't know if I will be shining among the stars anytime soon, but if my children and grandchildren do, it would sure make my day. Love you all.

DAY 281

*Lord, our Lord, how majestic is your name
in all the earth!*

PSALM 8:9

HELLO FAMILY: I read this scripture and am shamed at how our culture, our language, and our attitude towards our Creator has become. I remember on the few occasions growing up where a foul word slipped from my lips, I was immediately found foaming with a bar of soap in my mouth as a result. If there was no soap to be had, it was a stinging slap across the cheek. In today's world that would be warranted as child abuse. When we are faced with the **truth** when Jesus comes again in all His glory and every knee shall bow down, this very scripture will ring loudly across the earth. Do take the time to recognize where each breath comes from and praise the name of God Almighty in your daily walk. Love you all.

DAY 282

*Do not merely listen to the word, and so deceive yourselves.
Do what it says.*

JAMES 1:22

HELLO FAMILY: I really appreciate direct and to-the-point guidance. "Do what it says." I recall and know that parents tell their kids many things to do and not to do. At times I recall telling my boys, "Do what I say and don't worry about what I do." Imagine that grand guidance coming from your dad. We all can predict what our children are going to do. They are likely to do exactly what they saw being done in their home, at school, and everywhere else examples are being set. Our flesh is very accustomed to following examples, and if we are smoking cigarettes, drinking beer or wine or whiskey, or cursing our way through the day, note the behaviors being played out day in and day out for our children to observe. Our physical bodies are subject to many "feel good" amenities out there in the world today, and it's critical to explain these temptations to our children in order to prepare them for what exists and how to deal with those temptations. We have heard before we are what we eat. That's the physical side of this concept. But what about spiritually? Spiritually, we are what we see and what we hear. What words we read, what music we listen to, and what books we read form our spiritual being. I hope that by putting this book together, children out there will have these scriptures read to them by a loving parent, guardian, or friend who will be able to explain in compassionate detail why God inspired these scriptures to be written. So, do what I say and read the Bible to our kids. Love you all.

DAY 283

Do not love the world or anything in the world. If anyone loves the world, love for the Father is not in them. [16] For everything in the world—the lust of the flesh, the lust of the eyes, and the pride of life—comes not from the Father but from the world. [17] The world and its desires pass away, but whoever does the will of God lives forever.

1 JOHN 2:15-17

HELLO FAMILY: Reading this scripture can be a real kick in the kisser when you take it all in and recognize how much we really want to live in this world. Let's be honest—our entire health care system is designed to keep people alive at all costs. We have spent billions and trillions on keeping people alive and there is no end in sight. Spiritually, the mere mention of a chronic health condition warrants the deployment of priests, pastors, clergymen and clergywomen to deploy prayer warriors on behalf of the victim. Holy water, holy oil, and the lighting of candles is a common theme in our local churches for a person who is not healthy. Thankfully, some preachers express some joy when there is the mention of someone passing away. They are to be with the Lord! Yet we all want to stay alive, whatever the cost, especially us well-off Americans. We have health care options to keep us going. This scripture emphasizes the importance of recognizing that "things" of this world pass away, including us. This is critical to a relationship with our Lord. Our spiritual preparations should be a daily walk and not a crisis to prayer when sickness or tragedy intrudes our lives. Do take the time to have that relationship established, the communications lines open with our Creator and Savior Jesus Christ. Love you all.

DAY 284

He has shown you, O mortal, what is good. And what does the L<small>ORD</small> require of you? To act justly and to love mercy and to walk humbly with your God.

MICAH 6:8

HELLO FAMILY: "Requirements" are something we deal with on a daily basis in society. There are requirements to be a loyal employee. Showing up to work on time every day, being collaborative with your associates, and following instructions are all essential. From the moment our children are able to comprehend our words, we teach them how to follow the rules, the guidance of their teachers, and the acceptable classroom behaviors. Why should it be any different as a child of God? So many of us now just go to church, and that is not every Sunday either. There are available Bible studies, Sunday school classes, and other service-oriented fellowship activities where prayer is engaged and godly work gets done. This is "what is good" as mentioned in this scripture, to grow in Christ gaining a better understanding of where we all will end up sooner or later—with our Shepherd. Love you all.

DAY 285

Jesus answered, "I am the way and the truth and the life. No one comes to the Father except through me."

JOHN 14:6

HELLO FAMILY: When I read this, I recall a number of conversations with family members about our faith in Jesus Christ. Some have mentioned that they agree there is a creator or supreme being managing humanity (they must watch *Ancient Aliens* on the History Channel). But they truly struggle with the concept of Jesus Christ being here on earth and rising from the dead, then returning again. They have reviewed the great miracles of life, our earth, and the universe. These are educated people and yet when it comes to the details of our Lord and Savior, there is a spiritual wall. Sometimes I wonder if it's a commitment thing, that once you accept Jesus as your Savior there is some kind of "work" that you are committing to, and some folks want no part of that. The life of Jesus fascinates me. Of all the religions in the world, none compare to Christianity. Not even close! Jesus performed so many miracles in front of thousands of people. He raised people from the dead! Jesus foretold His resurrection. Then Jesus came back to His disciples and other people after His death on the cross. For the life of me, there is no other than our Lord and Savior Jesus Christ! Key point: Jesus quotes here that "No one comes to the Father except through me." I say no more. Love you all.

DAY 286

Direct my footsteps according to your word; let no sin rule over me.

PSALM 119:133

HELLO FAMILY: This scripture implies that the request comes from someone who is familiar with the "Word" of God. "Footsteps" is a reference to making decisions even in a very fast-paced world, a world that can be deathly cruel and unforgiving no matter who we are or where we come from. I think of the pressures on our young people today from social media. Every single letter, chat, picture, and video sent or received can now be brought up to haunt our future endeavors. That's why it's important to stay in God's Word, the BIBLE: Basic Instructions Before Leaving Earth. Reading God's Word will gleam an immense amount of wisdom to guide decisions and guide our footsteps for years to come. Reading the book of Proverbs with our children at bedtime can create all kinds of discussions and explanations that can help them stay out of trouble in the future big time. Love you all.

DAY 287

"Peace I leave with you; my peace I give you.
I do not give to you as the world gives.
Do not let your hearts be troubled and do not be afraid."

JOHN 14:27

HELLO FAMILY: On so many occasions as I would mentally prepare to deploy as a member of Special Forces, I would put a wall up between my family and me. I would be short and to the point, not wanting to get emotional or softhearted. Looking back, it was a horrible thing to do. There was a tense cloud that overshadowed the very time my family needed the confidence that this scripture provides. Fortunately, not that long ago I realized what was happening to me and how my character would change during these pre-deployments. The sad part was that I realized this after my time in the military. I was still getting curt with my loved ones prior to going on business trips that were only going to last a few weeks or so. This scripture is the exact promise to take to heart when we find ourselves getting uptight. Our children need to experience that "peace" of mind, that confidence of knowing all is going to be totally fine in their homes. "Do not let your hearts be troubled and do not be afraid." This peace is coming from our Lord and Savior to all of us. We are to share to all who will listen. Love you all.

DAY 288

Jesus looked at them and said, "With man this is impossible,
but not with God; all things are possible with God."

MARK 10:27

HELLO FAMILY: When I look back on my life, I wonder how much more I may have accomplished if I had included God in the equation. Even today, as I look at the work that needs to be done in the back woods, I recognize already that more work has been done, more than I ever could have imagined being accomplished because I called upon God for help. I dare say, we sell ourselves short by not getting God involved in every plan we put together. Recall the scriptures that call for us to be courageous and to fear nothing. How many times will we take the safe plan and not venture out for the Promised Land? For that matter, me putting together all of these daily scriptures and thinking about putting them into an actual book is reaching the Promised Land. I can hear the critiques now. "All things are possible with God." That needs to be the battle cry when we face new horizons and challenges that test our every skillset. No worries. Be brave and know that God has you in His hands. Love you all.

DAY 289

*For it is by grace you have been saved, through faith—
and this is not from yourselves, it is the gift of God—*

EPHESIANS 2:8

HELLO FAMILY: I remember growing up and wondering how much work I would have to do to get to Heaven. We altar boys would talk with one another about the activities we should be doing on behalf of our church, you know, for "extra points." We boys always mumbled under our breath that it was just plain "church work" we had to do to really get to Heaven. We had no concept of being nice to others and helping others outside our church grounds and in our families. Now that I am grown, I have realized that I am called to serve everyone, whether they are members of my church or not. The most important aspect of this service is to do it with joy. That's right, if we are going to work for the Lord, we best have a great attitude about it or we are not really going to receive the blessings of the entire process. The gift of grace from God has no strings attached. This is really hard for our culture to accept, because everything we get has a price attached to it. Many times my father expressed to me, "Nothing is free in this world." Serving on behalf of the Lord is an exuberant daily walk, working or not, so relax and enjoy the journey. Love you all.

DAY 290

*When I am in distress, I call to you,
because you answer me.*

PSALM 86:7

HELLO FAMILY: I write my two cents' worth every day and I am the first one to resort to primal instincts when in distress. Distress is an event that can trigger a "flight or fight" response that releases hormones on our bodies that fire us up. It is a survival mechanism God created for us to get through potentially bad times. Depending on how we evaluate the situations we find ourselves in, this can result in doing more harm than good even though we survived. Relationships with doctors, nurses, the police, work associates, and, most importantly, the ones we love can be fractured big time. Do call for help. Thankfully, a voice has reminded me on more than one occasion that God is in control and has a handle on this. Many times, I have had to come home and say, "I am sorry. Will you forgive me?" Yes, even say "I am sorry" to health professionals. So far so good with the police. Having a moment to find peace and replay what just happened in the distressful moments is key, especially when life has its shocking moments. I love you all.

DAY 291

"For the eyes of the Lord are on the righteous and his ears are attentive to their prayer, but the face of the Lord is against those who do evil."

1 PETER 3:12

HELLO FAMILY: I recall years ago reading an article about a discussion between a teacher and a student. The student made the point that darkness was the absence of light, the absence of energy, the absence of God. God is energy. He is the light. Without God, there is darkness. When the face of the Lord is upon you, the energy is with you. The light guides your steps. The light exposes the truth. Nothing will be hidden. How do you want to live your life? There is a choice to be made, so choose wisely. Prefer to walk in the light and not stumble through darkness. Love you all.

DAY 292

So if you faithfully obey the commands I am giving you today— to love the LORD your God and to serve him with all your heart and with all your soul—[14] then I will send rain on your land in its season, both autumn and spring rains, so that you may gather in your grain, new wine and olive oil.

DEUTERONOMY 11:13-14

HELLO FAMILY: I was just chatting with friends about how hot and dry it has been this month. Leaves are falling from the trees. The grass crunches under our feet and the smell of dry debris fills the air. Just as I began reading this scripture, the clouds opened up. Now it is pouring down rain as I write. Water is life. It brings the fruits of the earth to our tables for a feast to be had. Drought brings panic, distress, and even, in some cases, death. God is in control and our country has favored well as a Christian nation. We are the world's breadbasket feeding millions across the entire globe. Keep the waters flowing in our lives with a healthy and robust passion for our Lord and Savior, Jesus Christ. Our gardens will be fruitful forever. Love you all.

DAY 293

Be perfect, therefore, as your heavenly Father is perfect.

MATTHEW 5:48

HELLO FAMILY: Perfection can be something that we give up on pretty fast. Let's face it, who is "perfect"? With that said, much of the military training I attended demanded it—training for Jump Master, Dive Med Tech, and Dive Supervisor just to name a few. Perfection in testing was mandatory. If you failed, you got sent home, a humiliation to your unit. These military skills requiring perfection saved lives in training and in combat. The pressure was on big time. This scripture declares God's standards are even higher. These standards save souls for eternity. So we need to get with the program and perfect ourselves. In the military, you may find yourself "recycled" back a time period to be retrained and tested again. You pound away at the skills to be tested until perfection is reached. You don't ever just quit on yourself or your unit. Just like we don't want to quit on ourselves in regards to our faith and our family. Final testing is not until our last breath. We just don't know when that will be. So study hard children. We don't want to be a recycle. Love you all.

DAY 294

When hard pressed, I cried to the LORD; he brought me into a spacious place. [6] The LORD is with me; I will not be afraid. What can mere mortals do to me?

PSALM 118:5-6

HELLO FAMILY: "Mere mortals" can make your life pretty darn miserable. Watching the news and seeing how cruel, even lethal, we are to each other is absolutely frightening. Million dollar companies make commercials of people falling victim to crooks just to sell security systems. Now insurance companies have commercials that feature a thief stealing your car! "Does your insurance company cover this?" All instilling fear in order to extort our money. This scripture calls out, "**Stop** the madness!" If we are in concert with our Lord and Savior Jesus Christ, will He not listen to our cries, as is promised in this scripture? Take control of the fear impulse button and free yourselves to a spacious place with Christ. Experience the calmness that will come over you as you communicate with the Almighty and come to terms with the challenges ahead. Love you all.

DAY 295

In the same way, the Spirit helps us in our weakness.
We do not know what we ought to pray for, but the
Spirit himself intercedes for us through wordless groans.

ROMANS 8:26

HELLO FAMILY: I love this scripture, "wordless groans." Listen to ourselves today and note how many grunts, groans, and moans we make. Every time I get up from sitting and even when I do a plop to the couch, I hear the groans under my breath, especially after a full day of being on my feet walking up and down stairs. The knees will groan on their own, too. Mornings are prayer time for Carol and me. We get really focused and talk to God. Yet for me in the early morning, there are times I don't actually have a subject to pray about. I may just engage God and let Him know I am on the line. Then after I ponder through a couple cups of coffee, the Lord guides me to pray for the people who may be dealing with weaknesses. We don't have to ponder too long to think of friends and associates, perhaps even family members, that are dealing with weaknesses of various forms. Love you all.

DAY 296

If you falter in a time of trouble,
how small is your strength!

PROVERBS 24:10

HELLO FAMILY: Failure is not an option! I recall that theme being driven into my head on numerous military training events. Whether it was a grueling road march, an overnight patrol to ambush the enemy, or swimming 10km in a set amount of time, we pushed ourselves until we dropped. Many did drop, some to their deaths. They gave everything they had until their hearts just stopped. Others would make it to the objective and need medical attention. They pushed their bodies too far and were unable to complete the mission. Mental toughness is as important as physical toughness. Do we have the strength to finish college, to say no to drugs, to say no to booze, or to give up our keys and not drive drunk? This is "faltering" in times of trouble, in times of being tested, and in times of needing to make the right decision. We need wisdom. The book of Proverbs is the book of wisdom. Paul proclaims that if you don't know what to pray for, pray for wisdom. Don't falter in times of trouble. Love you all.

DAY 297

You, my brothers and sisters, were called to be free. But do not use your freedom to indulge the flesh; rather, serve one another humbly in love. [14] For the entire law is fulfilled in keeping this one command: "Love your neighbor as yourself."

GALATIANS 5:13-14

HELLO FAMILY: On my last return trip home from Germany, I prayed for an upgrade to have a little extra room to work on this book. I was shocked when I received it. First class at that! Now, first class is no joke—all the drinks, awesome food, headphones, movies, a seat that spread out to a bed, fluffy pillows, and blankets to boot! To top it off, a flight attendant is constantly checking on every need that a person can imagine. They will even provide you with a fully stocked travel hygiene kit! Every indulgence your flesh desires is on call in first class. I laugh because my prayer was to have a little more room to get a big start on this book. Immediately the prayer was answered. I was tempted to indulge big time in beer, food, sleep, and movies. Don't worry, I did work on the book. There are many temptations all around us to soak in and indulge. Food is an easy one. We use it as a comfort, and we have great cooks all around us serving up plenty of portions. I am guilty of eating after 8 p.m. while watching TV. Salted popcorn, chips and dip, cheese and crackers, and let us not forget the cold beer. The only thing I am gaining is high blood pressure from the salt and high cholesterol from the cheese and pepperoni. We are "called to be free." But we are called to be free to focus on serving others, not ourselves. To do that, we must take great care of ourselves first and be aware of indulging ourselves. Love you all.

August 2021: Kim, me, and Lynn in Germany.

DAY 298

Consequently, you are no longer foreigners and strangers, but fellow citizens with God's people and also members of his household,

EPHESIANS 2:19

HELLO FAMILY: We had a wonderful church sermon this week. Our pastor Brother Kenny Rogers really got me thinking when he mentioned our "spiritual family." We have a physical family that can be something we are proud of, or not. We have a physical family that does not stay close to us. The kids move on when they grow up, and sometimes relationships grow apart for various reasons. Then we have physical family members that at some point pass away and go on to the spiritual world. Reading this scripture clarifies the relationship of being a "fellow citizen with God's people" with those we serve and worship together at our church. Think about this for a moment. In and with our church family, we may already be with our spiritual family. At church we share our happiness, sorrows, work responsibilities, and all other experiences in serving God. We sing together, pray together, and study the Bible together. Our values are one in the same. We get along because our lives are centered on a relationship with Christ. This belonging to the household of God provides great security, warmth, and a sense of purpose to live life to its fullest. I pray my whole family grasps the opportunity to get together and enjoy life with their spiritual family just as much as we do when we all get our physical family together. Love you all.

July 2007: My parents with Lynn, Shane, and Blake.

DAILY DEVOTIONALS | 179

DAY 299

For we live by faith, not by sight.

2 CORINTHIANS 5:7

HELLO FAMILY: The best time in our church service is when we have a children's sermon. You just never know what a child is going to ask or how they will respond when the teacher gives them the opportunity to get involved. One Sunday, a young boy asked, "How do you know?" to every statement about Jesus that the teacher was speaking about. Finally, the teacher asked the little boy what he needs to breathe in order to stay alive. After a brief science lesson, it finally came out that "oxygen" was the answer. Then the teacher asked the boy, "Do you see the oxygen? How do you know it is there? Do you know that you are getting enough oxygen? How do you believe that the air is okay to breathe?" With every answer the boy gave, he started with "I believe." He said, "I believe it's because I can live. I believe there is enough oxygen in the air because I can run fast." The teacher recognized they boy's repetition and responded with, "So you have faith that there is oxygen in the air?" The little boy paused and smiled. "Now I get it," he said. Our faith is in what we believe, not what we see, just like this scripture reads. Family, we must believe and allow our faith to grow. Love you all.

DAY 300

"Many will say to me on that day, 'Lord, Lord, did we not prophesy in your name and in your name drive out demons and in your name perform many miracles?' Then I will tell them plainly, 'I never knew you. Away from me, you evildoers!'"

MATTHEW 7:23

HELLO FAMILY: Jesus explains that there are those out in the world driving out demons in the name of "Jesus" and that even these people will be told, "I never knew you." Talk about getting the door slammed right in your face! There we are at the judgment seat. We are either headed to the light or down into darkness. I pray no one hears the words "I never knew you." This scripture is all in red ink in the NIV translation. These are the words coming from Jesus Himself. It doesn't get more serious than this. In this world, much of what we have and do is in direct relationship with who we know. Most of us understand the concept of preferential treatment—being treated better because "you're in good with the boss." Who have we invested in, who have we maintained a relationship with that helps our career, our financial worth, and our spiritual growth? It all has to do with who we know. It won't be any different when we pass away. Now is the time to get to know Jesus Christ and get to know Him very well. No one knows when our last breath is about to happen, so what are you waiting for? Love you all.

DAY 301

> *I have much to write you, but I do not want to do so with pen and ink.*
>
> 3 JOHN 1:13

HELLO FAMILY: Many books in the New Testament share different versions of the Gospel of Jesus. To read this scripture, John basically has plenty more to write about but wants to give the information in person. This is revealing in and of itself. As many of you know, I love to embellish my fishing and hunting stories. Just a little. You can't write about the excitement of reeling in a six-pound monster bass. You have to physically see the excitement in the eyes and body language of the storyteller. I have even been known to take pictures of the same monster fish at different locations along the lake at different times of the day to claim that I caught ten monster bass! One can surely relate in having to share face to face the excitement of Jesus Christ from personal accounts, rather than writing it all down. This is the same for John when he was writing this scripture. He desired to share these great miracles and experiences in person! Each of us has our own story to share about our salvation in person. Allow others to see the excitement in your eyes, the enthusiasm in your tone, and the kick in your step. Love you all.

DAY 302

> *When the day of Pentecost came, they were all together in one place. [2] Suddenly a sound like the blowing of a violent wind came from heaven and filled the whole house where they were sitting. [3] They saw what seemed to be tongues of fire that separated and came to rest on each of them. [4] All of them were filled with the Holy Spirit and began to speak in other tongues as the Spirit enabled them.*
>
> ACTS 2:1-4

HELLO FAMILY: As our faith grows and we share our faith boldly with other Christians, we may find ourselves visiting other churches, hearing others speak in tongues we don't understand. I have been there. I have also taken "tongues" in this specific scripture to mean other languages being spoken freely and fluently. No matter how it is interpreted, the key point of this scripture is to show the power of the Holy Spirit. The Holy Spirit is a reality which we must acknowledge with immense respect. The Holy Spirit is here for us to seek counsel and mentorship in our spiritual growth. The Holy Spirit imparts truth upon us so we can make wise decisions and recognize when we are getting snowballed. Call upon the Holy Spirit to help us with understanding and forgiveness when feeling frustrated with loved ones and friends, get guidance, and handle situations with grace. Love you all.

DAY 303

> *To them God has chosen to make known among the Gentiles the glorious riches of this mystery, which is Christ in you, the hope of glory.*
>
> COLOSSIANS 1:27

HELLO FAMILY: I have news for us. We are the "Gentiles." We are not the Jews and we are not going to the Promised Land, per say. So, when we see "Gentiles" written in scripture, we fall into that category. What we have here described as a "mystery" is accepting Jesus Christ as our Lord and Savior. We too are going to receive the "glorious riches" of eternal salvation. Just as God rescued the Jewish nation from the Egyptians, so too are we rescued from our sins through Jesus Christ as Gentiles. This grants us eternal paradise, in the light of the Lord, forever and ever. This gives us great hope in our day-to-day challenges that test our temptations and gives us great strength to overcome adversity. Love you all.

DAY 304

> *Do nothing out of selfish ambition or vain conceit. Rather, in humility value others above yourselves, [4] not looking to your own interests but each of you to the interests of the others.*
>
> PHILIPPIANS 2:3-4

HELLO FAMILY: There is that word "selfish." That word should be right at the top of our Holy Spirit guidance list. The Holy Spirit will smack us with that word just about every single day! What is the most expensive item that everyone has? You can't buy it back. Yet you can share it with others, and no one can take it away from you. It is time! How we spend our time will tell the truth of where we are spiritually. When we see where we spend our time, the truth will be told. It is a hard pill to swallow when it is all said and done. When we look at how much time is spent in prayer, reading God's Word, and participating in worship services, the cards are all laid out. The Holy Spirit will move us during our prayer time, perhaps in church when we are made aware of where our time may need to be spent to help others. Spending time, where we put others first ahead of our own interests is a positive sign to godliness. Especially when there is no thought of, "What is in it for me?" We may find ourselves putting our hobbies and golf games on the backburner. Yes, even our time in the tree stands waiting for the big buck. Yes, a challenge indeed and well worth it. Love you all.

DAY 305

> *Now Thomas (also known as Didymus), one of the Twelve, was not with the disciples when Jesus came. [25] So the other disciples told him, "We have seen the Lord!" But he said to them, "Unless I see the nail marks in his hands and put my finger where the nails were, and put my hand into his side, I will not believe."*
>
> JOHN 20:24–25

HELLO FAMILY: Let me tell you the rest of the story! One week later while the disciples were in the house again, guess who showed up? Jesus showed up and busted out "Doubting Thomas," immediately telling him to put those fingers in Jesus' holes and side. Needless to say, it was a very telling moment, a moment we all need to think about. What does it take for us to believe? Historians and archeologists more than ever are validating Bible references with other government documents of that time period. We have the Dead Sea Scrolls. We have references in ancient Chinese scrolls that speak of a voyage by three kings at the time of the birth of Jesus. I want us all to focus on the word "believe," just like in the Christmas show we watch every year about the little boy who doubted whether or not Santa Claus was real. His ticket read "Believe." Jesus even said that Heaven will be filled with those who believe like children. Sometimes we get a little too smart for our own good, so let's not miss that Christmas train. Riding on that train of faith, we will learn in due time the mysteries of our faith. Love you all.

DAY 306

> *What is more, I consider everything a loss because of the surpassing worth of knowing Christ Jesus my Lord, for whose sake I have lost all things. I consider them garbage that I may gain Christ*
>
> PHILIPPIANS 3:8

HELLO FAMILY: We are going to know God when **we** want to know Him. Once we know God, our belief systems change. We actually enjoy church, Bible study, and being with our spiritual family. Our spiritual families are those who know God and have attained similar values as ours. We become a team. I refer to it as the Army of God. The priorities of the past become forgotten as we are filled with a spirit of joy. We find immense pleasure in helping and doing things for others. The relationships we have in our very own families will improve because we will naturally think of others first. We will reach out to each other like we have never done before. Get to know God and experience the great joy He has planned for our lives. Love you all.

DAY 307

Consequently, faith comes from hearing the message, and the message is heard through the word about Christ.

ROMANS 10:17

HELLO FAMILY: What puzzles me to no end is why a highly educated person wants to beat up on my faith when they never took the time to actually learn or experience it. The book titled *The Case for Christ* by Lee Strobel is about his time as an atheist reporter who set out to prove that God was not real. In this book, he invests a great deal of his personal time learning about Christ to try to prove that Christ and God's Word are a giant hoax. He writes of the evidence found over the century and comes to a pretty big revelation himself—that Jesus Christ is real! Y'all can read the book (or watch the movie). Get ready for some shocking evidence! Lee Strobel is now a well-known author and speaker who proclaims that Jesus Christ is Lord and lives. Listening to the word of God means we are willing to learn something new, that we are willing to hear what God is saying. This listening requires a very concentrated focus with a clear mind in a place of peace with no distractions. Find this place. Learn and experience our faith. See what God has in store for us. Love you all.

DAY 308

"I tell you that in the same way there will be more rejoicing in heaven over one sinner who repents than over ninety-nine righteous persons who do not need to repent."

LUKE 15:7

HELLO FAMILY: Well, first we need to understand what it means to "repent." To repent means to feel sorry about a way of life and to take action to change it. This does not mean we give up beer for Lent only to replace it with vodka! If alcohol has taken over our lives, it means that we stop drinking alcohol altogether—not just for Lent. It is an easy example to use. Many preachers and other clergymen and clergywomen do because alcoholism is such a serious problem in many relationships. There are many other hidden little secrets or idols that can get us in deep trouble. Pornography, seeing or dating someone outside of our committed relationships, taking drugs we should not be taking, gambling, and the list can go on and on. All of these temptations are out there and can destroy our lives very quickly. But Heaven will rejoice when we repent from these temptations. We are basically saving ourselves and, more importantly, others around us from great misery and embarrassment. Love you all.

DAY 309

The simple believe anything, but the prudent give thought to their steps.

PROVERBS 14:15

HELLO FAMILY: The most fun I have is entertaining young kids with camping stories—the alligator man that lives in the bottom of the pond, the creek creature that lives in the fog by the lake, and many more. My neighbor and I just laugh until we cry as we plot on our grandchildren, making plans for the next camp out where we can make Big Foot tracks in the mud by the pond for the kids to see when they wake up. Now don't get fired up on me, but I love to watch the Big Foot shows. These folks are out in the middle of the night with cameras in their faces. I have even been known to do some tree knocks deep in the woods at night just to stir the lake folks up when they have their grandkids in town for the holidays. Young kids have great imaginations and a trusted grandparent can just about convince them of anything. Afterwards, we just return them to their parents and prep for the phone calls coming in from our upset children because the grandkids won't sleep in their rooms alone. Those of us who take the time to study, read, pray, and worship with others learn from those who have chosen to study and share even more knowledge, and we tend not to make the same mistakes that someone else has shared. Or better yet, we copy a successful process that was prosperous for someone else. Love you all.

Kim and Lynn's first visit to my parents' home in New York before meeting me.

DAY 310

Blessed is the one you discipline, LORD, the one you teach from your law; [13] you grant them relief from days of trouble, till a pit is dug for the wicked. [14] For the LORD will not reject his people; he will never forsake his inheritance.

PSALM 94:12-14

HELLO FAMILY: This is a very powerful statement, a promise of our Lord's commitment to those who have accepted God as their Father. There is the declaration of being disciplined and it being a blessing. In any family group, there are behaviors that are acceptable and others that are not. For the most part, if a member of the family crosses that line, they are immediately called out. I recall a time at my parents' house when girlfriends of my sisters would spend the night and have a party. They would get "the speech" from Mom: they were to stay in the girls room and were warned not to cross a particular line heading to the boys room. Yes, the boys were warned also. When the boys were growing up, we had a cuss box that was in plain view, reminding us all to keep our language in check. When someone let their tongue slip into darkness, money had to be given up immediately. Our Lord is always providing for and protecting us children, many times from ourselves. What is at stake? Our godly character, for one. It is hard to convince others to come to church when we are out there cussing up a storm. There is an inheritance at stake, just as there is a will written by us parents with our children in mind on who will get what when we depart. God's inheritance is eternal and far greater than anything we humans can muster up. This scripture is a magnificent promise for our salvation, an inclusion into a great and glorious inheritance for eternity. Love you all.

DAY 311

"The promise is for you and your children and for all who are far off—for all whom the Lord our God will call."

ACTS 2:39

HELLO FAMILY: We were reading in the book of Acts yesterday at Bible study. We read that Christians scattered from Jerusalem because of persecution. Christians were being dragged from their homes and literally killed. As they scattered all over the country, they brought their faith with them. Christianity was on the move by land and sea. Christians settled far from their homes where they grew up—one can only imagine the uncertainty that followed—but they had their faith in Christ with them always. This scripture, this letter reassures all of us everywhere across this great world that God will call us home when the time comes. When I read this I ask myself, "How many will recognize God's call? How many seek God in their daily walks?" Make the time to be in God's grace. Don't miss the final call home. Love you all.

DAY 312

"The Lord your God is with you, the Mighty Warrior who saves. He will take great delight in you; in his love he will no longer rebuke you, but will rejoice over you with singing."

ZEPHANIAH 3:17

HELLO FAMILY: How many people do you know that take "delight" in you? How many people get visibly excited when they see you? We only get our family together, at best, a couple times a year. When we do, our voices elevate, there is excitement, and everyone is talking at the same time. It can get loud. Not to mention the big meals that are prepared. Supplies need to be gathered well in advance. The preparation is almost as much as fun as the actual get together. It's a big deal and everyone delights in it. Now imagine a great warrior who has won the great eternal battle. He has defeated death for His entire family. It will be a majestic homecoming. He knew in battle that He was fighting for loved ones, and now He gets to see them all upon His return. Rest assured that there will be plenty of song and dance, a great celebration to be had and for us to enjoy for eternity. Love you all.

DAY 313

Dear friends, now we are children of God, and what we will be has not yet been made known. But we know that when Christ appears, we shall be like him, for we shall see him as he is.

1 JOHN 3:2

HELLO FAMILY: So many times I hear people's opinions on what happens when we die. I read books about people who had died and returned. The most common theme: "Come with me, it is beautiful." My favorite book to read is *Heaven is for Real*. "And what we will be has not yet been made known." Numerous hints are in the scripture readings and every one of them is promising an eternal paradise, a place Jesus himself has prepared for each one of us. When I do get in these discussions with doubters, I merely express, "What if I am right? What if these Bible scriptures that have lasted thousands of years are correct? I will tell you what, I will be there celebrating. Where will you be, ignoring all this evidence of **God**?" Love you all.

DAY 314

He guides the humble in what is right and teaches them his way.

PSALM 25:9

HELLO FAMILY: There is nothing worse than a student who knows it all already. Teachers and instructors get immediately turned off by a know-it-all student's pride. Many times these type of students will be allowed to flutter on their own. Carol and I love to watch *Master Chef*. At times, a contestant will actually try to tell one of the judges (true master chefs) that their advice is not best or make a smarty pants reply. Immediately, Carol and I will look at each other and note that this person is doomed for failure and won't last long. Is it not the same with God? We are created in His likeness and we know it pays well to be humble and take instruction from our teachers. We are called to be humbled students, joyfully willing to read, listen, and learn. This will please God, and His blessings will flow into our lives. Love you all.

DAY 315

I know that there is nothing better for people than to be happy and to do good while they live. [13] That each of them may eat and drink, and find satisfaction in all their toil—this is the gift of God.

ECCLESIASTES 3:12–13

HELLO FAMILY: The pictures we share of our family reunions, our family trips on vacations, and even the great food and drink we enjoy are what this scripture references. We truly find great joy and satisfaction when we are together with family and friends. The energy of the food preparation and the anticipation of guest showing up, these are the best memories we hold onto as we grow. These are going to be the best memories for our children as well. My granddaughters told their moms at our last reunion, "This was the best day I ever had." It was a big day with lots of hiking, super great food, riding in a canoe, and playing ball and freeze tag in the yard! It just doesn't get any better than that. What a wonderful gift from God that we get to experience these best of times together. Love you all.

DAY 316

He mocks proud mockers but shows favor to the humble and oppressed.

PROVERBS 3:34

HELLO FAMILY: What a wonderful family day we had! Uncle Dave and Aunt Laura came to town and brightened our weekend. There was golf with the boys, great food, and yes, card games. During our games, snicker remarks are just part of the play, except from Carol. She could be hundreds of points ahead (and she was) but won't say a word in prideful spite. Carol just grins and says, "Pride comes before the fall." Carol says this every single game at least once because score updates are read by the score keeper and someone (Aunt Laura) always has a comment or two. **And** Dan (me) won the spades game this time! First time in 30 years! I did the victory dance in my room alone; it just came out. Here in our home and in our lives, each day starts humbly with Bible reading and prayer. We are keenly aware that these blessings mentioned above along with all of the others come from our Lord. Being in God's favor, wanting to stay in God's favor, is a conscious effort. We continue our daily walks humbly, going about our days looking forward to future blessings and pray for others and their blessings to come also. **All** from God. Love you.

DAY 317

Jesus said to them, "A prophet is not without honor except in his own town, among his relatives and in his own home." [5] He could not do any miracles there, except lay his hands on a few sick people and heal them. [6] He was amazed at their lack of faith. Then Jesus went around teaching from village to village.

MARK 6:4-6

HELLO FAMILY: So true. As I recall, most all prophets were banned, rejected, and even killed by the very people they had known their entire lives. There sure isn't much gratitude for the Christians enthusiastic about sharing their faith in this world, even in their family circle and home towns in many cases. Some would say life gets tougher when we become Christians because we are being challenged in every word, act, and decision by the Holy Spirit, to do what is right in all matters. If we make a mistake, everyone in the town is going to be talking about it and then we hear others accuse us of being hypocrites behind our backs. For Christians, many choices are not the most "popular" in today's culture. At least that is what is being played out in today's media world of political correctness and promotion of sexual freedoms. Today's culture boils over with selfishness, pride, drama, and stubbornness, all of which can be seen on many Facebook pages. This scripture speaks of honor to those who keep the faith and humbly pray, read, and worship sincerely. This is how we seek God daily. This is an honorable life that will bring us great glory for eternity. Love you all.

DAY 318

For the LORD is good and his love endures forever;
his faithfulness continues through all generations.

PSALM 100:5

HELLO FAMILY: There may be times in our days when we just don't feel the love or the gratitude from the ones who we have cared for. I am talking about people in our own families, our close friends, and people who are close to us. People can really let us down, making us consider shutting them out of our lives. We see it all the time in many families, neighborhoods, and at work to name a few places. Then this scripture pops right in there, just at that moment. God doesn't need a single item from us. He doesn't need our money. He doesn't need our company, our prayers, our text messages, our time, our gratitude, our phone calls, or a "Like" on His Facebook page. Nothing! But, as the scripture reads, "the LORD is good and his love endures forever." We are called to be godly and good and to love forever with everyone, especially our family and friends. I encourage us all to continue doing that in all of our relationships. Love you all.

DAY 319

The Lord will rescue me from every evil attack and
will bring me safely to his heavenly kingdom.
To him be the glory forever and ever. Amen.

2 TIMOTHY 4:18

HELLO FAMILY: Just as there is good in this world, so there is evil. There are many people who feel they solely exist to destroy everything in their paths. They totally enjoy it. The evil is premeditated. It is preplanned, and there are victims all around us. We see it daily in the news and in our hometowns. It has no limitations on where it strikes. When we read "rescue" from "every evil attack" in this scripture, God is making a bold claim and promise. Protection from sex offenders on our children, rapists from our wives, burglars from our homes, and any other threat out there. We need to stop and check ourselves. Are our faith and our beliefs in the Great Shepherd Jesus Christ? Our Great Shepherd defends His flock and His sheep with His life. It is very important to understand this and to be thankful for it. Praise God for the protection of our families from evilness and matters that we will never even be aware of. As our children grow and our travels expand across this globe, our faith in God Almighty provides the ultimate security. Love you all.

DAY 320

"See, I have engraved you on the palms of my hands; your walls are ever before me."

ISAIAH 49:16

HELLO FAMILY: When I read this, I immediately thought of the many tattoos I have seen of names that people have put on their bodies. Many of which are the names of children, loved ones, or other persons that they care to remember forever. Parents are proud to boast of their children. When asked, it becomes a platform to share their pride and joy. It can also have the opposite effect, too. There are tattoos that can be very heartbreaking. I recall a woman getting very emotional about a list of names (three) she had tattooed down her arm. She lost her children in a car accident, and when asked, she relives the entire horrible day. God has you on the palms of His hands in celebration. We belong to Him and no other. He knows every hair on our bodies, our thoughts, and heartbeats. We may lose a tooth, burn a hand, or have a two-day surgery, but find peace knowing that God is in control. Love you all.

DAY 321

For we did not follow cleverly devised stories when we told you about the coming of our Lord Jesus Christ in power, but we were eyewitnesses of his majesty. He received honor and glory from God the Father when the voice came to him from the Majestic Glory, saying, "This is my Son, whom I love; with him I am well pleased."

2 PETER 1:16

HELLO FAMILY: I never noticed until now the word "power" used in this scripture. "The coming of our Lord Jesus Christ in power"! Now that's a statement to hold onto! I don't read this and see Jesus arriving on a donkey like He did on His arrival into Jerusalem. More importantly, in this reading, Peter is telling us all that he and others were eyewitnesses to the great power and majesty that our Lord Jesus is fully capable of. He declares how he and others heard the majestic voice proclaim from the heavens, "'This is my Son, whom I love; with him I am well pleased.'" These statements are revealing who we serve in our Lord and Savior Jesus Christ. Many in our culture look at Christians and scoff, even laugh, at how weak we are to believe in such fairy tales. When the sky above opens and the great power of our Lord is revealed to this earth, as it is written in Romans 14:11, every knee will bow. Even the knees of those who scoffed and never believed. Love you all.

DAY 322

And without faith it is impossible to please God, because anyone who comes to him must believe that he exists and that he rewards those who earnestly seek him.

HEBREWS 11:6

HELLO FAMILY: Words cannot describe the battle between the worldly beliefs versus the godly beliefs. I just caught myself thinking of taking out the word "belief" in that last sentence because many people I cross paths with don't "believe" in anything. They just wake up every morning and go about their days taking care of themselves and circles of friends that share their common values. Many of them wrap themselves up in created drama—drama that is the focus of their daily conversations, their attitudes, and their personality for that day. We see the word "earnestly" in this scripture. This is the focus of our day when we seek God. It is an outward focus and not an inward self-focused approach that looks to be serving others in faith. Let's face it, we must have faith and it must be all in. Our lives are going to drive on with serving others, and we are going to need God's blessings to keep us joyful in our ventures. Stay focused on the cross and keep the faith, even when the world's distractions attempt to steer us away. Love you all.

DAY 323

When Judas, who had betrayed him, saw that Jesus was condemned, he was seized with remorse and returned the thirty pieces of silver to the chief priests and the elders. [4] "I have sinned," he said, "for I have betrayed innocent blood." "What is that to us?" they replied. "That's your responsibility." [5] So Judas threw the money into the temple and left. Then he went away and hanged himself."

MATTHEW 27:3-5

HELLO FAMILY: Guilt by far is a very dangerous emotion. We read here of a suicide because of guilt. I dare say that some who read this are aware of someone they knew who committed suicide. The ones who I am aware of may very well have had guilt as a motivator to the thought of taking one's own life. So, what is the cure for such guilt that drives us into alcoholism, drug abuse, personal abuse, and even death? Our God is the cure for guilt. Our God is the God of Grace. When we read through the scriptures (Romans 3:10, Romans 3:23, and Luke 12:3 to name just a few), we learn of grace and the healing that will come as our relationship and understanding of Jesus Christ grows. Yes, we have laws in our world that will punish us without mercy. But always remember, grace heals all. Love you all.

DAY 324

The Lord said to Moses, "How long will these people treat me with contempt? How long will they refuse to believe in me, in spite of all the signs I have performed among them?"

NUMBERS 14:11

HELLO FAMILY: I must declare when I was in my youth and even as a young man, I wasn't totally sold on the whole "God story" myself. Even growing up as an altar boy in a Catholic church and going to "church school" on Wednesdays, I still struggled with the interest or belief in and the focus on God. So, what happened to me in life (as it was being the first born of many siblings) was trial and error learning. Being number one in a crew of kids meant that I didn't have an older brother to learn from. Child number one isn't able to watch and see what he or she would get a spanking for. This is also the case for Christ in my pitch here. I am proclaiming that faith is a far better teacher than experience. We learn a great deal with both methods, but experience will hurt a great deal more. Growing in faith opens our ears and thoughts to what God expects from our behavior. We learn of the Holy Spirit guiding our decisions away from getting a spanking in life. We grow up being what God's plan is for our lives in Christ. Love you all.

DAY 325

"Come, follow me," Jesus said, "and I will send you out to fish for people."

MARK 1:17

HELLO FAMILY: To be a follower of Christ, what will we become? What will our friends think? Better yet, what will our friends **say**? I recognize as I am writing along here day after day that these questions have been ringing in my ears for a good time now. Have we ever really attempted to understand where a life following the very teachings of Christ will lead us? I will tell us this: the voice of the Holy Spirit will alert us throughout each of our days. There might be a time when we are out and about and we are tugged to secretly pay for a young family's meal. These nudges are the work of the Holy Spirit. That's when we know that we are hearing and listening to God's guidance through the Holy Spirit. We get big goose bumps. I will answer a few of those questions that I started with. We will find out pretty quickly who our true friends really are. We will be led to new friends in our newly found spiritual family. In following Christ, we will be set free in the most peaceful sense, ways that words cannot explain. The best part of all, we will see our priorities in life focused on bringing the Gospel to others. We will become fishers of people. Love you all.

DAY 326

> *"I am the true vine, and my Father is the gardener. [2] He cuts off every branch in me that bears no fruit, while every branch that does bear fruit he prunes so that it will be even more fruitful."*
>
> JOHN 15:1–2

HELLO FAMILY: Wow! This speaks to me big time and I believe it will to my youngest son, Blake, too. Recently, Blake and I cut down these big wild vines that crawl up our trees and weight them down. These vines keep pulling on the trees, making them grow crooked and falling in the windy storms. We left hundreds of these vines to die and rot back into the ground. The work was tedious to say the least. Up and down the ravines we climbed, and it seemed as soon as we finished one monster clump of vines, another clump would appear. The weather was hot, and we would say, "Let's get just one more." Then it became a joke because to this day you can go out there and keep cutting away because there are thousands more. Can you imagine God working day after day cutting and pruning away, cleaning up His woods and His vineyard in the same manner? I will say there is no mercy for the wild vines, and I don't see any mercy for the vines that bear no fruit. Later in this scripture reading Jesus explains clearly, "Apart from me you can do nothing." We are called to ask ourselves how we will work through Jesus Christ to bear fruit in our lives. Love you all.

December 2016: Our youngest son Blake; no resemblance there, right? He is special to us all and especially his mama, Carol.

DAY 327

He appointed twelve that they might be with him and that he might send them out to preach.

MARK 3:14

HELLO FAMILY: We have a Bible filled with actual quotes from our Lord Jesus. The quotes from Jesus are always written in red. The purpose of Jesus appointing 12 was to have eyewitnesses to document and share firsthand knowledge of the accounts to the world. These writings along with hundreds of years of documents from the earliest of times have been verified with the findings of the Dead Sea Scrolls. Our Bible has survived thousands of years, and what a splendid book this is. The Old Testament is a choreographed documentary of history preparing the human race for the coming of Christ. These writings have hundreds of very descriptive prophecies written hundreds of years before Christ was born that are spot on in describing our Lord's family lines and then His entrance into humanity. Our Lord Jesus knew that He needed eyewitnesses to capture every miracle, every sermon, every healing, every example, and every word He spoke. We rely on eyewitness testimonies in every courtroom today. People's lives can be changed immediately on the outcome of those testimonies. What is remarkable in these 12 being chosen is that they did not write their letters, their testimonies, or their books together in a room. They did not collaborate and make sure their stories matched up. Their writings spanned over decades, from locations hundreds if not thousands of miles apart from each other. Think about that when you hear about court cases ending because of collaboration between witnesses. Be confident in your faith! Love you all.

DAY 328

This day I call the heavens and the earth as witnesses against you that I have set before you life and death, blessings and curses. Now choose life, so that you and your children may live.

DEUTERONOMY 30:19

HELLO FAMILY: This is Old Testament tell-it-like-it-is scripture here. As we progress through our days, learning more and more about the processes of our bodies and the changes they go through, we come to terms with the fight to live on. Without question, most of the people I can think of choose life, and they go through the most painful surgeries, radiation, and chemical procedures to try and extend their lives on as long as they can. Yet I call to question "most people" because I am keenly aware of a population of people among us that seem to be "cursed." We see them in the streets, homeless. In refugee camps, parentless and alone. At what point in a person's life are the choices being made to follow God or not and go it on our own? What does going out on your own lead to? What does that path alone without God mean for the children of those who do not choose a godly path? These questions are for us all to ponder and to keep in mind when sharing our faith with others. Many great wars have been fought with men and women giving of their lives and fighting for the lives of others. We are all called to recognize the value of life and how precious it is. God wants us to choose life through Him and all the joy it brings. Love you all.

DAY 329

Enter his gates with thanksgiving and his courts with praise; give thanks to him and praise his name. [5] For the LORD is good and his love endures forever; his faithfulness continues through all generations.

PSALM 100:4–5

HELLO FAMILY: "Enter his gates with thanksgiving." Enough said during this fine Thanksgiving season. Recognize that all good things come from God. Look hard at nature and know that God created all the intricate DNA that brings the earth's creation to life and supports the growth we see every day. The Bible has survived for thousands of years (the Dead Sea Scrolls come to mind, a miracle). Know that God is there for us all and be very thankful for this special season of Thanksgiving. Reflect on the goodness God provides. Love you all.

DAY 330

Be alert and of sober mind. Your enemy the devil prowls around like a roaring lion looking for someone to devour.
1 PETER 5:8

HELLO FAMILY: Good gracious! This is the get-real statement of the Bible right here. I love the reference to a "sober mind." Who out there can say that they are not vulnerable to making big blunders that can and may have affected the course of their lives while being under the influence of great beer, wine, and whiskey? I dare say, and not always from personal experience, that there are those times that alcohol has made us all poor choice makers. Without question, not being of sober mind can lead to very risky behavior that can have lifelong and even devastating results. That devil really is, as is described in this scripture, a roaring ruthless beast of a lion. Ever watch on TV those African documentaries and see a lion take down any animal? There is no mercy. There is no question what the end result is going to be. What a ruthless take down it is, and death immediately follows. And so it is when the devil has us in his sights. It is going to happen in a flash—that drunk driving horrific accident, that test of a drug that enslaves the rest of our lives, or that disease that comes with being promiscuous. "Stay alert, stay alive" was one of the calls to battle while I served in the military. It is also our in our call to serve the Lord. Love you all.

December 2019: Granna Carol & Opa Dan meeting adopted newborn grandson Colton.

DAY 331

> *On the evening of that first day of the week, when the disciples were together, with the doors locked for fear of the Jewish leaders, Jesus came and stood among them and said, "Peace be with you!"*
> JOHN 20:19

HELLO FAMILY: Just imagine for a moment what these disciples are going through. They are in a peaceful garden with Jesus. Evening comes along with a troop of angry priests, their servants, and guards. Swords are drawn, and a servant's ear gets cut off! Jesus heals the ear of the servant and is then taken prisoner, hauled off in shackles to trial, soon to be crucified. These disciples are a witness to the most cruel and tortuous death of their leader. Their teacher. Their Messiah. They know if they show their faces anywhere in town, they will meet the same outcome as Jesus. So there they huddle together in fear with the door locked. As we look back on our lives, do we recall a moment where such fear had us locked up in a room, a car, or a space where nobody could find us? I recall such a time with my fellow Special Forces teammates, hiding in a ditch far behind enemy lines as the Gulf War began. What do we do when we get caught? I know what I did. I prayed and I prayed and I prayed some more. I was making big deals with the Lord. "God, if you get us out of here, I will be in church every Sunday. I will be the best husband to my wife. I will be the best father to my children. I will take care of myself so I can be of service to others," and the prayers kept coming. Look now after all of these answered prayers, here I am writing my two cents' worth to God's Word in this book. Fear can have a paralyzing effect on the entire body. When we call on Jesus, our minds are able to process what is happening around us so we can perform under the most fearful conditions, even pain. God will recognize our voices, even if it is for the first time. Love you all.

DAY 332

"Now, LORD my God, you have made your servant king in place of my father David. But I am only a little child and do not know how to carry out my duties. [8] Your servant is here among the people you have chosen, a great people, too numerous to count or number. [9] So give your servant a discerning heart to govern your people and to distinguish between right and wrong. For who is able to govern this great people of yours?"

1 KINGS 3:7–9

HELLO FAMILY: How many times have we been given duties that immediately stress us out? I have watched my children grow a great deal over the past 20 years and observed them tackle the challenges of parenthood, multiple job interviews and changes, relocating their homes, management in retail, and going through an adoption process. They are growing their networks of influence in their churches, their neighborhoods, their workplaces, and among their many friends. We ask ourselves, what examples we are setting for others to follow when we get in these situations that challenge what is right and wrong. We see a prayer in this scripture where a very young king has a huge challenge ahead of him. What wisdom, to pray for "a discerning heart" and "to distinguish between right and wrong." This is a lesson for us all to remember. We can pray for this great wisdom to help us in our daily walks. We can be the light of Christ in our actions as well as our words. Love you all.

DAY 333

Some of you have become arrogant, as if I were not coming to you.

1 CORINTHIANS 4:18

HELLO FAMILY: Now this is one of those scriptures that leave no doubt of who it is for, "coming to you." Our hope and trust in Christ alone shall never falter, ever. A great price has been paid for the forgiveness of our sins and Christ did that for every single one of us. Jesus can never be taken away from us. No one can ever take Jesus away from you. Huge plans have been worked out to allow each of us to experience the grandest salvation, far greater than our minds can comprehend. Paradise will bring such great joy to all of us who have accepted Jesus Christ as our Savior and Lord. Lest we never forget, never let our pride get the best of us, thinking all that we are and have is of our own doing. Our Lord God has us in the palm of His hand and He is coming for you in the end. Love you all.

DAY 334

> "I am now a hundred and twenty years old and I am no longer able to lead you. The LORD has said to me, 'You shall not cross the Jordan.'"
>
> DEUTERONOMY 31:2

HELLO FAMILY: So, there you are at over 100 years old and the great event of crossing into the Promised Land (you have been through so much) is right before your eyes and God says no. Talk about disappointment. We cannot imagine what was going on in the mind of Moses, processing what he had just heard while speaking directly with God. I have to keep my thoughts in perspective here because Moses is talking directly with God. The God! Perhaps Moses just took it all in stride as the loyal servant of the Lord that he was. For example, say I was in line with the family to see the latest Star Wars movie and while Carol stepped away to get popcorn and soda, I turned to the kids and said, "Sorry, but work called and we have to head back to the house." I get a huge feeling that they would have told me, "Go ahead, Dad. We'll watch the movie without you!" Now this may not be the best example of having our dreams coming true only to be halted in a flash, but it does happen. There are painful occurrences when trying to obtain finances for a home, being accepted and getting approvals in an adoption process, or the death of a loved one that just stops the flow of joy altogether. Just remember, the plan that is going to happen is God's plan. We are here to serve the Lord and to follow His paths, not always ours. Love you all.

My oldest son Shane is all grown up! Shane and Blake enjoyed archery, competing on the Trigg County Team of archers winning a World Championship.

DAY 335

I think it is right to refresh your memory as long as I live in the tent of this body, [14] because I know that I will soon put it aside, as our Lord Jesus Christ has made clear to me.

2 PETER 1:13-14

HELLO FAMILY: The memories—who can keep track of them all? Better yet, who can recall memories with precise accuracy? We get a pretty good laugh when the family gets together and someone is sharing one of those family stories. As soon as the story line starts to "grow" a little, one of the ladies of the family jumps in to make it right. We poor guys can never get through a great deer hunting or fishing story to save our skins when the women are around. Our little dog Petie was in a golf cart accident many years ago. He now suffers on occasion from neck spasms in his old age. Even worse, every time he has a spasm, I am reminded by my wife that it is because of the golf cart accident. Did I forget to mention that I was the careless driver and didn't secure my passenger (Petie)? There are other memories we keep to remind us to not make the same mistake twice. Memories that caused great pain and scars are there in our heads and on our bodies to share with others the importance of not making the same mistakes we did and not repeating their own mistakes in life. Also, in this scripture we have the mention of our bodies being "tents." I have spent many nights in a tent and still enjoy it. Tents are known to tear, get punctured, rip apart along stress points, and the zippers always split. Sounds like my body as I age. That's because tents and bodies are one in the same when the term "temporary" comes to mind. We're each only given one tent in this life, and someday we'll leave it to be with the place the Lord is preparing for us. Love you all.

DAY 336

These people are grumblers and faultfinders; they follow their own evil desires; they boast about themselves and flatter others for their own advantage.

JUDE 1:16

HELLO FAMILY: The scriptures just prior to this one paint the picture of our Lord coming with thousands upon thousands of his holy ones to judge and convict humanity. It is the Judgment Day. I don't hear many sermons on this subject on Sunday mornings. This scripture points to the character of those who will receive the death penalty, the most devastating ending of any human. There will be no escape from this judgment for eternity. When we review these character traits, read and heed. Have we not all grumbled, found fault in others, and had selfish desire? My family tells me on occasion that I can embellish any occurrence making great campfire stories. Flattery? All we have to do is look at our social media sites and see how "flattering" we can make ourselves. What do we do then in regard to this scripture? How do we escape this brutal Judgment Day? First, we don't quit on ourselves. Keep reading the Bible. Keep saying our prayers and keep attending worship services. Allow God to work on our hearts, transform our characters, and hear the voice of the Holy Spirit. It won't happen overnight, and God knows this. When we accept Jesus Christ as our Lord and Savior, we have taken the most critical first step. We are safe in God's hands. Love you all.

Shane loves to go fishing, and God has blessed us with a pond so he can go anytime he wants!

DAY 337

Because of the LORD's great love we are not consumed, for his compassions never fail. [23] They are new every morning; great is your faithfulness.

LAMENTATIONS 3:22-23

HELLO FAMILY: There is a hymn — "Great is Thy Faithfulness" — that is a huge favorite at the assisted living facility where we have family residing. Playing this song on the piano brings great peace to all who are in listening range and is requested often. It is because of the Lord's great love, His compassion for us, and the Lord's constant watch over our lives, knowing that His love is always there waiting faithfully for us to turn to Him. Love you all.

50-CENT BONUS

We can immediately recall the moments when going through the daily grind when our joyful spirit can break down. I go through it. Sometimes I get so frustrated, I could go into the woods and just leave this crazy paced world behind. Just live out of my old rucksack and be in total peace with God in the forest. Carol sees me go through these episodes of frustrations and reminds me of the joy we bring to each other when we follow the guidance of the Holy Spirit. She is totally right.

I hadn't played the piano in over 30 years, but now I'm the one playing "Great is Thy Faithfulness" at the assisted living facility where Carol's mother, Barbara, lives. It's because of the Holy Spirit that I am even playing the piano these days.

The day I was first asked to play at this facility, I was attempting to read piano music and play from a Methodist hymnal. After a few minutes of playing the keys, I noticed a small group of residents had formed behind me. They shared with me that their piano player had moved and requested that I take her place. I was immediately overwhelmed with emotions. I listened to their stories and agreed to do my best. I prayed earnestly to the Holy Spirit to help me — I was in way over my head. Then, the residents even requested I play at 10 a.m. on Wednesday mornings. More pressure on me, because I currently had a full-time job and would have to make arrangements. Then, a commitment was made.

I have to practice a great deal — it takes many hours to prepare and get these old fingers to move again. Yes, it is a big challenge to try to play the requested songs that I had never heard before (music from the 1940s and '50s). Carol spends her time with Barbara during the day, so she has become the "receiver" of music requests, finding out what music to order for me to practice. This process alone has excited so many residents and even me. Everyone has a job to do now. The residents find music for me, and I practice and perform. No pressure, right?

Continued on next page.

DAY 337, *continued from page 197.*

I am in tears attempting to find the words to describe the joy we are having. The fingers, the feet, the clapping, taping of the toes to keep the beat, the soft voices singing the songs of their youth, and the shout of a 96-year-old woman yelling, "That was fun!"

"Blueberry Hill," "Rock'n Around the Clock," and "Let Me Call You Sweetheart" are just some of the titles of the new favorites now. All of this is a praise because of the **Lord's** great love. Recognizing the voice of God and having the confidence in knowing that the Holy Spirit will guide us along the way brings peace. The blessings are so overwhelming for so many. Just because He loves "every morning."

My daughter Kim with her husband Christian and children Philipp and Hannah.

DAY 338

When pride comes, then comes disgrace,
but with humility comes wisdom.

PROVERBS 11:2

HELLO FAMILY: Pride just happens to be a super huge and easy trap for many to fall into. We all have successes to be proud about (especially when you get lucky in picking the winning Super Bowl team year after year). Our country had recently boasted of having the strongest economy ever, record unemployment across all racial divides. There were construction projects all over the country. America was moving, led by a very "proud" president. Although we are not dependent on oil or gas anymore, we fall victim to cyber-attacks stopping the flow of abundant fuel in our pipelines. Our military is coming home and leaving a country potentially in great distress, especially for women. We see how quickly a year can change everything, with a pandemic to boot! As we celebrate every 4th of July, with all the fireworks and parades, I recall the memories. So many examples of "with humility comes wisdom." Humbly give God the praise, glory, and credit for the times of prosperity, and be wise to the trap of pride and what follows it — "disgrace." Love you all.

DAY 339

"No one can serve two masters. Either you will hate the one and love the other, or you will be devoted to the one and despise the other. You cannot serve both God and money." [14] The Pharisees, who loved money, heard all this and were sneering at Jesus. [15] He said to them, "You are the ones who justify yourselves in the eyes of others, but God knows your hearts. What people value highly is detestable in God's sight."

LUKE 16:13-15

HELLO FAMILY: Money, money, money. The song "Money" off Pink Floyd's album *Dark Side of the Moon* was my favorite song growing up. As a boy, I had my savings account book from the Bank of Castile. I would love to review the numbers, adding them up to see when I could get my brand-new Kawasaki 125 dirt bike. I worked hard on the farms around me and, little by little, the numbers grew. My faith was nothing to speak of back then. As I got older, the thought of giving away that hard earned money to a church was just plain nuts! Even as my faith grew, it was crazy difficult for me to give money to the church. Then a point came in my life where I was going to be all in or not in at all. Needless to say, Carol and I choose to be all in. Here is the really crazy part: God has taken our money worries away. It is called tithing. God knows how hard it is. Especially when we grew up knowing how hard it was to save money. To take ten percent and give it to God through a church takes straight up faith. Yes, it can be a serious challenge. It is a serious challenge for so many of us and our Lord knows it. This scripture knows that and calls it out directly, because money is clearly one of those "loves" that can be worshiped as a God. The love of money can and will alter our decisions, where and how we spend our time. The love of money can change our characters, just as the love of God changes our characters. Know the difference. Love you all.

DAY 340

*Praise the L*ORD*, my soul, and forget not all his benefits—*
[3] who forgives all your sins and heals all your diseases,
[4] who redeems your life from the pit and crowns you with love
and compassion, [5] who satisfies your desires with good things
so that your youth is renewed like the eagle's.

PSALM 103:2-5

HELLO FAMILY: Wow, what a great scripture to memorize and always remember. The Lord has healed my hand in record time. New skin is already there. My hand was burned by hot oil. I had a big second-degree blister covering the back side. We also had a crisis with our dryer. As many of you know, Carol does a good bit of laundry for our family along with her mom's laundry, too. We are very satisfied with our new Maytag dryer. The old one burned out Saturday. We are also getting a new modem for our high-speed internet! The old modem quit too. And, I get a new tooth molded this week! The implant for my tooth broke off a couple of weeks ago. These are just some examples of things that can happen in one week of life that can alter and shake up your plans. Health, injuries, broken down cars, and equipment can happen real fast, as seen in our week above. I will say this: our prayers, our music, our worship, and our reading the Bible never stopped. Our godly service to others never faltered, either. Just keep marching forward no matter how hard the winds and rain hit us. By marching forward, I mean pursuing our love for God. Carol and I woke up this morning refreshed, healthy, and ready to take on our new week. I pray this same energy fires you up as well in your faith of Jesus our Lord! This scripture is a home run! Love you all.

Another precious picture of my daughters together, Kim with Hannah. I must share that on one of our first get-togethers in Germany after we had "found" each other, we held hands one very late night around a little fire behind the house where they were staying. We held hands and prayed. We had a long journey ahead, and God was now invited in to help us with many years of separation that we had endured.

DAY 341

To do what is right and just is more acceptable to the LORD than sacrifice.

PROVERBS 21:3

HELLO FAMILY: We will never ever really know all the blessings we have received from God for living an "acceptable" life. In the same manner, we may never know the grief we have been spared by doing what is "right and just," like taking on massive additional responsibilities in life and not getting paid a nickel. These godly responsibilities may take up as many hours in our week as a full-time job. They may take up time that could have been spent doing other fun things. Doing what is right in the eyes of God and still being joyful in the process has rewards yet to be seen. A life dedicated to answering God's call to service, putting others first, and doing what is right takes faith. We must believe! It takes prayer, power, motivation, and help from others in all kinds of ways, and God will send it all. Living a righteous and just life is noticed and appreciated by God. He witnesses this feat of faith and goodness. All I can say is, in this family we don't have to look far to be witnesses when it comes to Carol in caring for her mom. Love you all.

DAY 342

Then he said to them, "Watch out! Be on your guard against all kinds of greed; life does not consist in an abundance of possessions."

LUKE 12:15

HELLO FAMILY: They have this show on TV that I really enjoy called *Pickers*. Basically, these two guys travel the country collecting old things—old cars, motorcycles, oil cans, toys, big signs, gas pumps, and glass globes to name a few. They meet the most interesting people who many have collected and piled up thousands of possessions. In some cases, guests on the show call in these two buyers to come and buy their parents' massive collections and possessions. The volume of things these people have piled up it is astounding! Sometimes the buyers literally have to climb over the tops of these piles to see what is really in there. They are hoping to find a jewel, a piece from the past. On the flip side, I see homes, residences, sheds, yards, and barns filled to the top with possessions that have taken over people's lives. The possessions have consumed lifetimes, perhaps generations. It is seen in the expressions of the family members who have realized that they need to reclaim their space and their lives. This scripture reads like a warning, because it is. I have this secret policy: if I did not use something in over a year, out the door it goes. It will go to Goodwill, a church auction, the recycle place, or a person who could use it. It is hard to keep the clutter down, like when I got rid of all my Army gear (sentimental value, perhaps). Well worth it when we free ourselves from lugging it around, trying to find places to store it. Love you all.

DAY 343

> Lord my God, I called to you for help,
> and you healed me.
>
> PSALM 30:2

HELLO FAMILY: When I think about the miracles that Jesus performed, it is the healing miracles that come to mind first. Jesus was always looking to heal people even right up to His arrest in the garden, healing the ear of the servant. Jesus was healing people that reached out just to touch Him—the woman in the crowd comes to mind (Matthew 9:20–22). Jesus gave the blind sight and the crippled new limbs. Jesus is the greatest doctor ever recorded! Jesus raised the dead and gave them life again. How anyone can deny our Lord when they actually take the time to learn about Him just puzzles me to no end. When we are sick, we call upon our Lord to help the doctors, nurses, and caretakers to make the right decisions in order to get us healed up and working again. These are the prayers to rely on when you are down. I know I have said it before. Be sure our voices are recognized when we call out for help. Love you all.

DAY 344

> "Give us today our daily bread."
>
> MATTHEW 6:11

HELLO FAMILY: What I love about this early morning venture with everyone is that I never know what the scripture will be until I open up my Bible app. Sometimes the scriptures take a good bit of thought. Then there are those so to the point that there is only one thought—food. Are we thinking the food we eat? This scripture speaks of the nourishment we receive from God's Word. The Word of God is a daily requirement for our mental, spiritual, and yes, physical wellbeing. Without God in our lives, what is our purpose for living other than a self-centered and self-serving daily grind? God's Word physically gives us security and will guide our physical bodies along a path of righteousness. Mentally, we will be planning the tasks ahead with our brains focused and engaged. Spiritually, we will be filled with joy. Blessings will abound throughout our days in all we do. The Word of God will feed us more than plain bread ever will. Love you all.

DAY 345

This is what the LORD says: "The people who survive the sword will find favor in the wilderness; I will come to give rest to Israel."

JEREMIAH 31:2

HELLO FAMILY: Words will never describe the great peace I have had in the woods, talking to God and having the best of conversations in the midst of His creation. Many of my veteran friends also find immense peace in the woods. We call it deer hunting. Go ahead and laugh. We laugh because the best part of deer hunting is the preparation phase in the woods before the hunting begins. Picking out that best tree for a tree stand. Setting up a camera or two to see what critters are passing by and just being out there when the sun is just about to rise. Out there in the woods, we are a witness to God's creation coming to life very early in the morning. We really experience the majesty of it all. It is not just what you see, it is also the smell of the leaves, the songs of the birds waking up, and the cool morning breezes whispering by our faces. And, just maybe, seeing that big buck. Either way, I am a witness to this scripture as a survivor of battle. I find the Lord's favor in His creation—the wilderness in all its glory. I know you will, too. Love you all.

DAY 346

I keep asking that the God of our Lord Jesus Christ, the glorious Father, may give you the Spirit of wisdom and revelation, so that you may know him better.

EPHESIANS 1:17

HELLO FAMILY: As we grow older and our families' careers take us farther and farther away from each other physically, we may find ourselves wishing for the "good old days." I do, at least! I also recognize that the communications that occur now between families' members were clearly established when our children were growing up. My sisters call their mother four or five times a week. My sons call or text their mother three of four times a week. As for me, good old Dad here, I may get a call or text once every two weeks if I am lucky. I blame no one. I merely reflect on the compassion and communications shared between children and their mothers as has happened in our family and perhaps yours. This relationship situation can be twisted around to where the dad takes it very personal and retracts deeper into what some may describe as a form of isolation. I caught myself in this pity party and I have discussed this many times with my fellow dads of the world. This scripture speaks of wisdom and revelation, true blessings to pray for. It's not that our children don't care to speak or text their dads. They have grown up watching their dads take work calls, go on deployments, or work two jobs at the same time. When I do get the chance to chat, visit, or text with my children, it is Heaven on earth. Everything in my life stops just to give my children undisturbed attention. You can rest assured that it is the same when we reach out to God in prayer. Love you all.

DAY 347

> *Do not be deceived: God cannot be mocked. A man reaps what he sows. [8] Whoever sows to please their flesh, from the flesh will reap destruction; whoever sows to please the Spirit, from the Spirit will reap eternal life. [9] Let us not become weary in doing good, for at the proper time we will reap a harvest if we do not give up.*
>
> GALATIANS 6:7-9

HELLO FAMILY: You reap what you sow! Growing up in a farming community, this passage has been at the forefront of our lives. The blessings of recognizing very early in life that the decisions, the efforts, and the commitments we make at a young age will have a resounding effect on our fortunes or misfortunes down the road. More so, we bring praises to our Lord God for the blessings and fortunes in our lives. We still give praise even when we are met with the many challenges of life. When we plant our seeds in a Bible-reading church, we can rest assure that our commitments in life will be in doing good and spiritually grounded activities that will be pleasing in the eyes of God. Many times, our "flesh" will not want to participate in staying up late to "work" for the church activities planned. It is better to be awake doing this than in thousands of worse situations because you had not sown your seeds in a church many years ago. Love you all.

Philipp, Hannah, and Leonie with their auntie in Germany.

DAY 348

Then he said to them all: "Whoever wants to be my disciple must deny themselves and take up their cross daily and follow me. For whoever wants to save their life will lose it, but whoever loses their life for me will save it. What good is it for someone to gain the whole world, and yet lose or forfeit their very self? Whoever is ashamed of me and my words, the Son of Man will be ashamed of them when he comes in his glory and in the glory of the Father and of the holy angels. Truly I tell you, some who are standing here will not taste death before they see the kingdom of God."

LUKE 9:23-27

HELLO FAMILY: In losing our lives to Christ, we save our lives for eternity. There have been times I have seen people take some very dramatic measures in reference to these scriptures. Jesus is not asking us to drop who and what we are. Rather, we are to take that step to establish a "daily" relationship of prayer and study into His life. What I believe happens is that a transition takes place in our priorities. We become more aware of our surroundings. We respond generously with compassion to the needs of others around us. In this process, as we age like fine wine, we are engaged in doing good and great things in the name of God. There will be no time to sit alone in an empty home, watching endless hours of TV and getting crazy mad about the politics or comments made on Facebook. Life takes on a whole new meaning. We see ourselves as being vessels of joy to others involved in godly work and service that everyone will appreciate. Love you all.

DAY 349

For if you live according to the flesh, you will die; but if by the Spirit you put to death the misdeeds of the body, you will live.

ROMANS 8:13

HELLO FAMILY: Living "according to the flesh" is a reference used in many scriptures that can create some uneasiness for sure. What we are referring to is all the big and small desires our body craves. We can indulge to the point it hurts us. These cravings, otherwise referred to as "temptations," can consume our lives. Many of these temptations are evil. So many of us are addicted to various cravings such as pornography, alcohol, and different prescription drugs as well as illegal drugs, just to identify a few of the common ones. When living according to the flesh, we may find ourselves in situations where death can appear to be the only escape. When we see the reference to the Spirit, we are applying the lessons of the Bible. We are treating our bodies as temples, temples fit for the Holy Spirit. Our souls, some like to say. This is the power received when receiving Jesus as Lord and Savior. We become aware of the temptations that need to be put away. Love you all.

DAY 350

"But seek first his kingdom and his righteousness, and all these things will be given to you as well."

MATTHEW 6:33

HELLO FAMILY: What is the very first thought that comes to mind when the alarm goes off and I wake up? We have pets—a little dog that sleeps on the bed with Carol and me and a cat that could just about be anywhere. These pets also respond to that alarm. It generally means that we must get them out of the house for their morning business. As funny as this may be, this is the very first thought each morning I wake up with when I am home. After the critters get taken care of, it is time to get a cup of coffee and have that quiet time with the Lord, seeking first His guidance on the challenges of the day. We have a saying: "What would Jesus do?" After asking this, I open my phone's Bible app to see what is in store for deep thought and prayer. Then, I pray this prayer: "Lord, have the Holy Spirit fill me this day with the best words and actions so that I can be the light of Christ to others around me." Great peace comes upon a person knowing in their heart that they are in God's hands, seeking His guidance at the start of each day. I pray everyone gets to experience this. Remember to invite the Holy Spirit into your heart, body, and soul. Love you all.

DAY 351

Blessed are those who find wisdom, those who gain understanding,

PROVERBS 3:13

HELLO FAMILY: On any day of worship, take a moment to count our blessings. Recognize the "wise" decisions we have made that placed us where we are today. Recognize the decisions we made that kept us from being in prison or getting addicted to drugs and alcohol. What stopped us from making very poor choices? Identify and be thankful for the decisions we made to get us where we are today, the wise decisions that had to be made and the actions that were put into play. Know that our relationships with Christ brought us the voice of the Holy Spirit lighting the wise path to take. Be thankful and continue in our faith with great trust in our Lord. Love you all.

DAY 352

Above all, love each other deeply, because love covers over a multitude of sins.

1 PETER 4:8

HELLO FAMILY: There is the "love" word again. What is this morning's interesting point? Love covers sin! I had never captured this in all my years. Love is an action. We have to do it for someone—give them our time, a gift, a kind word, a soft touch, and perhaps be of service to them. All of these activities are multiplied immensely when we apply our God-given talents in the process. Each of us has been given specific gifts or talents to serve God in some capacity. Just like different parts of our body have specific jobs, so does the family of God. When this church body comes together and loves the world in this way, good delightful things happen, like baptisms in the lake with an enormous singalong and food to follow. We each experience our God-given talents when we love each other. Like Lynn my daughter did yesterday. She took the time to video call her dad. Or me using a God talent to play the piano at a facility for seniors. There is great joy to be experienced by many when we take action to love. Love you all.

DAY 353

The LORD is good to all; he has compassion on all he has made.

PSALM 145:9

HELLO FAMILY: "Compassion on all he has made." God is the creator of all life, all things that live. God put humans in charge of it all on earth. I remember a few family stories where my brothers and I would pick on my little sister and tell her she was adopted. I later learned that in my wife's family, they also did the same thing, picking on their youngest sister in the same way. As if the "adopted" sister was of less value. Yes, this was very mean to say the least. I am thankful our little sisters are doing very well and have forgiven us all for our sibling teasing. The point to make here is that everyone alive was created by God and meant to be treated with compassion. Life is very precious. You are precious. We are all one family under God. We are all also adopted into God's family. We should live our lives treating others with kindness and compassion always. Love you all.

DAY 354

You need to persevere so that when you have done the will of God, you will receive what he has promised.

HEBREWS 10:36

HELLO FAMILY: During my military days, the word "persevere" would usually mean that some event was going to be painful, miserable, or both. I recall seeing a military poster of a soldier crawling through an obstacle course in sloppy mud under barbed wire. The soldier was cold, miserable, and just pushing through to finish the task at hand for each event along the course. "Persevere" was written across the top of this poster as a character trait to be proud of. These images of perseverance are of those who volunteered to crawl through mud, road march 20 miles with a rucksack, and go through these events with a cheerful attitude to boot. From experience, I will share that these events with other troops build a lifelong bond of brotherhood. A similar brotherhood can be found serving as a member of a church. This, my spiritual family, is why we serve the Lord and persevere through the challenges. We are the troops in God's Army. We persevere through orders given by God to serve on behalf of His Kingdom on earth. These who we serve with will be the Christian comrades we will keep for eternity. Love you all.

DAY 355

The prospect of the righteous is joy, but the hopes of the wicked come to nothing.

PROVERBS 10:28

HELLO FAMILY: The first part of this scripture, righteousness resulting in "joy," is a prospect to be attained. When we fulfill our commitments, things we say we will do, we feel great about it. Especially if it pertains to making others happy. Now, what is "wicked," you may ask. Perhaps this is the guilt felt when we are focused inward, taking care of our selfish motives. We get what we want knowing full well that we left others stuck with a mess or extra work to do because we took care of ourselves. This can pertain to work relationships, church relationships, and the big one—marriage relationships. Being righteous in our relationships is key to having joyful lives. We will feel great knowing in our hearts that we are team players in our family and especially in the Body of Christ. Love you all.

DAY 356

> *His divine power has given us everything we need for a godly life through our knowledge of him who called us by his own glory and goodness.*
>
> 2 PETER 1:3

HELLO FAMILY: When these morning scriptures come up, they really are a mystery until I actually read them. After I pray for help from God to guide my thoughts, key phrases immediately present themselves. This one jumped out this morning: "through our knowledge of him." This phrase is the action we need to take to get "everything we need for a godly life." How do we gain this "knowledge" so we are blessed with a godly life? We listen to the word of God. We pray and talk to God. We choose our friends very wisely, and we attend church. Remember, church is not the building. Church is God's people together in worship, belief, and service in Christ. This is referred to as the "body" of Christ. By serving with the church body, we are among a group of people with godly values. Rest assured, our days are secure in a flock protected by Jesus Christ our Shepherd. Love you all.

DAY 357

> *May the favor of the LORD our God rest on us; establish the work of our hands for us— yes, establish the work of our hands.*
>
> PSALM 90:17

HELLO FAMILY: "The work of our hands" can be the most rewarding of experiences. Throw some sweat and elbow grease in there and it is a party. Our hands are also great for healing. That soft touch or hug is magical. Hands are great communicators, too. We have heard clapping, we have seen thumbs up, and other finger forms for getting a point across. Hard work and hands feed us all, serve us all, and protect us all. Blessed are those who seek the favor of the Lord in the use of their hands. I almost forgot, playing music with our hands will bring peace and joy to all in hearing range. Love you all.

DAY 358

> "Which of you, if your son asks for bread, will give him a stone?"
>
> MATTHEW 7:9

HELLO FAMILY: Those rascal kids of ours. We are created in God's image and likeness. When we accept and receive Jesus as our Lord and Savior, God has adopted us as His children. God, as a parent so to speak, hears our prayers, our requests, and our complaints. God recognizes our joys and fully knows our needs, just as parents today know these things of their children. Just as parents do, God will respond to our requests. God has no limits to His resources. God is the biggest dad on the block. Sometimes we get what we want. Sometimes we have to wait. Then there are times when we just get plain spoiled and smothered with blessings. What is important to know is that our requests are heard. The question is this: Are you one of God's kids? Is God your dad, with all the goodies at His disposal? Love you all.

DAY 359

> For to us a child is born, to us a son is given, and the government will be on his shoulders. And he will be called Wonderful Counselor, Mighty God, Everlasting Father, Prince of Peace.
>
> ISAIAH 9:6

HELLO FAMILY: This scripture was written about 700 years before Christ was born! Think about that. Seriously, we are not on "our" timeline here. Well, enough said, Merry Christmas to all and we pray the celebration will last a lifetime. Love you all.

DAY 360

My dear brothers and sisters, take note of this: Everyone should be quick to listen, slow to speak and slow to become angry, [20] because human anger does not produce the righteousness that God desires.

JAMES 1:19-20

HELLO FAMILY: If you want to be remembered as the one who spoils the party, be the one who gets mad about something and starts cursing up a storm. These anger issues can really damage a relationship with family, friends, work associates, and church members. Real anger is nothing to toy with, either. It can spread fast and furiously as tempers flare. What is really unfortunate is when that real anger exposes itself. It turns others off quickly and has a lasting effect. Most people don't care to associate with a hothead. It sucks the joy of life right out of the room, big time. And, if people do choose to associate with this person who has temper tantrums, everyone lives on pins and needles waiting for the next eruption. When we listen, we learn a great deal. We are filling our hard drives with information to be wisely used in the future. When we are fast to speak, we are not really paying attention to who we are speaking with. A good listener is a teacher's dream, the student with whom the teacher will invest greater compassion and time because the teacher knows their efforts are being appreciated and applied by the student. God likes a good listener, too. That's our prayer time. It is the silence used to ponder what the Word or God is pouring into our hearts. Love you all.

My son Shane and his wife Katie visiting where they adopted Colton in Utah.

DAY 361

"For those who exalt themselves will be humbled, and those who humble themselves will be exalted."

MATTHEW 23:12

HELLO FAMILY: I just sent out a message of how great Carol's football team, the Texans, are doing. I was talking them up and all of a sudden, the Saints came marching in! Oh when the Saints come marching in! The Saints marched right over those poor Texans and beat them. Yes, our family so enjoys football season. A time of fantasy football. A time of big-time trash talk and bragging rights as fans dress up wild and crazy to support their teams. I don't recall this time of year ever being a humble one (unless it's your team getting pummeled real bad). One year, a particular team was so bad for so long that the fans wore brown paper bags over their heads with eyeholes cut out to see. They wore the paper bags over their heads while wearing the team's jerseys. Talk about humility. You guessed it—it was the New Orleans Saints! They used to be horrible. That year in particular, the city of New Orleans was devastated by a hurricane. The NFL team was on its knees and its young quarterback, Drew Brees, had recently signed on. What many did not know was that Drew Brees was a godly faithful man of prayer. Throughout the season without a stadium to play in (it was used to shelter the homeless after the storm), he would be seen with his teammates on their knees praying prior to the start of each and every game. That season, Brees led his team on to win the Super Bowl and the brown paper bags were never to be seen again. He was recently attacked on social media for being featured in a commercial where he encouraged kids to bring their Bibles to school. You can rest assured that Drew Brees was not shaken by these attacks. With God on your side, what can mere mortals do? Make sure you are on the right team, too. Love you all.

DAY 362

Through Jesus, therefore, let us continually offer to God a sacrifice of praise—the fruit of lips that openly profess his name. [16] And do not forget to do good and to share with others, for with such sacrifices God is pleased.

HEBREWS 13:15-16

HELLO FAMILY: The holiday season is here! A few days ago, we read in James how our words can poison one another. Today we read how we can use our words to please God by praising Him. So do it! Praise God for being alive and able in all circumstances, able to get up and go. Do something. Do good things today. Smile at others and be cheerful. Love you all.

DAY 363

He came to that which was his own, but his own did not receive him. [12] Yet to all who did receive him, to those who believed in his name, he gave the right to become children of God—[13] children born not of natural descent, nor of human decision or a husband's will, but born of God.

JOHN 1:11-13

HELLO FAMILY: Understand that Jesus was born with a Jewish bloodline. This is the same Jewish nation along with their high priests that crucified Jesus. They did not receive him well. Now we read that "Yet to all who did receive him," keyword being "receive," and "to those who believe in his name," keyword being, "believed." How many of us believe in God, in Jesus, and that there is the Holy Spirit? How many of us boldly declare that we will go to Heaven because we believe? I ask, will Satan and his demons go to Heaven also? They too believe fully that God and Jesus exist. Yet they were tossed out of Heaven by God, Jesus, and His Angels. Satan knows fully firsthand and believes that God and His Army exist. Now back to the other keyword, you must "receive" Jesus Christ as your Lord and Savior. Not only must you believe Jesus is who He is, but you must also receive Jesus Christ as Lord. I pray everyone who reads this really takes the time to grasp. This is how we gain the right to become children of God, our Father. Every single one of us, whether planned or not. We are not mistakes. We are not accidents. We are not Fatherless. Love you all.

August 2021: Me with my granddaughters Hannah and Leonie.

DAY 364

> *"You shall have no other gods before me. [4] You shall not make for yourself an image in the form of anything in heaven above or on the earth beneath or in the waters below. [5] You shall not bow down to them or worship them; for I, the Lord your God, am a jealous God, punishing the children for sin of the parents to the third and fourth generation of those who hate me, [6]but showing love to a thousand generations of those who love me and keep my commandments."*
>
> EXODUS 20:3–6

HELLO FAMILY: Reading this Commandment spoken and written by God Himself in stone for Moses to take to the people, key words immediately capture our attention. Think about our experiences in life and the broken people we have seen. We read this Commandment and we all know what jealousy is. Have we not all experienced jealousy? People have killed one another over jealousy. We read further and see the "punishing [of] the children for sin of the parents to the third and fourth generation" of "those who hate" God! On the flip side, we see a "showing [of] love to a thousand generations of those who love" God and keep His commandments. A thousand generations—how many years can that be? Carol and I have home videos of her grandparents praying and praising God, Jesus our Savior during prayers said before our meals. My parents are both still alive and serve earnestly in their church with great passion and love for God. We the children of these parents and grandparents are witnesses to God's blessings. Perhaps, it is because of the love our parents and grandparents demonstrated. Reading this scripture is a family affair for generations to come, with great rewards and yes, very bad consequences as well. These words are by no means something to disregard and take lightly. Each of us has a responsibility as a member of our family. Again, God wrote these words Himself. Love you all.

DAY 365

"This, then, is how you should pray: 'Our Father in heaven, hallowed be your name, [10] your kingdom, your will be done, on earth as it is in heaven. [11] Give us today our daily bread. [12] And forgive us our debts, as we also have forgiven our debtors. [13] And lead us not into temptation, but deliver us from the evil one.'"

MATTHEW 6:9-13

HELLO FAMILY: This project of writing 365 days (and many more) started with a sermon from my preacher telling of his experience not being able to give away a single Father's Day card during his prison ministry. Just to refresh, our pastor gave away hundreds of Mother's Day cards for prisoners to write in and he would send to their mothers. But when Father's Day came, not one of the prisoners wanted to send a card to their father. To end this journey with the Lord's Prayer is a must. This prayer comes directly from the Son of God. Jesus taught us to start this prayer this exact way: "Our Father in Heaven." Jesus didn't tell us to pray to "my" Father in Heaven. This is "our" Father. Our Creator and our Provider. Our God is everything to us all. He is **ours**! Love you all

Epilogue

While working on this book for the past couple of years, a key theme kept resounding in my thoughts. Why me?

Do you ever get upset about life and ask, "Why me?" How many times in a gaffe of frustration do you ask God, "Why me?" How many situations do we get into where they just aren't going our way? Our health or our abilities fall short. Or our physical abilities become impaired and unable to perform or fulfill an expectation from others or to ourselves? Perhaps our mentality in thinking through situations may not be keeping up with the rest of the world. Even after a Google search and a YouTube video talking us through each step, our plans can and will get disrupted. Hard life-changing choices may have to be made. So, "Why me?" All of these situations happen to each and every one of us at some point in our lives. As our Heavenly Father, God will impress upon us to get specific "chores" done to further the benefit of the family, to further God's Kingdom here on earth. Completing this book has been a challenge with many disruptions, many doubts, many gaffes, and potential excuses to just quit! We must not quit as Christians. When God impresses upon us to do something, it is for the good of humanity. It is good for us all.

Remember this: You are not alone!

When we are in God's hands, rest assured, our lives will never be the same. We must be bold and recognize that in every single second, God has us in the palm of His **very mighty hand**! This is why so many scriptures call for the praising of our Lord under all circumstances, **all** of them! The acute changes in our lives are for the future good. I know that's a hard pill to swallow when tragedy is in our midst. What is most critical is our attitude. We must teach our children about attitude and remind them every single night the message of a positive attitude. We must remind ourselves, our co-workers, and our friends too. God is with you! You are loved! Be secure and be joyful in all circumstances. These changes in our plans are going to lead to glorious times in which we will be able to share as witnesses to the world God's great love for humanity.

As the title of the book proclaims, absolutely no one is Fatherless. Even as messed up as mortal fathers can be, cruel, careless, and meaningless in our lives. God the Father is all loving all the time, always. What I pray is for this book to open the hearts of fathers, sons, mothers, and daughters across the world to a fresh start. A start that will begin with forgiveness in a very overpowering way that is difficult to articulate, yet the examples are all around us and written for us in the Bible. Forgiveness is the single key to release the most ever-bearing chain that brings us down hard, a chain that hurts us in ways we will never know mentally, physically, and spiritually. Not forgiving others makes us miserable in so many ways we may never understand. It destroys our ability to experience full joy. Joy is the key that I look for when I observe my children wherever we may be. I look into their souls to witness if they

Continued on next page.

EPILOGUE, *continued from page 223.*

are experiencing joy and determine if they are really happy. Then my wife and I discuss our findings together. This drives our prayers of thankfulness, and perhaps focuses our prayers on concerns. Remember, we all have situations that need prayer, divine guidance, and praises.

I recall a very deep discussion in Germany with a father figure in my daughters' lives. He asked me, "Why are you here, and what do you look for when you visit?"

I didn't even have to think about the answer. I merely said, "I want to see if my daughters are happy. Are my daughters loved by their husbands? Are they treated with respect and dignity? Is God in their lives, and is joy a daily experience for them in their relationships?"

This father, who I greatly respect, responded with a big German smile and a bear hug to boot. This again was another moment in life to thank God for along this earthly journey, but more importantly to recognize that we are created in the likeness of God. Therefore, I conclude this is also what God our Father desires for each of us also, as His adopted children through Jesus our Lord.

No one is Fatherless.

Sincerely,

Daniel R. Kostrzebski